Design, Innovation and Intellectual Property

Nan Jiang

Design, Innovation and Intellectual Property

Toward a New IP System—Lessons from China

Springer

同濟大學出版社
TONGJI UNIVERSITY PRESS

Nan Jiang
Shanghai International College of Intellectual Property
Tongji University
Shanghai, Shanghai, China

ISBN 978-981-95-2041-1 ISBN 978-981-95-2042-8 (eBook)
https://doi.org/10.1007/978-981-95-2042-8

Jointly published with Tongji University Press Co., Ltd.

The print edition is not for sale in Mainland China. Customers from Mainland China please order the print book from: Tongji University Press Co., Ltd.

This work was supported by State Natural Science Fund project (72274137).

This Springer imprint is published by the registered company Springer Nature Singapore Pte Ltd.
The registered company address is: 152 Beach Road, #21-01/04 Gateway East, Singapore 189721, Singapore

Preface

Design, innovation, and intellectual property (IP) are the triad that powers modern creativity and economic progress. They are not isolated concepts but interconnected forces: design gives form to innovation, innovation breathes life into design, and IP ensures that both can thrive sustainably. Over years of engaging with designers, innovators, legal experts, and policymakers, I have witnessed a recurring truth: without a clear understanding of how these three elements interact, even the most brilliant ideas risk being undervalued, copied, or lost. This book, Design, Innovation and Intellectual Property, is born from that observation—an attempt to map the landscape where creativity meets protection, and where innovation meets its potential.

The need for such a work became evident through countless conversations. A product designer once asked, "How do I stop competitors from copying my chair's unique curve without stifling the evolution of seating design?" A traditional craftsman wondered, "Can my family's centuries-old weaving patterns be protected without cutting them off from cultural exchange?" A tech entrepreneur queried, "How do I safeguard the user interface of my app when code and visuals blur together?" These questions revealed a gap: existing resources focused narrowly on either design theory, innovation strategy, or IP law, but rarely wove them into a single, actionable narrative. This book seeks to bridge that gap.

What follows is a comprehensive exploration of design in all its forms from physical products to digital services, from urban landscapes to brand identities—rooted in the reality that innovation cannot flourish in a vacuum. It is not enough to create, we must also ensure that creators can reap the rewards of their labor, and that society can benefit from the diffusion of good ideas. This balance is at the heart of every chapter.

The Vision: Why This Book Matters

This book is structured to guide readers from foundational concepts to real-world applications, ensuring that theory is always grounded in practice. It begins by defining design and innovation, then examines how IP law safeguards them. It proceeds to apply these principles to specific design disciplines, from product and environment design to visual communication and services. Finally, it looks to the future, addressing how emerging technologies are reshaping the rules of the game.

Chapter 1: Overview of Design and Innovation lays the groundwork. It defines design as a purposeful practice that transforms ideas into solutions—one that draws on art, science, and economics. It explores design principles (artistry, innovation, functionality, cost-effectiveness) and distinguishes between types of innovation (technology-driven, market-driven, design-driven). Crucially, it introduces IP as the backbone that turns creative effort into lasting value: protecting designers from imitation while encouraging the sharing of ideas that drive progress.

Chapter 2: Design and Intellectual Property delves into the legal frameworks that protect design. It explains how copyright, patent, trademark, and anti-unfair competition laws each play a role: copyright guards expressive elements, patents protect novel, industrial designs, trademarks secure brand identity, and anti-unfair competition laws fill gaps. It also traces the evolution of international IP cooperation—from the Paris Union to the WTO—showing how global standards balance national interests with cross-border creativity.

Chapter 3: Product Design and Intellectual Property focuses on tangible creations: industrial designs, traditional handicrafts, furniture, and apparel. It argues that product design is inherently human-centered, blending function and aesthetics. Through case studies—such as disputes over copied furniture designs or the challenges of protecting traditional crafts—it offers strategies: navigating patent timelines for fast-changing fashion, or safeguarding artisanal techniques without stifling cultural exchange.

Chapter 4: Environment Design and Intellectual Property shifts to the spaces we inhabit, from buildings to public art. It explores how IP protects architectural drawings, landscape plans, and installations, addressing questions like: When does a building's aesthetic qualify for copyright? How can public art be shared without infringement? It also examines "fair use" for outdoor art, ensuring public access while respecting creators' rights.

Chapter 5: Visual Communication Design and Intellectual Property examines the visual languages of communication—typography, logos, packaging, posters. In a world of global branding, these designs carry immense commercial weight. This chapter unpacks IP challenges: protecting logo distinctiveness, preventing packaging imitation, and judging "substantial similarity" in posters. It uses cases (e.g., font copyright disputes, trade dress conflicts) to show how courts balance creativity and competition.

Chapter 6: Service Design and Intellectual Property explores intangible innovations—digital platforms, public services, and product-service systems. Service design—rooted in user experience—redefines industries (e.g., telemedicine, ridesharing). This chapter addresses a critical gap: how to protect service innovations, which rely on processes, data, and interactions. It covers copyright for user interfaces, patents for service methods, and trade secrets for proprietary data.

Chapter 7: Design Innovation and the Future of Intellectual Property confronts emerging disruptions—AI, 3D printing, IoT, and the digital economy. These technologies blur lines—between human and machine creation, physical and digital goods. It asks: Who owns IP in AI-generated designs? How to regulate 3D printing to prevent counterfeiting? What new frameworks are needed for data-driven services? It argues that future IP systems must be adaptive, encouraging innovation while addressing ethical concerns.

Core Principles: What Makes This Book Unique

Three principles guide this work: they are integration, relevance, and global perspective.

The first one is Integration. Design, innovation, and IP are not siloed. A furniture designer cannot ignore patent law, a lawyer cannot grasp IP disputes without understanding design processes. This book weaves insights from design theory, economics, and law to offer a holistic view.

The second one is Relevance. Theory matters only if it solves real problems. Each chapter includes case studies from global disputes, industry practices, and legal precedents. Whether it is a Chinese apparel brand fighting copycats or a European architect defending a landmark's copyright, these examples show how IP works in practice.

The third one is Global Perspective. Design and innovation are borderless, and IP challenges cross nations. This book examines Chinese IP laws alongside international treaties (e.g., TRIPS, the Hague System) and comparative approaches from the U.S., EU, and Japan. It acknowledges no "one-size-fits-all" solution, highlighting how cultural and economic contexts shape IP strategies.

For Whom This Book Is Written

This book speaks to a diverse audience. They are designers and innovators, legal practitioners, policymakers, business leaders, and students.

Designers and Innovators: Industrial designers, craftspeople, service designers—anyone creating value through design—will find guidance on protecting their work, managing legal risks, and using IP to turn creativity into impact.

Legal Practitioners: Lawyers, patent agents, and IP consultants will gain clarity on design-specific challenges—judging similarity in visual communication, protecting intangible services, or navigating cross-border disputes.

Policymakers: Those shaping IP laws will find analysis of global best practices, with recommendations for balancing protection and innovation—especially in emerging areas like AI and digital services.

Business Leaders: Executives in design-driven industries will learn to integrate IP into innovation strategies, turning design into a competitive advantage.

Students: This book serves as a textbook for courses in design, innovation, and IP, offering a foundation supported by real-world examples.

The Heart of the Matter: Stories Over Jargon

This book prioritizes clarity and relevance over jargon. Technical terms are defined when first introduced, and complex legal concepts are illustrated with stories. For example, when discussing design patents, we do not just explain legal criteria—we examine a dispute over a chair's silhouette, showing how courts determine "substantial similarity." When exploring traditional handicrafts, we do not just outline IP rules—we follow a weaver's journey to protect a family pattern while allowing it to evolve.

These stories matter because they humanize the concepts. Design is not just about aesthetics, it is about people—their needs, their creativity, their livelihoods. IP is not just about legal technicalities, it is about ensuring that creativity is rewarded, so that more creativity can flourish.

Acknowledgments

This book would not exist without the contributions of countless individuals, they are as follows: The designers who shared their struggles and successes, reminding me that IP is not an abstract concept but a tool for survival and growth. The legal experts who walked me through complex cases, helping translate legalese into practical insights. Colleagues and students who tested early drafts, asking tough questions that sharpened every chapter. The publishers who supported this project, ensuring it reaches those who need it most.

I am equally indebted to the National Natural Science Foundation of China for its generous support through General Program Grant No. 72274137, "Research on the Optimization Mechanism of Key Core-Technology Innovation Chains in Patent-Intensive Industries Driven by Digital Intelligence." This funding provided the empirical foundation and analytical depth that enriched every discussion of innovation and intellectual property within these pages.

To all of them—and to the creators and innovators who will use this book—I offer my gratitude. This book is for you: the designer sketching a better future, the entrepreneur turning an idea into a service, the policymaker shaping a world where creativity thrives. May it equip you to protect what you create, innovate boldly, and leave a legacy that endures.

Shanghai, China
22nd July, 2025

Nan Jiang

Contents

Chapter 1
Overview of Design and Innovation

Design plays an increasingly important role in the world economy. Industrial design filings worldwide have seen continued growth over the last decade, often at double digit rates, notwithstanding the global economic down turn. The look and feel of devices—their design—helps drive consumer choice, as it determines the ease of use and influences consumer experience of a product. Design enables firms to differentiate their products and foster a particular brand image, ultimately establishing a competitive edge in the marketplace. Firms are therefore sensitive to the copying of their designs, as it may lead consumers to purchase other products and result in a loss of market share.

In innovation studies, design is sometimes treated on the same footing as a firm's expenditure on research and development (R&D), software, training and other knowledge-based investments. As a result of this emerging evidence and the above-mentioned court cases, policymakers have shown greater interest in "industrial designs" as a form of IP.

Today, design accounts for a substantial share of firms' investments in intangible assets and innovation. There has been marked growth in the use of IP to protect product designs. Product designs and electronic user interfaces are also at the center of legal disputes in the high-technology industry. As a result, policymakers have shown greater interest in better understanding the role of design in innovation and economic growth. This special section has discussed a number of the conceptual and definitional challenges that exist on this front. For a start, there is need to agree on a statistical definition of design for the purposes of innovation measurement; such a definition would need to capture the economic relevance of design activity. New measurement tools could then be developed based on that definition (WIPO 2012).

N. Jiang, *Design, Innovation and Intellectual Property*,
https://doi.org/10.1007/978-981-95-2042-8_1

1.1 Introduction to Design

1.1.1 The Concept of Design

Design is a planned and purposeful idea and practice that plays a very important role in promoting social progress. At the same time, research of design covers an extremely wide range of content and fields. Before learning about the relationship between design, innovation and intellectual property, we must first understand the concept of "design."

Scholars have discussed the concept of "design" from a variety of perspectives, including the following:

From the perspective of behavioral processes, Victor Papanek (1985), an American design theorist, believes that design is basic to all human activity. The planning and patterning of any act towards a desired, foreseeable end constitute the design process. Furthermore, design is the way we plan and create actions, services, and all of the other humanly shaped processes of public and private life, striving to meet their needs and desires and facilitating the exchange of information and ideas that is essential for civil and political life (Buchanan 2001). Linda Le Phan (2022) argues that achieving good design takes clarity around a specific goal, and when a larger team is involved, collaboration and alignment. The design process is crucial because it's the disciplined approach that guides creative teams towards a clear and meaningful goal for their design work.

From a philosophical point of view, Eekels (2000) argues that, design is a science concerning an important area of action. It has a subject performing the action, and there is an object that has to be changed by the action. The subject of design generally refers to the person who carries out intelligence or thinking activities, which is usually called the agent. The object of design refers to the object or result of design, which is usually called artifact or technical system (Eekels 2001).

Linguistics, especially in terms of lexicality, is also discussed. Ralph and Wand (2009) proposed a conceptual model of design, in which design is both a noun and a verb. As a noun, design is a specification of an object, manifested by some agent, intended to accomplish goals, in a particular environment, using a set of primitive components, satisfying a set of requirements, subject to some constraints; As a verb, design is to create a design, in an environment where the designer operates.

Finally, the concept of "design" can be studied from the perspective of innovation. According to the Design Council, Design is the connection between creativity and innovation. Design shapes ideas to become practical and attractive propositions for users or customers. Design may be described as creativity deployed to a specific end (Indianapolis Council 2011).

Scholars engage in discussions from various perspectives that collectively enrich the concept of "design." Although scholars hold differing views on the surface, their understanding of the essence of "design" is remarkably similar. Generally, "design" refers to the development of plans, schemes, or strategies aimed at achieving specific goals or requirements through appropriate processes or technical means. In other words, "design" can be defined as tools and methods transforming ideas and technologies into outcomes and products satisfying people's needs, a process to create new things.

1.1.2 Principles of Design

Design is both a social practice for the benefit of mankind and the transformation of nature, and an important humanistic activity involving science, technology and art. Principle of design is a fundamental rule or law, derived inductively from extensive experience and/or empirical evidence, which provides design process guidance to increase the chance of reaching a successful solution (Fu et al. 2015).

Design should adhere to the following fundamental principles:

(1) The Principle of Artistry. Though practical function of a product is always the industrial designer's main concern, aesthetic effect is still a critical issue for the development of a new product (Lin et al. 2019). Creators should take into account the artistry of the product or work they are designing, ensuring that its form possesses appropriate aesthetic characteristics and artistic taste, thus providing the public with a sense of aesthetic enjoyment. The goal of design is to create a product of utilitarian, cultural and aesthetic value, which can satisfy both consumers' material and spiritual needs.

(2) The Principle of Innovation. Design is a creative activity, and its essence demands innovation. With economic growth and technological advancement, people's material and spiritual needs are constantly evolving, rendering traditional design concepts and methods insufficient to keep up with the rapidly changing demands. Therefore, creators must stand on the shoulders of their predecessors, engaging in appropriate innovation in design theory and practice, ensuring that the final products and outcomes can meet people's needs and enhance their material and spiritual lives.

(3) The Principle of Functionality. "Functionality" is the most fundamental attribute of an item as a useful object. Creators must formulate differentiated design objectives based on personalized needs of different user groups, making targeted and purposeful design decisions. The products and outcomes produced by creators must meet specific physiological or psychological needs of a particular group to achieve utility maximization.

    As Krippendorff (2011) said, form should not follow function but meaning and design has to make sense to others. Acknowledging meanings as a primary target of design considerations is saying that the diversity of individual (user) conceptions matters as much as if not more than the (techno-)logic of designers and engineers.

(4) The Principle of Cost-effectiveness. In a sense, the purpose of design is to bring added value to products and outcomes. The products and outcomes created are the culmination of their knowledge and effort, possessing both aesthetics and practicality, and are thus inherently high in added value. However, during the

creative process, creators must consider the manufacturing costs. On the basis of controlling costs, they must also ensure the quality and aesthetics of the final product.

1.1.3 Types of Design

Due to the interdisciplinary nature of design, there is a wide variety of design categories, including industrial design, product design, handicraft design, architectural design, furniture design, textile and fashion design, graphic design, service design, UI design, illustration design, animation design, and more. For better understanding, a brief introduction to several design types covered in this book will be made, and later chapters will delve into the concepts, characteristics, and legal protection related to these design types in detail.

(1) Product Design

Product design is the process of transforming a certain purpose or need into a concrete physical form or tool. In this process, creators present the shape of the product in two-dimensional or three-dimensional forms by combining various elements such as lines, symbols, numbers, colors, and more. The total product design concept consists of three elements, namely functionality, aesthetics, and meaning, each of which arises from more elemental product characteristics. Functionality arises from a product's features that deliver the specific benefits that customers realize from using the product. Aesthetics arise from the product's sensorial characteristics, including its appearance, sound, touch, smell, and feel. Meaning refers to the significance and memorial associations about a product that is shared by its customers (Srinivasan et al. 2012).

Product design is a creative activity that harmoniously integrates scientific, artistic, economic, and social aspects, with the aim of creating products that have a positive affinity and compatibility with the physical and mental well-being of users. Among numerous outstanding product design works, one of Marc Newson's most famous early works is the Lockheed Lounge designed in 1990. It achieved international recognition when Madonna was spotted reclining on it in the music video for her 1993 track "Rain." It stands as one of the most iconic pieces in modern furniture design.

(2) Environment Design

Environmental (Art) Design is one of the most dynamic and studied design disciplines in China, derived and developed from Interior Decoration and Design. "Environmental Design"and "Environmental Art Design," two naming variations for the same discipline, coexist within the Chinese cultural context, in which many Chinese scholars developed their own comprehension of the nature of "Design". Therefore, these two names are often misused in Chinese academia and industry. The broad concept of "Environment" led to an ambiguity in the core, boundary, and scope of the discipline. Within this background, the discipline of Environmental (Art) Design is facing confusion and challenges.

In the latest discipline directory of the Ministry of Education of China, the following descriptions can be found: "The focus of this discipline is to study the environmental relationship between nature, artifacts, and society, with the main purpose of optimizing the quality of human life and living environment (Yang and Zhu 2020)."

(3) Visual Communication Design

Visual communication design, seen as an activity, is the action of conceiving, programming, projecting and realizing visual communications that are usually produced through industrial means and are aimed at broadcasting specific messages to specific sectors of the public. This is done with a view toward having an impact on the public's knowledge, attitudes, or behavior in an intended direction (Frascara 2004). Visual communication is the practice of using visual elements to get a message across, inspire change, or evoke an emotion.

Visual Communication exists in two parts: communication design and graphic design.

- Communication design refers to crafting a message that educates, motivates, and engages the viewer.
- Graphic design uses design principles to communicate that message in a way that is clear and eye-catching to the intended audience.

What visual communication is really about at its core is selecting the elements that will create the most meaning for your audience. These elements usually include text, icons, shapes, imagery, and data visualizations.

(4) Service Design

Service design is the activity of planning and organizing the people, infrastructure, information communication and material components of a service in order to improve the quality of the service. Service design is concerned with systematically applying design methodology and principles to the design of services. It assumes the customer/user as the starting point or lens into a specific service and through the use of creative, human-centered and user-participatory methods models how the service can be performed. At the same time, service design integrates the possibilities and means to perform a service with the desired qualities, within the economic and strategic intent of an organization (Holmlid and Evenson 2008). Service design can be the modification of existing services or the creation of entirely new service. It can be both tangible and intangible. The purpose of service design is to construct a holistic service framework by exploring the needs of various stakeholders within the system. It involves designing various touchpoints within the service framework to create a better service experience for users and other stakeholders within the system.

1.1.4 Tools for Design

As a famous Chinese proverb goes, "A workman must first sharpen his tools if he is to do his work well." In the context of design, the right design tools are indispensable for successful creative work. With the development of modern technology, design tools continue to evolve and improve, leading to a situation where traditional and modern tools coexist. They collectively serve the creative activities of designers. Here is a brief introduction to several common design tools.

(1) Unassisted sketching

Unassisted sketching is one of the most traditional methods of hand-drawn design. They are typically loose and informal conceptual sketches rather than a complete and precise set of design plans. It is a design approach to develop designers' creative thinking. Meanwhile, it serves as the most explicit design tool for expressing ideas, conveying emotions, and presenting the visual effects of a design.

Unassisted sketching can utilize various techniques based on the tools used, including pencil sketches, pen drawings, oil painting techniques, marker renderings, and more. Unassisted sketching forms the foundation of the following design activities. However, it also has its drawbacks, which are, primarily, the complexity and low efficiency of hand-drawing, and difficulties in modifications.

(2) Computer Software and Programs

The advent of computers and the internet has ushered humanity into the digital age, with a plethora of practical and efficient computer design software and programs emerging rapidly. Traditional unassisted sketches are gradually being phased out. With the support of design software and programs, designers no longer need to do cumbersome manual works as they did before. Instead, they utilize various convenient and efficient design tools. They can create a personalized working space with different software and hardware tools based on design fields, user requirements, personal preferences, etc. Common design software tools include Photoshop, AutoCAD, CorelDRAW, and others.

(3) Mind Maps

Mind map is an effective graphic tool for expressing divergent thinking. It helps designers overcome the information chaos by figuring out the relationship between different messages as well as sparking inspiration and generating new ideas and concepts. When creating a mind map, designers first establish a core idea and expand and elaborate outward from that central idea, allowing for free extensions without deviating from the initial core idea. Each node represents a connection to the central theme, and each connection can become another sub-central theme, branching out into thousands of nodes, creating a radial three-dimensional structure. These interconnected nodes function similarly to neurons in the brain, eventually forming the designer's personal creative repository.

(4) Persona

Table 1.1 Example of Persona Models

Persona: Mona Hall, Secretary of Trading Company
Mona, 22, is currently a small white-collar of a trading company. She is more concerned about new book information. Reading is an important part of her life. She spends a lot of time reading her favorite books. She likes to surf the Internet on her mobile phone and enjoy the joy that reading brings her anywhere.
The goals of Mona using mobile reading application are to: Learn about new book information, inquire about author information, book discount information, book souvenir information. Interact with book friends, write book reviews at any time, and update reading dynamics. Explore unknown areas, expand horizons, etc.

The term "Persona", first introduced by Alan Cooper (1999), is an early "user modeling tool" in design activities. The persona is a "hypothetical archetype of real users" (Pruitt and Adlin 2006) that can be imagined as a real person (name, age, personal habits, hobbies, emotions), and serves to express a specific user need. When designers or design thinkers form such a persona, they use it in subsequent ideation, prototyping and testing phases as a point of reference (Kouprie and Visser 2009). Because the act of creating Personas has helped us make our assumptions about the target audience more explicit. Once created, the Personas have helped make assumptions and decision-making criteria equally explicit (Pruitt and Grudin 2003). Based on user research data, creating virtual persona models helps to better reflect the characteristics, goals, and behaviors of real user groups. This further assists designers in gaining a deeper understanding of users' actual needs, reducing subjectivity, and facilitating the design of user-centered products or services tailored to specific groups.

The specific persona models are shown in Table 1.1.

1.2 Innovation in Design

1.2.1 Introduction to Innovation

(1) The Concept of Innovation

The word innovation is originated from Latin word, innovare, which means "to make something new." Back in 1985, Drucker (1985) had defined innovation as the entrepreneurs' specific tool to exploit change for a diverse business or service. He added, this innovation can be presented as a discipline which can be learned and practiced. In other words, innovation is also said as "an idea, practice, or object that is perceived as new by an individual or other unit of adoption (Grawe 2009)."

Meanwhile, Tidd and Bessant (2020) defined innovation as a process of transforming an opportunity into fresh ideas and being widely used in practice. The OECD (2005) also has a definition of "innovation"—an innovation is the implementation of a new or significantly improved product (good or service), or process, a new marketing method, or a new organisational method in business practices, workplace organization or external relations.

In summary, "innovation" refers to any new practice for an organization, including equipment, products, services, processes, policies and programs. This broad definition of an innovation encompasses a wide range of possible innovations. An innovation can be more narrowly categorised as the implementation of one or more types of innovations, for instance product and process innovations (OECD 2005).

(2) Types of Innovation

① Divided by innovation object

Since innovation involves various aspects of a company's products, processes, and organizational methods, from the perspective of innovation objects, "innovation" can be divided into four categories: product innovation, process innovation, marketing innovation, and organizational innovation. According to The Oslo Manual (OECD 2005), these four main types of innovation are defined below:

A product innovation is the introduction of a good or service that is new or significantly improved with respect to its characteristics or intended uses. This includes significant improvements in technical specifications, components and materials, incorporated software, user friendliness or other functional characteristics. Product innovations can utilise new knowledge or technologies, or can be based on new uses or combinations of existing knowledge or technologies. The term "product" is used to cover both goods and services. Product innovations include both the introduction of new goods and services and significant improvements in the functional or user characteristics of existing goods and services.

A process innovation is the implementation of a new or significantly improved production or delivery method. This includes significant changes in techniques, equipment and/or software. Process innovations can be intended to decrease unit costs of production or delivery, to increase quality, or to produce or deliver new or significantly improved products.

A marketing innovation is the implementation of a new marketing method involving significant changes in product design or packaging, product placement, product promotion or pricing. Marketing innovations are aimed at better addressing customer needs, opening up new markets, or newly positioning a firm's product on the market, with the objective of increasing the firm's sales. The distinguishing feature of a marketing innovation compared to other changes in a firm's marketing instruments is the implementation of a marketing method not previously used by the firm.

An organisational innovation is the implementation of a new organisational method in the firm's business practices, workplace organisation or external relations. Organisational innovations can be intended to increase a firm's performance by reducing administrative costs or transaction costs, improving workplace satisfaction (and thus labour productivity), gaining access to non-tradable assets (such as non-codified external knowledge) or reducing costs of supplies. The distinguishing features of an organisational innovation compared to other organisational changes in a firm is the implementation of an organisational method that has not been used before in the firm and is the result of strategic decisions taken by management.

② Divided by the level of innovation

According to the level of innovation, "innovation" is divided into two types: radical innovation and incremental innovation.

Schumpeter (2017) described radical innovation as the key to economic development, through a process of creative destruction, a revolutionary "change"—a breakthrough—in product, process, or organization. In other words, this type of innovation breaks with previous structures, procedures, activities and products in a firm (Schumpeter 2013). A radical innovation, then, is an innovation with a high degree of novelty, which breaks with what existed previously and is the result of non-obvious paths or ideas. Consequently, a radical innovation involves great challenges and opportunities (Teece 2010).

In contrast, incremental innovation is an innovation with a low degree of novelty, as well as less risk and cost than radical innovation (Martínez-Ros and Orfila-Sintes 2009), though with considerably less potential for positive impact on firm performance. Thereby, incremental innovation does not break with previous products, processes or organizational methods, because it is a significant improvement of previous products, processes or organizational methods, as this carries a lower degree of novelty. Nonetheless, consecutive incremental innovations could result in a radical innovation.

(3) Strategies for Innovation

Since the Industrial Revolution, the tremendous progress of human technology has always been accompanied by continuous development of innovation, and the path, scope, and depth of innovation have also been continuously expanded. The three common innovation strategies currently available are technology push innovation, market pull innovation, and design driven innovation.

① Technology-driven innovation

Technology can be defined as a scientific method or process that converts inputs including knowledge, labour, material, capital, energy and information into outputs (Tushman and Anderson 2018). This broad definition of technology refers to all strategies of innovations including technology-push and market-pull innovations that involve a technical process to create a new product, new process and new business model or to improve existing ones.

Technology-driven innovation is the innovation led by the development of new technology or the application and conversion of the original technology, which is one of the most basic innovation strategies. Technology-push innovation occurs where R&D experimentation precedes market opportunity analysis and the development of a business model (Souder 1989). Technological breakthroughs have a disruptive impact on industries and are often the source of long-term competitive advantage, which can be considered a type of radical innovation.

Technology-push innovation can be divided into two types, namely high-tech innovation and low-tech innovation. High-tech innovation refers to a product or process created by utilizing very sophisticated and complex operations with significant R&D involvement, while a relatively low-tech innovation implies the opposite (Khandwalla 1976).

CONCEPT-X is a state-of-the-art unmanned construction machine solution announced by Doosan Infracore in 2019 (Hyundai Doosan Infracore 2023). The system consists of an excavator, a wheel loader, an ADT (adjective dump truck) and X-CENTER, a control center that controls the construction machinery. Our flagship model, the excavator, can solve various problems in construction sites in connection with drones and X-CENTER. By minimizing human intervention in construction sites where many risk factors exist, safety factors and work efficiency can be improved, because these machines can operate 24 h a day. The failure prediction system also minimizes maintenance costs.

② Market-driven innovation

Market-driven innovation is the innovation of technology or product application from user needs. It does not take technology as the origin of innovation, but innovates by discovering users' needs in life and work, and innovates to meet this need. Market-pull innovation starts with an analysis of user needs and then searches for technologies that can better satisfy them, or updates product languages to respond to existing trends, thus market opportunities as a source of innovation precedes a firm's likely investment in R&D (Souder 1989). It aims not to question and redefine dominant meanings but rather to better understand and satisfy them. It falls within the domain of incremental innovation.

Mastercard extends its commitment to inclusivity by introducing a new accessible card standard for blind and partially sighted people (Purchase 2021), called the Touch Card. The new Touch Card credit cards have a squarish notch; debit cards have a rounded notch; and prepaid cards have a triangular notch. The standard has been designed to work with point-of-sale terminals and ATMs, ensuring it can be deployed at scale.

③ Design-driven innovation

Roberto Verganti (2009), an authoritative expert in innovation management, first proposed a third strategy: design-driven innovation—that is, radical innovation of meaning. He interpreted it as "the novelty of the information and product language transmitted by the product is far greater than the novelty of the technical achievements contained in it." Design-driven innovation is propelled by a firm's vision about possible breakthrough meanings and product languages that people could love, whose core is to give product meaning and connotation through design.

He believed that people do not buy products but meanings. People use things for profound emotional, psychological, and sociocultural reasons as well as utilitarian ones. Every product and service in consumer as well as industrial markets has a meaning. Firms should therefore look beyond features, functions, and performance and understand the real meanings users give to things.

A typical example is the camping kit co-designed by Yiche (BITAUTO) and Hermès, which emphasizes communication with consumers featuring the expression of trendy art in the trend of refined camping. This kit includes dinner plates, scarves, and woven baskets. The dinner plates are crafted with intangible cultural heritage techniques, presented in a material of ivory white (also known as "Oriental White"). The design, using stylized techniques, abstractly interprets nature through elements, bodily lines, and other characteristics, revealing the most fundamental element-vitality, and accentuating the true beauty of nature. This elicits emotional and lifestyle resonance among consumers. Yiche's camping kit does not fall under the category of technology-driven or market-driven innovation. Instead, it is a new product resulting from design-driven innovation, which gains a sustained competitive advantage by satisfying consumers' underlying emotional, psychological, and socio-cultural needs.

1.2.2 Design Innovation

(1) The Connotation of Design Innovation

According to Mutlu, "Design innovations" comprise "(a) the incremental novelties in the design of an existing product or service, or (b) radically new products or services obtained by design effort with no or minimal technical novelty." The "design effort" mentioned in this definition refers to "a design activity with a central role of 'industrial design', and contributions of a variety of design practices." The "technical novelty" mentioned here refers to "novelty in a product or service attained by the use of sole scientific methods or practices (Mutlu and Er 2003)."

Meanwhile, Oakley's (1990) definition of design also includes the definition of "design innovation": design effort is devoted to "help turn an invention into a successful innovation – or to extend the usefulness of an existing innovation." He describes this effort as a "fine-tuning to achieve a result that suits our needs more accurately". He also points out that 99 percent of the new products in the market are a derivation of an existing application, thus emphasizes the importance of design effort in terms of introducing novelties by extending the usefulness of the existing innovation.

In general, "design innovation" includes both incremental innovation in existing products or services, as well as newly designed products or services. Design innovation is different from traditional linear processes, and it does not correspond to a straight set of stages that commonly start from research and end with product distribution. Design is iterative and recursive, people-centered, constantly diverging and converging. It delineates an approach to define problems with a special focus on people's needs, which has caused the progressive expansion of the concerns of design innovation (Mortati 2015).

(2) Approaches to Design Innovation

Generally speaking, the methods of design innovation mainly help designers to obtain ideas by widening design ideas or eliminating thinking barriers to form more satisfactory works. The methods of design innovation mainly include the following:

① Brainstorming

Brainstorming is an individual or group method for generating ideas, increasing creative efficacy, or finding solutions to problems. Participants generate ideas on a particular topic or problem in a nonjudgmental environment following a set of ground rules about appropriate behaviors (Wilson 2013).

Designers viewed brainstorms as one of the best ways to get help and give help to others because, compared with e-mails or brief conversations, richer information was exchanged and attention was focused narrowly on the problem. They asserted that no person can consistently design good products alone; the process requires knowledge about too many things and making too many trade-offs between constraints (Sutton and Hargadon 1996).

The group of people selected for a brainstorming session should be diverse. It should not just be experts or those knowledgeable in the problem area, but should include a wide range of expertise and even laypeople if they have some familiarity with the problem area. The group must be non-hierarchical, although one person does need to take an organisational lead.

Brainstorming is often used in the early to middle stages of product development; however, this method is applicable any time that new ideas or solutions to problems are required. If designers have an unexpected and difficult problem just before they release a product, brainstorming would be an appropriate method for generating potential solutions.

The basic procedure for group brainstorming involves (Wilson 2013):

- Selecting a group of three to ten participants with different backgrounds.
- Posing a clear problem, question, or topic to the group.
- Asking the group to generate solutions or ideas with no criticism or attempts to limit the type and number of ideas. This is the "divergent" phase in which you want as many ideas as possible without any censorship.
- Discussing, critiquing, and possibly prioritizing the brainstorming results for later action. This last step is often called the "convergent" phase where there is a winnowing of all the ideas into the ones that are judged as most applicable to a problem.

② Synectics

Synectics is a systematic problem solving methodology that stimulates thinking processes via metaphor and analogy and emphasizes the importance of integration of individual opinions. It was developed by George M. Prince and William J.J. Gordon in the 1950s (Gordon 1961). The methodology has evolved substantially in the ensuing 50 years (Nolan 2003).

The main idea is to link initially unrelated issues together to change thinking models and then produce new concepts. During the process, random text tables, dictionaries and newspapers could be utilized as aids to provoke associations and multiple links. These associations and links originated from mostly physical objects. Synectics enables every member of a team to contribute to the results with his/her own background.

Like brainstorming, synectics is a group activity in which criticism is ruled out, and the group members attempt to build, combine and develop ideas towards a creative solution to the set problem. Synectics is different from brainstorming in that the group tries to work collectively towards a particular solution, rather than generating a large number of ideas. A synectics session is much longer than brainstorming, and much more demanding.

The major process for synectics involves (Duin et al. 2009):

- Describe the topic. The moderator selects a topic and then asks all participants to describe it. Then, the words are collected either on the board or the overhead; all words are accepted.
- Create direct analogies. The moderator selects another word or topic and then asks the participants to create a list that would have the same characteristics as those words or phases listed in the predecessor step.
- Describe personal analogies. The moderator asks the work-group members to select one of the direct analogies and create personal analogies. The participants become the object they choose and then describe what it feels like to be that object.
- Identify compressed conflicts. The moderator asks the participants to pair words from the list generated in the last step that seem to contradict one another. Then the members are asked to choose one by voting.
- Create a new direct analogy. With the compressed conflict pair voted on by the participants, the moderator asks the members to create a different direct analogy by selecting something that is described by the paired words.
- Re-examine the original topic. Now the group returns to the original idea or problem so that the participants may produce a product or a description that utilises the ideas generated in the process.
- Evaluate. Led by the moderator the group reflects on the outcome and evaluates the usefulness of the results. This may include some ranking of the ideas.

③ Focus group discussion (McDonagh-Philp and Bruseberg 2000)

Focus groups involve gathering target users together for a relatively informal discussion on a specific topic or issue. A moderator promotes the discussion amongst the group, while carefully ensuring not to direct, but to guide the group through the issues of importance to them.

Focus groups are a useful tool in terms of the design and development of new products. They are a valuable technique for sounding out people on new ideas and enabling relevant ideas and preferences to be explored without making assumptions about respondents' views. The designers will allow insights into their lifestyles, their values, their reasons for choices, and various pieces of background information. And the content of the discussion might take unexpected directions or open up new topics.

Focus groups may be utilised for a variety of new product development projects prior to initial concept generation. This enables the product development team to become immersed in the user experience prior to the designing process. Once the concept generation stage has begun, preconceived design solutions may cause barriers to effective new product development. Therefore, employing Focus Group activities as early as possible in the product development process provides evidence on which to base the initial concept generation.

Major phases involved in focus group interview are as follows (Dilshad and Latif 2013):

- Planning the focus group. The researcher must be clear about the objective of the focus group. The participants should be contacted in advance and be made aware of the objective of the activity.
- Group composition. The members of the focus group are not selected randomly. Rather a purposive sampling method is normally used. The individuals who suit the topic/ problem under study are selected by the researcher.
- Conducting the focus group. The moderator introduces the questions one by one. To facilitate the interaction between the group members, he constantly provides probes and pauses, and involves people in discussion without expressing any value on the answers received.
- Recording the responses. Moderator or assistant moderator may record the discussions in written notes.
- Data analysis. Look at first for big ideas and making list of them, considering words and context of their use, trying to examine the strength of the reactions/ feelings, and striking balance between detail and conciseness (Anderson 1990).
- Reporting the findings. Combine narrative summaries with actual quotes that explain the participant's opinions in his or her own words.

④ Scenario

Scenario is time-based narrative used to describe process, action, and snapshots of events (Campbell 1992). It uses personal experiences to express the structure of a story through which designers can absorb and transfer related information internally or externally. It can be used to depict the implementation of advanced technology in fulfilling the users' life in the future (Nardi 1992). It can play roles of communication and guidance to assist the coordination of the design process and situation (Carroll 2000), and thus it is often used in industrial and service design to establish product image and bridge designers and managers in communication. It provides links and language for multidisciplinary collaborative design team.

The use of scenario often includes information collection through observation, establishing user needs and product insights through understanding user behaviors and intentions that they are not even aware of, and having empathy to place oneself into someone's shoes to design product, service, system and interaction (Brown 2009). Storyboards, snapshots, 5W1H are often used to illustrate the context where users interact with designed artifacts.

The brain basically functions as a scenario generating organ. In that sense it constantly scans the environments, tries to make sense of what it perceives, identifies alternative future developments, alternative goals and actions, decides what to do—and makes sure that necessary steps are taken. Transformed into a scenario planning framework, we could talk about the brain's "TAIDA process" (Lindgren and Bandhold 2003):

- Tracking. The main purpose of this step is to trace and describe changes in the surrounding world that may have an impact on the focal question.
- Analysing. With the tracking done, the next step is to analyse changes and generate scenarios.
- Imaging. After gathering insights about plausible futures, it is time to create images of what is desired: visions.
- Deciding. In this phase of the process we identify development areas and strategies to meet threats and achieve visions and goals.
- Acting. Plans in themselves rarely give results. Acting is about taking action and following up. We will show how scenario planning can be followed up.

1.3 The Relationship Between Design and Innovation

1.3.1 Linkage Between Design and Innovation

(1) Design dominates innovation

The role of design in organisational innovation has been the subject of much research—particularly in the design and development of new products (Dorst 2011; Verganti 2008). More recently, it has become widely understood that design can add significant value to a firm's strategic capabilities beyond the development of a product or service (Borja de Mozota 2010). Design has redefined itself from a purely downstream, manufacturing-related activity, to one which adds strategic value to business (Battistella et al. 2012; Martin and Martin 2009). This union of design and strategy is referred to as design-led innovation (DLI). DLI is a process for business transformation, providing a mechanism where businesses are able to create an alternative competitive advantage in the fast-paced global marketplace (Bucolo et al. 2012).

Design-led innovation is broadly defined as a method which allows a company to consider and evaluate radically new propositions from multiple perspectives, typically spanning user needs, business requirements and technology demands. The final design solution is not presented as an artefact in isolation, but as an integrated product and service concept which anticipates future user needs, builds future proposals and encourages feedback. Key to this process is that design is core to a company's vision, strategy, culture, leadership and development processes (Bucolo and Matthews 2011).

Design-led innovation is positioned at the intersection of design, innovation, and business—and thus serves as a viable and necessary tool in transitioning from artifact design to business model innovation (Dorst 2011). It is a "cross-functional, iterative approach to innovation that aligns organizations and generates business value each step of the way (Nieters and Pande 2012)."

Being design-led is defined as embodying a culture of design as the "dominant logic (Prahalad and Bettis 1986)." Indicators of a company-culture embodying design as a dominant logic include a culture that values curiosity, cross-functional empathy, individuals having broad observational insight, and design as a physical manifestation of the brand. Moreover, it is insufficient for companies simply to embed design at the styling stage; rather, design must be embedded throughout and begin at the opportunity identification and strategic setting stage (Beverland and Farrelly 2007).

(2) Design Inspires Innovation

Design-inspired innovation mainly promotes innovation by creating new product languages (the meaning of the product). In addition to functionality, what really matters to users is the emotional and symbolic value and meaning of the product. If functionality is designed to meet the actual needs of customers, the meaning of the product will stimulate people's emotional and sociocultural needs.

Design-inspired innovation balances the property of new meaning with commercial value and technological feasibility. "In design-inspired innovation, the balance among technology, market, and meaning is unique. None can be neglected."

Design-inspired innovation requires creativity of a higher order, whether the products are professional tools, machinery for production, consumer goods, or services. It is, in essence, a synthesis of technology and users' experiences—boundaries that we observe blurring. Increasingly, products succeed because they have associated software and services that enhance their value.

What is peculiar in design-inspired innovation is that designers act as brokers of knowledge about languages rather than technology. Of course, technological competence is still crucial (as a means of speaking new languages), but the greatest value comes from their ability to understand the subtle dynamics of values and meanings in society and the impact these have on product language. They facilitate their manufacturing clients' access to the ongoing discussion about these dynamics and languages. They bring bits of knowledge, helping their clients interpret the design discourse, and position themselves in this discourse (Utterback et al. 2006).

(3) Design: the heart of innovation

Some studies refer to "design" as the core of the innovation process. These studies emphasize the role of "design" as the innermost part of the innovation process. Aubert (1982) defines design as "the very core of innovation, the moment when a new object is imagined, devised and shaped in prototype form." Design is considered as set of deliberate activities to create new products (goods and services) that are novel and significantly valuable.

Innovation entails resources such as R&D and design (Freeman 1982), because design activity extends the usefulness of a new or existing innovation and helps the products suit user needs more accurately (Oakley 1990). Design introduces technology into the social fabric (Aubert 1985). So even the most radical technological innovation has to be embodied in usable form via the design process.

Design clearly plays an important role in the realisation of the radical invention as an innovation; in particular, systemic innovations need a great deal of design co-ordination in development and commercialisation because systematic adjustments to other parts of the system have to be made (Walsh 1996).

1.3.2 Distinction Between Design and Innovation

(1) Design does not always seek something new

Design aims to identify needs and solve problems, but not necessarily to seek new things, because there are many ready-made design solutions that can be applied to different scenarios and solve different problems. And to achieve innovation, we usually need to break the rules and look at certain types of problems from a new perspective.

All products are designed, even though they may not be designed by a professional designer, and even though they may not incorporate any technological innovations (Walsh 1996), for example the new styling for a car body or a new pattern on a toaster or arrangement of controls on a cooker. Fashion design has been described as the creation of "non-innovative novelties (Piatier 1984)."

While this business of innovation requires Design, it is not Design, as Design is about more than the development of new or inventive artifacts. Design as a pure area of research, just like science as a pure area of research, is not necessarily interested in the application of its study, nor should it be. Instead, it is interested in discovery, which at some point might be applied in valuable, pragmatic, new ways (Kolko 2007).

Design aims to find needs and solve problems, but does not necessarily involve innovation (especially technological innovation), because there are many ready-made designs that can be applied to different scenarios to solve different problems. However, when we achieve innovation, we usually need to break the rules and look at some kind of problem from a new perspective.

(2) Innovation results are not necessarily in the form of design

There are products or services that are essentially the reassociation and integration of resources, creative problem solving solutions that do not take the form of "design". These products or services contribute to sustained beneficial social change.

Traditionally, designers focused their attention on improving the look and functionality of products. Classic examples of this type of design work are Apple Computer's iPod and Herman Miller's Aeron chair (Brown and Wyatt 2010). In recent years design professionals have been pushing design beyond being just engaged with consumer culture and exploring new forms of practice. This is particularly evident when design is used to tackle social issues to create innovative solutions (Margolin and Margolin 2002).

There is growing consensus that design can be a mode of innovation that provides a set of skills, tools and methods that guide people to new socially innovative solutions or improvement of existing ones. Social innovation is "innovation that is explicitly for the social and public good. It is innovation inspired by the desire to meet social needs which can be neglected by traditional forms of private market provision and which have often been poorly served or unresolved by services organised by the state (Murray et al. 2010)."

A famous example is the Slow Food Movement from Italy, which calls on people to oppose standardized, homogeneous fast-food like hamburgers and promotes individualized, nutritionally balanced traditional cuisine. In this process, consumers and producers share the cost of producing high-quality food while jointly shouldering the responsibility in society. It represents a reintegration of resources, a creative solution to problems, and is a typical case of social innovation. It also embodies a human-centered design thinking, even though it may not be explicitly expressed in the form of "design".

Slow Food is an organization that promotes local food and traditional cooking. It was founded by Carlo Petrini in Italy in 1986 and has since spread worldwide (Slow Food 2022). Promoted as an alternative to fast food, it strives to preserve traditional and regional cuisine and encourages farming of plants, seeds, and livestock characteristic of the local ecosystem. It sees globalization as a process in which small and local farmers and food producers should be simultaneously protected from and included in the global food system.

1.4 Intellectual Property Protection for Design and Innovation

1.4.1 Intellectual Property Rights Safeguard Design and Innovation

According to the World Intellectual Property Organization (2022), Intellectual property (IP) refers to creations of the mind, such as inventions; literary and artistic works; designs; and symbols, names and images used in commerce.

The term intellectual property gained ground in the nineteenth century but only became popular in global legal systems in the twentieth century. The various types of intellectual property include copyrights, patents, trademarks and trade secrets industrial designs, models software, data base rights etc. Intellectual property is an asset, a creation of the mind, a unique ingenuity belonging to the owner, who is like a creator. There are two broad classes of intellectual property, namely; Copyright is concerned with protection Literary, musical and artistic creations whilst industrial property is concerned with protection of trademarks, industrial designs, patents, models, plants and animal varieties etc (Anyogu and Ozioko 2022).

The IP rights relate not to the physical machine, painting, book, or logo but confer certain privileges over "aspects of the ideas, expressions, knowledge, or information contained in these things" (Prager 1944). It provides ownership, irrespective of where it has derivatives from, in the "exclusive right to use, possess, and dispose of property..." that has economic value (Jonas et al. 2010). The rights given under intellectual property are usually protected to ensure that these rights enable the owner or the authorized person to have to themselves the economic and proprietary value of the assets and to be able to alienate same (Anyogu and Ozioko 2022). The rights and interests deriving from IP are often time-limited such as patents and copyrights (Anderson 2012).

In terms of technological innovation, intellectual property system itself is a product of technological innovation. In order to protected the legitimate interests of technology innovators and brought due interest returns which were obtained from the huge investment on innovation and invention, the intellectual property system came into being as the times require. Currently, more than 150 countries around the world have established their own intellectual property rights system in varying degrees. Intellectual property right system has become the most important laws for the innovation of science and technology. Technological innovation is difficult and has huge investment, but it is easy to be copied and imitated. Technological imitators or plagiarists do not invest in technological innovation, but can but can benefit from it, and technological innovators have fewer profits, even they can not recoup their investment. If there is no intellectual property system, the driving force of interests for technological innovation will disappear and technical innovation will impossible (Li 2020).

Technical innovation drives overall industry upgrades, and design innovation increase added value of products (Fan 2008). For certain categories of products with mature techniques, such as smartphones and clothing, design innovation is the direct basis upon which consumers decide whether to make a purchase and, to some extent, has already become a competitive advantage for many companies. Because industrial design and its innovations entail certain costs and are susceptible to imitation or replication, innovative-leading companies must protect this advantage by utilizing intellectual property laws and regulations (Lin and Wu 2016).

1.4.2 Design Companies Must Value Intellectual Property in International Competition

With the development of the digital economy and the implementation of the Belt and Road Initiative proposed by China, intellectual property rights (IPR) issue involved is more complex and problematic for Chinese design enterprises in the process of internationalization. At present, the intellectual property disputes faced by Chinese design enterprises in international trade mainly involve the United

States, the European Union and Japan, etc. The following is an overview of the frictions between China-US, China-EU and China-Japan respectively.

(1) China-US Intellectual Property Disputes

During the transformation and upgrade of China's manufacturing industry, the international trade that imports China's products with advanced technological level and added value have exposed U.S. domestic firms to tougher product market competition. At the same time, the intellectual property friction between China and the U.S. is heating up, mainly at the government level and enterprise level.

At the government level, as early as the late 1980s, China and the U.S. had held negotiations on the protection of intellectual property rights and drafted a memorandum on intellectual property rights protection. Around 1992, when China's IPR laws had not been made compliant with international IPR treaties, the U.S. strongly suggested that China should accelerate legislation on IPRs, and the two sides signed the Memorandum of Understanding between the Government of the People's Republic of China and the Government of the United States of America on the Protection of Intellectual Property. In 1994, the U.S. and China negotiated again on IPR issues and agreed to sign the Action Plan for the Effective Protection and Enforcement of IPRs. From 1995 to 2001, emphasis had been placed on the effective judicial enforcement of IPR in China (Zhang and Meng 2022).

After China's accession to the WTO in 2001, with international market conditions changing and U.S. trade policies adjusted, intellectual property issues once again became a major issue to be resolved in Sino-U.S. trade relations. In 2004, the U.S. raised its concern regarding IP protection in China, claiming that China's progress on intellectual property protection after its accession to the WTO was lagging behind compared with achievements in other fields (Zhang and Meng 2022). In 2005, China was placed on the Priority Watch List by the U.S. In 2006, China was on the top of the Priority Watch List. In 2007, the U.S. filed WTO lawsuits against China with respect to the deficiencies in China's legal structure to enforce intellectual property protection. Since then, the friction between U.S. and China on IPR issue has continued, featured by the former one frequently launching Section 301 Investigation and Section 337 Investigation against China.

In August 2017, the Office of the United States Trade Representative announced the launch of the sixth round of investigation into China's acts pursuant to Section 301. Findings showed deficiencies in China's intellectual property system, legislation, market legal environment, and the ineffective enforcement of IPR, which hinders the development of the international market. The United States required China to strictly protect U.S. intellectual property rights and provide fair market access for American citizens; while in fact, it was a form of strategic containment and suppression implemented by the U.S. which refers directly to Made in China 2025 Plan, especially regarding China's intellectual property-intensive industries, such as microchips, electric vehicles, etc.

It was followed by the issue of a ban on China's ZTE by the US Department of Commerce, leaving it in an unprecedented dilemma. Ostensibly, ZTE was accused for reselling American chips to Iran, which was currently under the U.S. embargoes.

But some experts believed that this accusation was actually great cover to suppress China's scientific and technological innovation. Soon, Huawei, China's leading high-tech enterprise, was also suppressed by the United States. For many years, Huawei used Google's Android system to promote products, and a large number of chips needed to manufacture products were also procured from global suppliers such as the United States. This means that once the United States announces to stop or reduce the supply of key parts of Huawei products like chips and operating systems, then Huawei will face huge risks in global operations. In 2019, Huawei was sanctioned by the United States for developing 5G technology. The shortage of parts for Huawei 5G communication equipment even forced the company to sell 4G mobile phones in the 5G era. In August 2022, the U.S. government promulgated the CHIPS and Science Act, aiming to provide huge subsidies and tax incentives for the U.S. domestic chip industry. The bill attempted to attract semiconductor companies to set up factories in the United States through investment subsidies, and to prevent semiconductor companies from increasing production in China by limiting the eligibility of subsidies, thus containing the development of China's chip industry.

At the enterprise level, Section 337 Investigation has become an important measure to restrict the entry of Chinese enterprise products into the US market. Since China's accession to the WTO, with a large number of Chinese products exported to the United States, China's mainland enterprises have replaced China's Taiwan region and Japan, and become the priority target of the investigation initiated by the United States. From 2002 to 2017, China has been the largest victim of the US Section 337 Investigation for 16 years. The average annual proportion of Chinese firms sued was up to 33.25% (Feng and Zhang 2019). In the past 10 years, the number of investigations involving Chinese enterprises remains high. According to the relevant data released by China Trade Relief Information Network and the official website of the United States International Trade Commission, from 2012 to 2021, of the 599 concluded cases in Section 337 Investigations, 558 Chinese enterprises faced charges from the U.S. commission. Only 29 Chinese companies were found non-infringement, and the non-infringement winning rate of Chinese enterprises was only about 5.2%.

In addition to the Section 337 Investigation, since 2006 the Office of the United States Trade Representative (USTR) has also identified a Notorious Markets List in the Special 301 Report. In 2010, USTR announced that the Notorious Markets List would be listed separately from the annual Special 301 Report as an irregular review report. In 2005, USTR pointed out in the Special 301 Report that China's Internet piracy problem turned out a primary threat to the US copyright industries and that service providers were still not held liable for infringing material due to loopholes in existing regulations throughout China. In September 2005, Baidu was sued by an American music company because its MP3 search engine violated copyright. In 2006, Baidu was included in the Notorious Markets List by the United States. Since then, Taobao, Alibaba, Tencent, Thunder, Sohu and many other domestic online platforms have been added to the list one after another. The latest 2022 Review of Notorious Markets highlights 9 physical markets in China. Although the list has no legal significance, its impact on corporate reputation cannot be underestimated.

In recent years, U.S. courts have frequently extended their reach by imposing long-arm jurisdiction in transnational intellectual property litigation between Chinese companies and western companies, which sets Chinese companies against lawsuits and hinders overseas business development. The term long-arm jurisdiction refers to a concept in the American judicial system, which mainly appeared after the Second World War. In the narrow sense, long-arm jurisdiction is the power of a court to assert personal jurisdiction over an out-of-state defendant, provided that the defendant has a sufficient connection with the state. In a broad sense, long-arm jurisdiction refers to the extraterritorial jurisdiction of the United States government (including the executive, legislative and judicial departments) over foreign citizens, corporate legal persons and even government departments under its domestic law (Wang 2020).

At present, Chinese enterprises are the main target of the US courts to implement long-arm jurisdiction, which covers export control, financial sanctions and intellectual property rights. With the intensified competition between China and the United States, the U.S. Department of Commerce began to sanction Chinese high-tech enterprises more frequently by abusing the U.S. Export Administration Regulations, International Emergency Economic Powers Act, etc. Huawei, DJI, Hikvision, IFLYTEK, BGI, CGN and other leading Chinese technology enterprises from various industries have been included in the Entity List by the U.S. Department of Commerce's Bureau of Industry and Security on charges that activities of these companies may harm the interests of U.S. national security and foreign policy, prohibiting U.S. and other national enterprises from supplying materials containing U.S. technology, equipment, parts and raw materials. According to these laws, regardless of whether Chinese enterprises have direct links with the United States, as long as the operations involve US products and technologies, the US Department of Commerce shall have the right to impose long-arm jurisdiction and cut off US technology and product supply at any time (Zhang et al. 2021).

(2) China-EU Intellectual Property Disputes

As one of China's largest trading partners, the bilateral trade friction between China and European Union in goods, services, technology and other fields has grown increasingly intense. Among them, emerging trade friction caused by intellectual property has become an important part of trade friction between China and Europe. The friction between China and Europe over intellectual property rights is mainly manifested at two levels: government and enterprise.

On the government level, since our country acceded to WTO, the EU has repeatedly required our country to strengthen IPR protection and fulfill commitments on IPR protection (i.e., Agreement on Trade-Related Aspects of Intellectual Property Rights (TRIPS Agreement)). Then, in July 2003, the EU promulgated the Council Regulation (EC) No 1383/2003 of 22 July 2003. This regulation is the main IPR regulation for international trade, which indicates that the EU has formed a relatively mature and complete IPR system. In developing economic and trade relations with China, the EU has begun to pay more attention to the protection of IPR. Between 2004 and 2006, the EU Trade Representative Lord Mandelson visited China four times and focused throughout on the protection of IPR. In 2004, the European Commission conducted research of the EU companies in China and found that 70% of those companies believed that China's IPR protection was poor implemented. It also submitted a proposal on IPR Protection to the Ministry of Commerce of China (Zhang et al. 2012), which suggested lowering the threshold for infringement investigations and increasing penalties. In June 2006, the EU and the US jointly launched anti-counterfeiting operations against global IPR infringement. According to EU statistics, 80% of counterfeit products seized at EU borders in 2006 came from China (Chen 2008), which seriously threatens the competitiveness of EU products. In November 2006, China and the EU signed the Memorandum of Understanding on Strengthening Cooperation on Intellectual Property Protection. However, EU governments continually pressured China, urging the Chinese government to take concrete actions to clean up the retail and wholesale markets where shoddy products are suspected of being sold, strengthen the protection of EU countries' intellectual property rights while introducing technology, prevent Chinese companies from illegally obtaining EU technology, and create a fairer environment for EU technology transfer.

On the enterprise level, Wenzhou lighters were challenged by Child Resistance Law of the EU in 2001, which fostered the conflict of intellectual property protection in bilateral trade between China and Europe. In 2002, DVDS exported from China to the EU were detained by British and German customs because of intellectual property issues. In the same year, European color TV producer Thomson sued China for patent infringement, which blocked Chinese color TV exports to the EU for a long time. In 2004, Hamburg Customs destroyed 10,000 Chinese-made tea cups in accordance with the EU's new customs protection law on intellectual property. As the first case after the EU new Customs intellectual property protection Act came into force, it has strong demonstration effect (Wu 2011). In 2005, the Chinese company HiSense's trademark "Hisense" was registered in advance by Siemens in Germany, which resulted in Siemens suing the company for trademark infringement when its products entered German market. In 2006, the EU Agreement on the Trade in Counterfeit Goods was adopted, which means the EU will further strengthen the protection of IPR and stricter controls. At the 2007 and 2008 CEBIT in Germany, Chinese booths were seized by German police for multiple times, which had very bad effects on the international image of Chinese companies. In 2010, more than 85 percent of the ships and products stopped by EU customs were "infringing products" from China.

In addition, European enterprises also challenged China's enterprises through various means. Since 2017, the dispute between Huawei and Conversant over standards-essential patents has continued. The two sides disagreed over patent licensing rates and had taken to several courts in China and abroad. In 2020, the non-infringement lawsuit initiated by Huawei against Conversant in the first instance judgment, and the Supreme People's Court issued the first injunction in the field of intellectual property rights in China, safeguarding the legitimate rights and interests of Chinese enterprises.

In 2018, GuangDong OPPO Mobile Telecommunications Corp., Ltd. officially entered the European market. The following year, Sisvel, an Italian patent litigation and licensing organization, launched a large-scale patent war against OPPO in the

United Kingdom, the Netherlands, Italy and other places. In April 2019, Sisvel launched another patent infringement lawsuit against Xiaomi, OPPO and other Chinese manufacturers in the UK, involving 3 communications patents. In June of that year, Sisvel filed a patent infringement lawsuit against OPPO, OnePlus and Xiaomi in the Hague, Netherlands. On May 27, 2020, the Hague Court ruled that the patent Sisvel used to Sue OPPO in the Netherlands was invalid due to the lack of creativity. As a result, Sisvel lost its Dutch patent case against OPPO, and the threat of a sales ban on OPPO in the Dutch market was lifted.

Despite the constant friction over IPR between China and the EU, the EU does not ignore the measures China has taken to strengthen IPR protection and open wider to the outside world, but rather adopts an active attitude to China. In the Joint Statement of the 20th China-Eu Summit, the EU recognized China's recent efforts to improve market access and investment environment, strengthen intellectual property rights protection and expand imports, and looked forward to the full implementation of these measures and further actions. In addition, on 15 July 2018, the leaders of China and the EU reached an agreement on cooperation, in which the two sides planned to explore the possibilities of strengthening cooperation based on current situation, safeguard multilateral mechanisms and measures to promote trade and investment, and coordinate positions on addressing major international challenges (Bai 2019). With the continuous and rapid development of China's economy and the continuous expansion and improvement of the integration degree of the European Union, the intellectual property frictions between China and the European Union will likely continue to be high for a long time, but the exchanges and cooperation between China and the European Union will not be absent.

(3) China-Japan Intellectual Property Disputes

As China boasts continuous advancement in science and technology and rapid economic growth, Japan's status as an economic powerhouse is being undermined by emerging economies and developing countries represented by China. A large number of Chinese products have entered the Japanese market. Inevitably, intellectual property friction between China and Japan intensified. The government and enterprise did the following:

At the government level, starting from the end of the nineteenth century, Japan established a relatively complete legal system and management agency to protect intellectual property rights, gradually forming a comparatively well-established intellectual property protection system. From the 1950s to the 70 s, the Japanese government adopted a patent strategy to build a patent network and protect the domestic market. After the 1970s, Japan's patent strategy focused on technological innovation and independent patents (Ma and Ma 2009). At the beginning of the twenty-first century, the intellectual property rights of Japanese companies were severely infringed abroad. In response, Japan formulated and published the "Intellectual Property Strategy Outline" in July 2002, aiming to enhance the industry's international competitiveness. The outline proposed intellectual property strategy slogans and established a comprehensive intellectual property strategy, including innovation and intellectual property protection (Wang and He 2007). Guided by this outline, Japan is highly concerned about the problems faced by domestic enterprises concerning intellectual property rights in the Chinese market. At the end of 2002, the Japanese Chamber of Commerce and Industry in China surveyed 2917 Japanese member companies invested in China. It showed that 53.4% of companies had suffered intellectual property infringement to varying degrees. Trademark infringement and design infringement were common types of infringement, with 71.8% and 68.5% of Japanese companies suffered, respectively. At the same time, Japan was asking for intellectual property negotiations with China, and on various occasions, it has called on China to strengthen the legal enforcement of intellectual property protection.

At the enterprise level, in 1997, Japan's Honda Motor Corporation began suing Shanghai Feiling Motorcycle Manufacturing Co., Ltd., Zhejiang Huangyan Huari (Group), and Henan Huangyan Huari (Group), Xinxiang Motorcycle Co., Ltd. for infringing on the patents for design and the invention of their motor scooters. In 2003, Omron Co., Ltd. also sued companies such as Beijing Sanhe Songshi Electromechanical Co., Ltd. for the infringement of design patents. In the same year, Japan's Kumamoto Agricultural Research Center passed DNA testing, believing that the bulrush used in Chinese tatami mats was "Hino green" developed by Kumamoto, which infringed on its "breeders' rights" (patent rights), and demanded a ban on importing this kind of bulrush from China and tatami mats made from it. In 2015, Japan's Panasonic Corporation filed an appeal against Zhuhai Kingdom Electrical Appliance Co., Ltd. and Beijing Likang Fuya Trading Co., Ltd., arguing that a beauty device it produced, sold, and promised to sell infringed on Panasonic's design patent rights, and demanded that the defendants stop the infringement and pay compensation for related economic losses and reasonable expenses. In 2017, the famous Japanese company Canon Co., Ltd. took it to court on the grounds that the toner cartridges manufactured, sold, and promised to be sold by Shanghai Mooming Electronic Technology Co., Ltd. infringed its patent rights.

Furthermore, Japanese companies have also used various means to launch an offensive against Chinese enterprises. In 2017, Shimano Co., Ltd. (Japan), a world-renowned bicycle parts manufacturer, sued China's Sensah Corporation for infringing its patent rights. The Court of First Instance found that the alleged infringing product fell within the scope of patent protection in this case, that Sensah Company constituted infringement, and ruled that it ceased infringement and compensated for losses. Sentah Company disagreed and appealed to the Guangdong Higher People's Court. The Court of Second Instance held that the corresponding technical features of the accused infringing product constituted equivalent to one of the technical features of the involved patent, but as the accused infringing product did not possess another technical feature of the involved patent, it did not apply to the scope of patent protection. Therefore, Sentah Company did not constitute infringement. As a result, the Court of Second Instance rejected all of Shimano Co., Ltd.'s lawsuits, settled disputes between world-renowned Japanese companies and domestic private enterprises in a relatively fair manner, and safeguarded the legitimate rights and interests of Chinese enterprises.

In January 2020, Sharp Corporation filed a patent infringement lawsuit with the Tokyo District Court, accusing OPPO Japan of infringing on its WLAN patent relating to mobile phone communication technology and requesting the court to issue a temporary restraining order(TRO) against OPPO Japan. OPPO immediately took a hard line against Sharp's patent lawsuit. At the end of February, in Tokyo, Japan, it countersued Sharp for infringing on its flash charging technology patent. At the same time, it sued Sharp at Shenzhen Intermediate Court for violating the FRAND principle, requesting the court to decide on the global rate for licensing OPPO's relevant standard essential patents owned by Sharp Corporation. Meanwhile, OPPO applied for behavior preservation, given the possibility that Sharp Corporation might use an "extraterritorial injunction" to coerce it into negotiations. The Court of First Instance ruled that Sharp Corporation may not file a new lawsuit or judicial injunction against OPPO concerning the patents involved in this case in other countries or regions until the final judgment, in this case, is made. Seven hours after the Court of First Instance issued an "anti-suit injunction," Sharp requested that Germany's Munich District Court No. 1 issue an "anti-anti-suit injunction" against OPPO, requesting OPPO to apply to the Chinese court to withdraw the injunction. The court of first instance conducted a court investigation on the "anti-suit injunction" and the "anti-anti-suit injunction", presented the facts and evidence of Sharp Corporation's violation of the preservation ruling, and explained to it the dire legal consequences of violating the Chinese court decision. In the end, Sharp Corp. unconditionally withdrew the application for reconsideration and the "anti-anti-suit injunction" applied to the German court in this case, and OPPO's interests were preserved.

Intellectual property friction between China and Japan is growing intense. The reason behind it, on the one hand, is that Japan pays special attention to the interests of domestic companies operating overseas. On the other, the US is playing a vital role. Since forming the US-Japan alliance, Japan has followed the United States and is keen to act as America's spokesperson in the Asia-Pacific region. Meanwhile, considering factors such as geographical importance, the US will also preserve the US-Japan alliance. Most of the time, Japan holds a similar position in international agreements with America. During Obama's administration, the US pushed for the signing of the TPP ("Trans-Pacific Partnership Agreement") in the Asia-Pacific region, excluding China. Later, when Trump took office, he pushed for the "America First" policy by abandoning the liberal internationalism advocated by the US after World War II, adopting trade protectionism, opposing other countries to continue "hitchhiking", emphasizing safeguarding national interests, so he chose to withdraw from the TPP. After the US withdrawal, Japan rejoined ten other member countries to sign the new free trade agreement CPTPP (Comprehensive and Progressive Agreement for Trans-Pacific Partnership, also known as TPP11). At the same time, the Japan-led CPTPP has also kept the door open for the US. The most obvious sign is that Japan persuaded the rest of the member countries to freeze rather than delete many of the provisions that the US is seeking so that the US can return as easy as possible when prepared (Zhang and Yang 2019). However, when China applied to join the CPTPP in September 2021, Japan clearly questioned it. Japan believed that if China were allowed to join the CPTPP as it was, the CPTPP would lose its value as it was designed to become a "high-level trade agreement." This shows that Japan still regards the US-Japan alliance as the cornerstone of its diplomatic policy and is trying to constrain China's development.

To sum up, in an evermore increasingly competitive international market, Chinese design enterprises, whether "going global" or "bringing in", should make all the necessary preparations before starting. They should actively encourage innovation, increase investment in intellectual property rights, improve research and development capacity, build their core technologies, attach importance to intellectual property protection, and adapt to foreign intellectual property environment as soon as possible, to make it easier to go abroad and achieve sustainable development. Furthermore, from the above cases, we can see the fundamental problem that Chinese enterprises lack originality in their designs. Before China joined the WTO, due to technical limitations and other factors, domestic enterprises generally drew on designs from other countries, then made improvements to form new products thereupon to win price competition. Very few enterprises innovated independently. After China joined the WTO, there were some improvements to this problem, but it has not been eradicated. It is hoped that in the future, China's design enterprises will increase their investment in scientific research and innovation to create their core patents and truly achieve "intelligently" manufacturing in China.

References

Anderson G (1990) Fundamentals of educational research. The Falmer Press, London

Anderson J (2012) Options for the future protection of GRTKTCES: the traditional knowledge license and labels initiative. J World Intellect Prop Org 4(1):73–82

Anyogu FA, Ozioko MVC (2022) Intellectual property and sustainability of global development processes in Nigeria. Int Rev Law Jurisprudence 4(1):125–128

Aubert JE (1982) Innovation in small and medium firms. Organisation for Economic Co-operation and Development, Paris

Aubert JE (1985) The approach of design and concepts of innovation policy. In: Design and innovation: policy and management

Bai M (2019) EU's situation and choice in Sino-US trade friction. Financ Manag Res 1:55–57

Battistella C, Biotto G, De Toni AF (2012) From design driven innovation to meaning strategy. Manag Decis 4:718–743

Beverland M, Farrelly FJ (2007) What does it mean to be design-led? Des Manag Rev 18(4):10–17

Borja de Mozota B (2010) Design management as core competency: from "design you can see" to "design you can't see". J Des Strateg 4(1):91–98

Brown T (2009) Change by design: how design thinking transforms organizations and inspires innovation. Harper Business, New York

Brown T, Wyatt J (2010) Design thinking for social innovation. Dev Outreach 12(1):29–43

Buchanan R (2001) Human dignity and human rights: thoughts on the principles of human-centered design. Des Issues 17(3):35–39

Bucolo S, Matthews J (2011) Design-led innovation-exploring the synthesis of needs, technologies and business models. In: Paper presented at the Participatory innovation conference proceedings. University of Southern Denmark, pp 351–354

Bucolo S, Wrigley C, Matthews J (2012) Gaps in organizational leadership: linking strategic and operational activities through design-led propositions. Des Manag J 7(1):18–28
Campbell RL (1992) Will the real scenario please stand up? ACM Sigchi Bull 24(2):6–8
Carroll JM (2000) Five reasons for scenario-based design. Interact Comput 13(1):43–60
Chen YJ (2008) Intellectual property protection in Sino-EU trade. Pract Foreign Econ Relat Trade 5:20–23
Cooper A (1999) The inmates are running the asylum. Macmillan Publishing Co., Inc.
Dilshad RM, Latif MI (2013) Focus group interview as a tool for qualitative research: an analysis. Pak J Soc Sci 33(1):191–198
Dorst K (2011) The core of "design thinking" and its application. Des Stud 32(6):521–532
Drucker PF (1985) Innovation and entrepreneurship practice and principles. Harper & Row Publisher, New York
Duin H, Hauge JB, Thoben KD (2009) An ideation game conception based on the synectics method. On Horizon 17(4):286–295
Eekels J (2000) On the fundamentals of engineering design science: the geography of engineering design science. Part 1. J Eng Des 11(4):377–397
Eekels J (2001) On the fundamentals of engineering design science: the geography of engineering design science. Part 2. J Eng Des 12(3):255–281
Fan QH (2008) The relation between industrial design and intellectual property. Art Des (Theory) 4:22–24
Feng XL, Zhang X (2019) China's intellectual property strategy under the background of Sino-US Trade Friction. Intertrade 1:44–51
Frascara J (2004) Communication design. Allworth Press, New York
Freeman C (1982) The economics of industrial innovation. Frances Pinter, London
Fu KK, Yang MC, Wood KL (2015) Design principles: the foundation of design. In: Paper presented at the International design engineering technical conferences and computers and information in engineering conference. American Society of Mechanical Engineers
Gordon WJJ (1961) Synectics: the development of creative capacity. Harper and Row, New York
Grawe SJ (2009) Logistics innovation: a literature-based conceptual framework. Int J Logist Manag 20(3):360–377
Holmlid S, Evenson S (2008) Bringing service design to service sciences, management and engineering. Springer, Boston, pp 341–345
Hyundai Doosan Infracore Concept-X excavator. https://ifdesign.com/en/winner-ranking/project/concept-x/309509. Accessed 7 May 2023
Indianapolis Council D (2011) Design for innovation. Design Council, London, p 27
Jonas H, Bavikatte K, Shrumm H (2010) Community protocols and access and benefit sharing. Asian Biotechnol Dev Rev 12(3):49–76
Khandwalla PN (1976) Some top management styles, their context and performance. Org Adm Sci 7(4):21–51
Kolko J (2007) The tenuous relationship between design and innovation. Artifact 1(3):198–203
Kouprie M, Visser FS (2009) A framework for empathy in design: stepping into and out of the user's life. J Eng Des 20(5):437–448
Krippendorff K (2011) Principles of design and a trajectory of artificiality. J Prod Innov Manag 28(3):411–418
Li MX (2020) Research on technological innovation and intellectual property protection of small and medium-sized enterprises in China. Int J Trend Res Dev 7(4):36–38
Lin XY, Wu S (2016) Present situation and trend of design innovation and intellectual property development. Globalization 2:104–119+134
Lin PH, Yeh ML, Lin HY (2019) Design for aesthetic pleasure. In: Rau PLP (ed) Cross-cultural design. Methods, tools and user experience. Springer, Cham, pp 519–530
Lindgren M, Bandhold H (2003) Scenario planning. Palgrave, London
Ma HZ, Ma H (2009) International experiences of intellectual property law enforcement in foreign trade and implications for China. Int Econ Trade Res 25(02):77–81

Margolin V, Margolin S (2002) A "social model" of design: issues of practice and research. Des Issues 18(4):24–30
Martin R, Martin RL (2009) The design of business: why design thinking is the next competitive advantage. Harvard Business Press, Boston
MartÍnez-Ros E, Orfila-Sintes F (2009) Innovation activity in the hotel industry. Technovation 29(9):632–641
McDonagh-Philp D, Bruseberg A (2000) Using focus groups to support new product development. Eng Des 26(5):4–9
Mortati M (2015) A framework for design innovation: present and future discussions. Des Issues 31(4):4–16
Murray R, Caulier-Grice J, Mulgan G (2010) The open book of social innovation. Nesta, London
Mutlu B, Er A (2003) Design innovation: historical and theoretical perspectives on product innovation by design. In: Paper presented at the 5th European academy of design conference, Barcelona
Nardi BA (1992) The use of scenarios in design. ACM Sigchi Bull 24(4):13–14
Nieters J, Pande A (2012) Rapid design labs: a tool to turbocharge design-led innovation. Interactions 19(3):72–77
Nolan V (2003) Whatever happened to synectics? Creat Innov Manag 12(1):24–27
Oakley M (1990) Design management: a handbook of issues & methods. Basil Blackwell, Oxford
Organisation for Economic Co-operation and Development (2005) Oslo manual: guidelines for collecting and interpreting innovation data. OECD Publishing, Paris
Papanek VJ (1985) Design for the real world. Academy Chicago Publishers, Chicago
Phan LL (2022) The design process and 5 reasons why it matters. Design delivery. https://blog.zeplin.io/the-design-process-and-5-reasons-why-it-matters. Accessed 27 Jun 2022
Piatier A (1984) Barriers to innovation. Frances Pinter, London
Prager FD (1944) A history of intellectual property from 1545 to 1787. J Pat Off Soc 26:711
Prahalad CK, Bettis RA (1986) The dominant logic: a new linkage between diversity and performance. Strateg Manag J 7(6):485–501
Pruitt J, Adlin T (2006) The persona lifecycle: keeping people in mind throughout product design. Morgan Kaufmann, San Francisco
Pruitt J, Grudin J (2003) Personas: practice and theory. In: Paper presented at the Proceedings of the 2003 conference on designing for user experiences, pp 1–15
Purchase NY (2021) Mastercard introduces accessible card for blind and partially sighted people. https://www.mastercard.com/news/press/2021/october/mastercard-introduces-accessible-card-for-blind-and-partially-sighted-people/. Accessed 7 Jun 2022
Ralph P, Wand Y (2009) A proposal for a formal definition of the design concept. Springer, Berlin, pp 103–136
Schumpeter JA (2013) Capitalism, socialism and democracy. Routledge, London
Schumpeter JA (2017) The theory of economic development: an inquiry into profits, capital, credit, interest, and the business cycle. Routledge, London
Slow Food. https://en.wikipedia.org/wiki/Slow_Food.Accessed 28 Jul 2022
Souder WE (1989) Improving productivity through technology push. Res Technol Manag 32(2):19–24
Srinivasan R, Lilien GL, Rangaswamy A et al (2012) The total product design concept and an application to the auto market. J Prod Innov Manag 29:3–20
Sutton RI, Hargadon A (1996) Brainstorming groups in context: effectiveness in a product design firm. Adm Sci Q 1996:685–718
Teece DJ (2010) Business models, business strategy and innovation. Long Range Plan 43(2–3):172–194
Tidd J, Bessant JR (2020) Managing innovation: integrating technological, market and organizational change. John Wiley & Sons, New Jersey
Tushman ML, Anderson P (2018) Technological discontinuities and organizational environments. Routledge, London, pp 345–372

Utterback JM, Ekman S, Sanderson SW et al (2006) Design-inspired innovation. World Scientific, Singapore
Verganti R (2008) Design, meanings, and radical innovation: a metamodel and a research agenda. J Prod Innov Manag 25(5):436–456
Verganti R (2009) Design driven innovation: changing the rules of competition by radically innovating what things mean. Harvard Business Press, Boston
Walsh V (1996) Design, innovation and the boundaries of the firm. Res Policy 25(4):509–529
Wang Z (2020) Re-thinking on the U.S. Long Arm Jurisdiction Policy to China in the new context of Sino-American relations. J Shanghai Univ Int Bus Econ 27(06):91–104
Wang X, He MH (2007) Study on state IPR strategy of Japan. East China Econ Manag 3:35–38
WIPO (2012) Special section the rise of design in innovation and intellectual property-Definitional and measurement issues. https://www.wipo.int/edocs/pubdocs/en/wipo_pub_941_2012-section1.pdf. Accessed 28 Jun 2022
WIPO. What is intellectual property?. https://www.wipo.int/about-ip/en/. Accessed 29 Jul 2022
Wu Y (2011) Analysis on the characteristics and development trend of economic and trade friction between China and EU. Stat Decis 17:141–144
Yang Y, Zhu D (2020) Environmental design vs. environmental art design: a Chinese perspective. J Hist Cult Art Res 9(4):122–133
Zhang H, Meng Y (2022) Impact of digital intellectual property rights friction between China and the United States on China-US trade. Jiangsu Sci Technol Inf 39(02):72–77
Zhang YT, Yang WD (2019) Japan's motivation for leading CPTPP and China's countermeasures. Contemp Econ Jpn 38(04):13–23
Zhang YL, Zhai XX, Zhou J (2012) Analysis of intellectual property friction in foreign trade of Chinese enterprises. Foreign Invest China 12:31–32
Zhang YR, Zhang XL, Yang JJ (2021) The extraterritorial abuse of US long-arm jurisdiction and China's countermeasures. Intertrade 3:36–43

Chapter 2
Design and Intellectual Property

2.1 The Relation Between Design and Intellectual Property

As a designer, inspiration is everywhere. Inspiration for design may come from the memories of a city, the reflections of a book, or the unique style of a work of art. In the design process, designers will inadvertently imitate the work of others. But there is a difference between being inspired by another work, between borrowing and copying, and the act of plagiarism is a violation of intellectual property rights, a wrongful infringement of intellectual property rights. Designers must be aware of the distinction between "being inspired by another's work" and "simply copying" in the design process. Even well-intentioned imitation or homage can infringe on the intellectual property rights of the original author and get you into considerable legal trouble. Therefore, it is important to always pay attention to the protection of intellectual property rights in the design process, not only by registering, registering and applying for your work in a timely manner, but also by being aware of the possibility of your work being considered as plagiarism and infringement of another's intellectual property rights. Only by having a deep understanding of the intellectual property system and keeping the concept of protecting intellectual property rights in mind can design be given new life.

Intellectual property, very broadly, refers to the legal rights which result from intellectual activity in the industrial, scientific, literary and artistic fields. Countries have laws to protect intellectual property for two main reasons. One is to give statutory expression to the moral and economic rights of creators in their creations and the rights of the public in access to those creations. The second is to promote, as a deliberate act of Government policy, creativity and the dissemination and application of its results and to encourage fair trading which would contribute to economic and social development (WIPO 2015).

Generally speaking, intellectual property law aims at safeguarding creators and other producers of intellectual goods and services by granting them certain time-limited rights to control the use made of those productions. Those rights do not

N. Jiang, *Design, Innovation and Intellectual Property*,
https://doi.org/10.1007/978-981-95-2042-8_2

apply to the physical object in which the creation may be embodied but instead to the intellectual creation as such. Intellectual property is traditionally divided into two branches, "industrial property" and "copyright."

The Convention Establishing the World Intellectual Property Organization, concluded in Stockholm on July 14, 1967 (Article 2(viii)) provides that "intellectual property shall include rights relating to:

- literary, artistic and scientific works,
- performances of performing artists, phonograms and broadcasts,
- inventions in all fields of human endeavor,
- scientific discoveries,
- industrial designs,
- trademarks, service marks and commercial names and designations,
- protection against unfair competition,
- and all other rights resulting from intellectual activity in the industrial, scientific, literary or artistic fields."

Please refer to Fig. 2.1. The areas mentioned as literary, artistic and scientific works belong to the copyright branch of intellectual property. The areas mentioned as performances of performing artists, phonograms and broadcasts are usually called "related rights", that is, rights related to copyright. The areas mentioned as inventions, industrial designs, trademarks, service marks and commercial names and designations constitute the industrial property branch of intellectual property. The area mentioned as protection against unfair competition can also be considered as belonging to that branch. The main intellectual property rights often encountered in design include copyright, patents, trademarks and unfair competition, which covers almost all branches of the intellectual property.

In all purposeful human activity, there are always two stages: design and implementation, and innovation is no exception. Only with the right design can there be successful innovation. This is the reason why innovative thinking and modern design can be linked to the need for it. Modern design is the development of

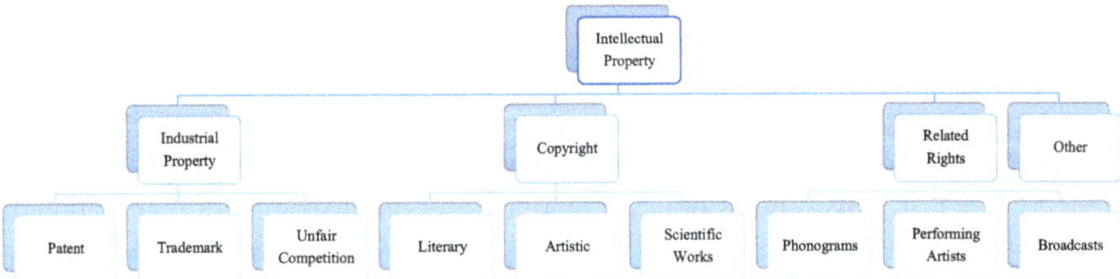

Fig. 2.1 Types of Intellectual Property. Note: Author independently created this figure based on the book content

traditional design, based on an awareness of the characteristics of the times, with a view to better supporting competition to win and innovation to succeed (Xie and Chen 2014).

2.1.1 The Importance of Design Intellectual Property in China

As China's economy enters a new normal and the role of intellectual property protection in promoting high-quality development becomes increasingly prominent, General Secretary Xi Jinping noted in an interview with Reuters that: "China's economic development is adjusting to the new normal and experiencing growing pains of shifting from old drivers of growth to new ones. Yet the fundamentals of a steadily growing economy have remained unchanged" (Reuters 2023). In the replacement process of the new normal economy development momentum, the innovation drive has replaced the scale drive as the primary driver of China's economic development. The guideline for IPR development (2021–2035) maps out a number of key tasks including establishing an IPR market operation mechanism that encourages innovation (Xinhua 2021), indicating that the concept that to protect intellectual property is to protect innovation is now ingrained in Chinese society.

The importance of design to the China economy is widely recognized. It is one of the key pillars of the knowledge economy, it plays an important role in the innovation process, and it is one of a number of specialisms that make China outstand from global competition. Despite this importance, the characteristic of intellectual property—intangibility—the ownership relationship is not as obvious as that of tangible property—makes intellectual property owners more likely to take the risk of IP infringement. This uncertainty renders it hard to analyze in advance, and makes it difficult to develop clear, consistent policies to support the designers.

2.1.2 Basic Attributes and Features of Design Intellectual Property

Before introducing design intellectual property, it is necessary to introduce basic attributes and features of intellectual property in order to have a comprehensive understanding of it.

As part of civil rights, intellectual property law has the nature of civil law.

(1) Private Rights

In the preamble of the Agreement on Trade-related Aspects of Intellectual Property Right, it states: "Recognizing the intellectual property rights are private rights." Private rights are generally understood as civil rights that a person has. Private rights are opposed to public rights.

(2) Human Rights

In 1976, Article 15 of the International Covenant on Economic, Social and Cultural Rights says: "The States Parties to the present Covenant recognize the right of everyone: To take part in cultural life; To enjoy the benefits of scientific progress and its applications; To benefit from the protection of the moral and material interests resulting from any scientific, literary or artistic production of which he is the author."

Human rights and private rights are fundamentally linked. With a logical knowledge and treatment of their relationship, it is conducive to a comprehensive understanding of intellectual property rights and to our thorough analysis of the values and social functions of the modern intellectual property system.

Compared to property rights, intellectual property rights are featured with the following characteristics:

(1) Intangible

It is obvious that intellectual property is a broad categorical description for the set of intangible assets owned and legally protected by a company or individual from outside use or implementation without consent. As a subset of intangible assets, intellectual property is not physical in nature as opposed to physical assets such as machinery (Kenton 2023).

(2) Exclusivity

Intellectual property rights holders shall have exclusive rights to their patents, trademarks, copyrights, etc., which means others, who are not owners, are prohibited from using the right (Bently and Sherman 2014). The creator or author of an intellectual property enjoys exclusive rights inherent in his work. In general, use without the authorization of the intellectual property rights holder is an infringement. This lack of knowledge of exclusivity is often a reason why some inventors have lost their entitlements.

(3) Territoriality

Intellectual property rights are of a territorial nature (Drexl et al. 2013). This means that the intellectual property rights generated in accordance with the laws of a certain country are valid within the territory where they are created. In accordance with the law having no binding force on other countries, foreign countries have no obligation to protect their rights.

(4) Timeliness

Knowledge should be shared, yet the exclusivity of specific products that have IP protection prevents others from exploiting them. If this effect is indefinite, societal innovation will be undermined; and if IPRs are protected for too little time, IP owners will find it challenging to realize financial goals or promote innovation.

Where design protection is not limited to the intended purpose of the underlying product or a particular dimension of the design, all prior designs are, in principle, to be considered as a relevant subject of comparison for testing validity of a design, irrespective of what purpose the prior design was or is intended to serve. When comparing prior art and the challenged later design all visible features which influence the overall impression of the prior art must be considered, the design's intellectual property rights typically include nature as followed.

(1) Novelty

The key date for assessing novelty is the date of filing of the application for registration or the date of priority. This appears to be common ground according to the law of numerous national jurisdictions. Designs examiners will not consider a design as new if they are aware of a prior publication of the same design and have some documentary evidence on which to base their objection to registration (Heath and Kamperman 2009).

(2) Individual character

The most difficult condition to determine for the design IP protection of a work is probably its individual character, because this always depends on the individual case. The work itself (and not the author) must show a certain degree of individuality or originality (CCdigitallaw 2022). This means it must stand out from what is considered usual and common. A work can still have an individual character even if similar works already exist, particularly if it stands out from existing works in terms of its content's own characteristics and unique aspects.

(3) Non-obviousness

An invention must be non-obvious to be patentable, and so do a design. The novelty and non-obviousness requirements work together. The former seeks to assure the public domain remains undisturbed, while the latter demands that the claimed invention be sufficiently removed from the prior art, meaning in most cases the invention reflects a leap forward (Nard et al. 2017). By way of exception from the scheme discussed above (novelty plus individual character), few countries established a specific standard requiring a certain degree of the link between the individual design at hand and the relevant prior art in order to find validity.

2.2 Legal Protection of Intellectual Property Rights for Designs

2.2.1 Copyright Law

(1) The Development of Copyright Law

The establishment of the copyright system in the People's Republic of China was greatly facilitated by the country's reform and opening-up policy. The "Copyright Law of the People's Republic of China" was deliberated and passed in 1990, officially coming into effect on June 1, 1991. Its primary purpose was to establish the basic framework for China's copyright system. In 2001, the "Copyright Law of the People's Republic of China" underwent its first revision. This revision reflected the interaction between international standards and China's specific circumstances. It played a crucial role in adjusting copyright creation, utilization, management, and protection in China after its accession to the World Trade Organization (WTO). This adjustment catered to the needs of China's socialist market economy while facing the challenges posed by new technologies, ultimately driving the development of China's copyright.

In 2010, the second decade since the implementation of the Copyright Law, the Standing Committee of the National People's Congress revised the law for the second time to comply with the WTO's ruling (WTO 2009) on the China-US intellectual property dispute. In 2020, the Copyright Law celebrated its 30th anniversary. Over the past three decades, it has played a significant role in promoting the development and prosperity of the economy, society, culture, and scientific endeavors. However, the rapid technological and social development has presented numerous new challenges concerning the creation, dissemination, utilization, management, and protection of copyright. Thus, the third revision of the Copyright Law came in 2020 and addressed several issues, including refining the definition of "works", strengthening copyright protection online, fulfilling obligations under relevant international treaties, and enhancing technical protection measures. These revisions demonstrated an open-minded approach to the categories of copyright subject matter within China's copyright legal system. However, the new amendment does not incorporate AI-generated outputs into the list of protectable subject matters, which means that AI-generated outputs can be protected in copyright only when they meet the relevant prerequisites for copyrightable works mentioned above (Wan and Lu 2021).

(2) The Relationship Between Copyright Law and Design

A copyright is an intellectual property right granted by a government to the author of an original literary, dramatic, musical, artistic, or other eligible creative work that gives them the exclusive right to control how the work is published, reproduced, performed, or displayed—as well as whether or not derivative works (e.g., a movie version of a novel) may be produced.

In China, the legal foundation for copyright is set forth in Article 1 of the Copyright Law of the People's Republic of China. This clause states the main legislative intent: "of protecting the copyright of authors in their literary, artistic and scientific works and rights related to copyright, of encouraging the creation and dissemination of works which would contribute to the construction of socialist spiritual and material civilization, and of promoting the development and flourishing of socialist culture and sciences."

Copyright covers a wide range of works, but copyright law only protects the expression of the work. As for the idea of the work, the medium of the work, and the materials used in the work, they are not included in the scope of copyright protection and shall be granted protection referring to other laws and regulations. "Works" mentioned in this Law shall refer to ingenious intellectual achievements in the fields of literature, art and science that can be presented in a certain form, including written works; oral works; musical, dramatic, quyi, choreographic and acrobatic art works; works of fine art and architecture; photographic works; audiovisual works; drawings of engineering designs and product designs, maps, sketches and other graphic works as well as model works; computer software; other intellectual achievements that meet the characteristics of works. Among them, the ones related to design specifically include fine art works, architectural works, abstract photographic works, graphic works, and model works, among others.

Copyright law outlines the rights possessed by copyright owners in an effort to inspire individuals to innovate. The ultimate goal of copyright legislation is to meet the public's spiritual and cultural needs. This is achieved not only by protecting the individual rights and interests of copyright owners, but also by fostering the advancement of social science, culture, and the arts through the protection of individual rights and interests.

The copyright restriction system is the result of this balancing of interests in copyright law between the private rights and interests of copyright owners and the general welfare. The term of protection for copyright, the fair use doctrine and statutory licensing are the main components of the copyright restriction system.

① The term of protection for copyright

The term of a work's legal protection under copyright is known as the term of protection. The length of protection is both the line between the private and public domains in copyright law and a crucial distinction between intangible and tangible property rights. The Copyright Law provides for unlimited protection of the moral rights of copyright such as the right of authorship, the right of alteration and the right of integrity, while the right of publication is for the lifetime of the author and 50 years after his death.

The purpose of limiting the term of protection for property rights is to promote the effective and exploitation of works and to ensure the transfer of works from the private to the public domain, thereby enriching the cultural life of society. The term of protection of property rights varies depending on the type of work.

The term of protection of property rights for "Works of Natural Person" shall be the lifetime of the author and 50 years after his death, expiring on December 31 of the fiftieth year after his death. In the case of a work of joint authorship, such term shall expire on December 31 of the fiftieth year after the death of the last surviving author.

Both the term of protection of property rights for "Works of a Legal Person or an Unincorporated Organizations" and "Audiovisual Works" shall be 50 years, ending on December 31 of the 50th year after the first publication of the work, but if a work has not been published within 50 years after the completion of the creation, it shall no longer be protected.

② The fair use doctrine

The fair use doctrine is the exception in the Copyright Law that makes it legal to use copyrighted works without obtaining their authors' permission in certain limited circumstances. Articles 24 and 25 of the Copyright Law of the People's Republic of China stipulate 13 circumstances of fair use.

③ Statutory Licensing

In accordance with the express provisions of the law, statutory licensing is a system that allows the use of another person's published work in a specific way without the permission of the copyright owner, so long as the copyright owner is compensated as necessary and no other rights of the copyright owner are violated.

The similarities between statutory licensing and fair use lie in two points: (1) both don't need the consent of the copyright holder; (2) both use the published works. The difference between statutory licensing and fair use lies in the fact that users under statutory licensing have to pay the copyright holder, while the users of fair use don't have to pay.

④ Service work

According to the Copyright Law of the People's Republic of China, service work is:

> A work created by a natural person when fulfilling the tasks assigned to him by a legal entity or another unincorporated organization shall be deemed to be a service work.

The copyright of a service work shall be enjoyed by the author, but the legal entity or unincorporated organization shall have a priority right to exploit the work within the scope of its professional activities, unless your work falls in:

> drawings, sketch maps, computer software and other service works created mainly with the materials and technical resources of your company;
>
> works for hire created by employees of newspapers, periodical presses, news agencies, radio stations, and television stations;
>
> service works of which the copyright is, in accordance with the laws or administrative regulations or as agreed upon in the contract, enjoyed by the legal entity or unincorporated organization.

In the situations above, the author of a service work shall enjoy the right of authorship, while your company shall enjoy other rights included in the copyright and may reward the author.

For service works, within 2 years of the completion of the work, the author may not give permission to a third party to use the work in the same way as it is used by the institution without the consent of the institution.

2.2.2 *Patent Law*

(1) The Development of Patent Law

As a combination of technology and law, the patent system is an integral part of the intellectual property legal framework. The reform and opening-up initiative marked the beginning of drafting patent laws in PRC history, and the strategic decision-making of socialist modernization propelled the formulation of patent laws.

March 12, 1984, the first Patent Law was passed by the Standing Committee of the People's Congress and came into force on April 1, 1985. The first Patent Law can be summarized in several parts: Types of Patents, Duration of Patents, Unpatentable Subject Matter, Publication and Examination, Rejections and appeals, Opposition and Invalidation, The definition of patent right, Non-infringing activities.

The first Patent Law tried to address problems including Foreign Filing License, Assignment, Ownership of patents, Patent Administrative Bureaus (Lin et al. 2004).

In 1992, to fulfill the commitments made by the Chinese government in the "Memorandum of Understanding on the Protection of Intellectual Property Rights between China and the United States", the Patent Law underwent its first revision. The focus of this revision was to align the law with the Agreement on Trade-Related Aspects of Intellectual Property Rights (TRIPS Agreement), which had already been formulated at that time.

The major amendments of the Patent Law can be summarized as follows:

① *Duration of patent*
② *Unpatentable subject matter*
③ *Definition of Patent Right*
④ *Opposition*
⑤ *Burden of Proof*

In the early twenty-first century, in order to align with the construction of China's socialist market economy system, enhance patent protection, and integrate with the international patent system, as well as to meet the requirements of joining the WTO, the Patent Law underwent its second revision in 2000. After China's formal accession to the WTO, characteristics of the patent legislation gradually shifted from being reactive to proactive. The main revisions included changes in the definition of patent right, non-infringing acts, damage calculation, preliminary injunction, opposition procedure, appealability of Board decisions, and so on.

The third amendment to the Patent Law in 2008 reflected the deep implementation of the scientific development concept and the systematic implementation of the "National Intellectual Property Strategy Outline" (Ma 2009). However, after the third amendment, the Patent Law faced prominent issues in patent protection practices, such as difficulties in obtaining evidence for patent rights protection, long legal processes, high litigation costs, and low compensation.

In January 2020, China and the United States successfully signed the "Economic and Trade Agreement between the Government of the People's Republic of China and the Government of the United States of America." The signing of this agreement promoted the process of the fourth amendment to the Patent Law. The fourth amendment was finally enacted on October 17, 2020, and it mainly included:

① Pharmaceutical Patents

patent linkage system

It enables an applicant or patentee of a pharmaceutical patent to challenge a generic drug for patent infringement by initiating a declaratory judgment action of patent infringement against the generic during its regulatory approval process with the China Food and Drug Administration (CFDA).

pharmaceutical patent term adjustment

It provides an opportunity for an applicant of a pharmaceutical patent to obtain patent term adjustment of up to 5 years to compensate for the regulatory approval process.

② Design Patents

Significantly, amended Article 2 allows protection of partial designs, i.e., design patents in China will cover a whole or a part of a product. This amendment aligns Chinese Patent Law closer to the rules in other major jurisdictions, such as the rules in the United States, European Union, United Kingdom, Japan, and Korea.

Amended Article 42 also prolongs the term of protection for design patents from 10 years to 15 years from the filing date of the application.

③ Infringement Damages

Amended Article 71 of the Chinese Patent Law promises that the rules on patent infringement damages are undergoing steady and patentee-friendly changes.

④ Domestic priority

The amended Article 29 specified that the right of domestic priority might be enjoyed only in inventions or utility models. The amended law stipulates that the right of domestic priority may also be enjoyed in the case of designs, which grants domestic applicants a remedy for mistakes if any. Since the term of examination of a design patent is very short, the timeframe of 6 months right of priority may be a window of opportunity for the applicant to resume his/her right in certain extreme circumstances. For example, when a design patent application is refused or withdrawn, the applicant may file the application again within the timeframe, after making necessary improvements.

⑤ Other Notable Changes

Some other notable changes include: (i) patent infringement disputes of significant national impact, (ii) a 6-month disclosure grace period for non-novelty destroying publications, and (iii) the statute extension of limitation for patent infringement lawsuits.

(2) The Relationship Between Patent Law and Design

Patent rights are a type of intellectual property that gives the owner the legal right to exclude others from making, using, or selling an invention for a limited period of time. The owner must sue someone infringing the patent to enforce their rights. There are different types of patents for different kinds of inventions or designs245. Patent rights are granted by a sovereign authority, such as the U.S. Patent and Trademark Office, in exchange for publishing an enabling disclosure of the invention125. Patent rights may vary depending on the industry, the country, and the ethical issues involved.

Types of Patent:

① Inventions

any new technical solution relating to a product, a process or an improvement thereof.

There are two significant characteristics of an invention patent. First is its technical characteristic, which refers to a new technical solution for addressing specific technical issues. Second is its legal characteristic, which requires examination by the patent office and meets the conditions specified in patent law before obtaining patent rights. In patent law, a new technical solution may be a technical concept that has not yet been directly applied to industrial production, but it should possess the potential for industrial application and the ability to solve specific technical problems.

② Utility models

> any new technical solution relating to a product's shape, structure, or a combination thereof, which is fit for practical use.

Like an invention, a utility model protects a new technical solution, but they are different. In terms of the scope of protection, the scope of a utility model patent is much narrower than that of an invention patent. It is limited to the protection of new products with a certain shape or structure, and does not protect methods and substances without a fixed shape, such as gaseous, liquid, powdered or granular substances or materials, processes, methods, etc. The so-called shape is a shape with a certain technical effect; the so-called structure refers to the internal structure of the product that expresses the interrelationship between the product or product parts in terms of technical characteristics and performance. In terms of technical level, a utility model patent is less demanding than an invention patent. Utility model patents protect "small inventions", which are less technically advanced and less difficult. In terms of the duration of protection, the term of protection is short. China's Patent Law stipulates that the term of protection for invention patents is 20 years, while that for utility models is 10 years. In terms of practicality, utility model patents are stronger. The technical solutions contained in utility models are applicable and practical in the industrial field, which is a major difference from patents for inventions. In addition, utility models protect inventions at a lower level of technology and are not subject to substantive examination during the approval process, which is characterised by short approval procedures and low fees.

③ Designs

> a new design of the shape, pattern, or a combination thereof, as well as a combination of the color, shape and pattern, of the entirety or a portion of a product, which creates an aesthetic feeling and is fit for industrial application

"Design" means a new design of the shape, pattern, or a combination thereof, as well as a combination of the color, shape and pattern, of the entirety or a portion of a product, which creates an aesthetic feeling and is fit for industrial application. Designs should have the following characteristics.

First, it must be a new design of the shape, pattern, color or a combination thereof. Shape refers to the appearance of product that consists of three-dimensional features. Pattern refers to the two-dimensional design, or the pattern formed with lines or with different colors, such as the patterns on carpet, bed sheet and so on. Color refers to the components that make up the pattern. Generally, design can be a three-dimensional work, a two-dimensional pattern, shape and color, or the combination of shape, pattern and color.

Second, it must be applied to specific products. For example, a picture can not be considered a design if it is not used on specific products. But if this picture is used as on a carpet, then it becomes a design, so design is also called industrial design.

Article 22 of the Patent Law of People's Republic of China illustrates that an invention or utility model for which a patent is to be granted shall be novel, inventive and practically applicable.

① Novelty

Novelty means that the invention or utility model is not an existing technology, and prior to the date of application, no entity or individual has filed an application heretofore.

② Inventiveness

Inventiveness means that, as compared with the technology existing before the date of application the invention has prominent substantive features and represents a notable progress and that the utility model has substantive features and represents progress.

③ Practical applicability

Practical applicability means that the invention or utility model can be made or used and can produce effective results.

Exclusions from Patentable Subject Matter are as follows:

All patented inventions fit into one of three categories: inventions, utility model, design. But not everything that fits in one of these categories can be patented. International treaties, as well as China's Patent Law and its Implementing Rules outlined the non-granting of patent rights, which can be summarized in the following four categories.

① Inventions that contravene any law or social moral or that are detrimental to public interests

Inventions that violate the law cannot be awarded patent protection. For instance, a tool or equipment that is used to gamble or drug use cannot be patented because the tool is illegal. However, if the invention is for an article that may be prohibited by law only in its use, such as various weapons, the technology of the invention may still be patentable if it qualifies.

Moreover, the excessive exploitation exclusive right may raise problems of economic justice and conflict of interest, which can raise tragedy of the anti-common (Heller 1998) and in turn it can threaten the sustainability of human life. So, inventions that are detrimental to technical progress or public interests cannot be granted as well.

② Scientific discoveries

Discoveries fall into the broad category of abstract ideas and are thus unpatentable. You cannot patent a mathematical formula. You cannot patent a law of nature, such as Einstein's $E = MC^2$, or patent natural phenomena like electricity (discovered by William Gilbert in 1600). These all exist independently of human intervention, whether we have discovered them or formulated their rules yet or not, and must be freely available to all of humanity for its understanding and betterment.

③ Rules and methods for mental activities

Mental activities mean the thoughts of human mind. The rules and methods for mental activities are judged on the basis of whether the implementation of the method relies on the intellectual activity of a person. So to speak, if human thinking can determine or influence the result, the process or method shall be categorized as rules and methods for mental activities.

④ Methods for the diagnosis or for the treatment of diseases

Diagnostic methods refer to the processes of identifying, studying and determining the cause or focus of disease in living human or animal bodies. Where a method involving the diagnosis of a disease complies with be practiced on a living human or animal body and immediate purpose to obtain the diagnostic result of a disease or health condition, it is a diagnostic method and cannot be granted a patent right (Zhang and Zhao 2021).

(3) Protection Principles of Patent Law

① The Rights of the Patentee

After the grant of the patent right for an invention or utility model, except where otherwise provided for in law, no entity or individual may, without the authorization of the patentee, exploit the patent, that is, make, use, offer to sell, sell or import the patented product; or use the patented process, and use, offer to sell, sell or import the product directly obtained by the patented process, for production or business purposes.

After the grant of the patent right for a design, no entity or individual may, without the authorization of the patentee, exploit the patent, that is, make, sell or import the product incorporating its or his patented design, for production or business purposes.

- Right of Exclusive Implementation

The right of exclusive implementation refers to the exclusive right of the patentee to make, use, license, sell or import his patented product or patented method in accordance with the law. The patent confers on its proprietor the right to prevent third parties from manufacturing, using, offering for sale, selling or importing for such purposes, without his consent, a product that is the object of the patent or the process.

- Right of Assignment

The right of assignment refers to the right of the patentee to transfer the ownership of his patent to another entity or individual. When transferring patent rights, the parties shall enter into a written contract and register it with the patent administration department, and the patent administration department shall announce it. The transfer of patent rights shall take effect from the date of registration.

- Right of License

The right of license is the right of the patentee to license others to implement his patent. Any entity or individual exploiting the patent of another shall conclude with the patentee a written license contract for exploitation and pay the patentee a fee for the exploitation of the patent. The licensee has no right to authorize any entity or individual other than that referred to in the contract for exploitation, to exploit the patent. According to the different content of patent implementation license, patent implementation license is divided into monopolistic license, exclusive license, ordinary license and sub-license.

- Right of Marking

The right of marking means the right of the patentee to indicate his patented product or packaging with the patent marks, patents type and patent number.

- Right of Pledging

The right of pledging means the right of the patentee, as pledgee, to pledge the property rights in his patent rights to secure the performance of his debts, and in the event of default or inability of the pledgee to perform his debts, the pledgee has the right to receive priority payment for the property in his patent rights.

② The Limitations of Patent Rights

While the granting of exclusive patent rights is considered as an incentive for investment in innovative activities and the production of knowledge, allowing the enforcement of the full scope of the exclusive rights in all circumstances may not always meet the ultimate goal of the patent system to enhance the public welfare. Therefore, in order to strike the right balance between the interests of the right holders, third parties and the public, the scope of the enforceable exclusive rights may be set under national patent laws according to certain exceptions and limitations to patent rights.

③ The Defense of Patent Infringements

According to the Patent Law of the People's Republic of China, following circumstances fall in the defense of patent infringements:

- Exhaustion Doctrine

Exhaustion refers to the doctrine that states once a product is sold by a patent owner, the patent owner can't sue the purchaser for having an authorized copy of the patented product. The patent owner's exclusive rights of the patented product have been exhausted once a sale has been made. Therefore, the purchaser can use the product and resell the product without restriction.

- Prior Use Doctrine

First of all, the second paragraph of Article 9 of the Chinese Patent Law stipulates the principle of "first application" for patent rights (in other words first-to-file). However, if an absolute monopoly is granted to the prior applicant, it will be unfair to the prior inventor or prior user.

Prior use doctrine paved the way for a third party to continue the use of an invention where that use began before a patent application was filed for the same invention. It should be taken into account that the main purpose of prior user rights is to strike a balance between the effects of the first-to-file principle on the one hand and third-party considerations on the other.

- Temporary Transit

The Patent Law provides that a foreign means of transport temporarily passing through China's territory shall not be deemed to infringe the patent right. This limitation on patent rights is aimed to secure the worldwide practice of international trade, as spelled forth in the Paris Convention for the Protection of Industrial Property. The Paris Convention for the Protection of Industrial Property provides for this.

- Using for the Scientific Research and Experiment

The use of the patent exclusively for scientific research and experimentation is not considered an infringement of the patent. The purpose is to encourage scientific and technological research. However, it is limited to "solely" scientific research and scientific experiments.

- Administrative Examination and Approval's Demand

The produce, use or import of patented medicine or patented medicinal equipment for the purpose of providing information required for administrative approval and the manufacture or importation of patented medicine or patented medical equipment exclusively for the purpose of such manufacture or importation shall not be considered as infringement of.

2.2.3 *Trademark Law*

Trademarks are the third main area of IP law. Trademark law seeks to protect consumers from unfair competition by preventing businesses from misrepresenting the source of goods or services, as well as encouraging brands to invest in the quality and consistency of their goods and services. In general, any "word, name, symbol, or device" may be used as a trademark to identify a particular business's goods or services. Trademark itself is design.

(1) The Development of Trademark Law

Trademark Law of China was enacted in 1982 and came into effect on March 1, 1983. The legislative purpose of trademark law is:

① To protect the exclusive rights to use trademarks;
② To maintain the interests of consumers, producers, and merchants;
③ To guarantee the quality of goods and services, and the success of trademarks with good standing;

④ To encourage fair competition and competition in the reputation of brands;
⑤ To improve the legal environment and maintain normal market operations;
⑥ To facilitate the development of the market economy in China.

In 1993, Trademark Law of People's Republic of China was first amended. After 10 years enactment, the law has become unsuited for the rapid development in the economy, trade and technology in China, failing to meet China's demand to further reform and open up to the world. The revisions essentially featured enhanced protection of 'service trademark' and 'geographical names'; strengthened regulation of authorized licensing; developed a system to 'revoke/cancel improperly registered trademarks'; altered 'categories of infringement' to identify infringing conduct.

In 2001, as China turned to a market-oriented economy and access into the WTO, China needed to adapt itself to new scenario and international treaties and convention. Hereby, the second amendment of China's Trademark Law is made. Expanded the scope of subject that natural person can apply for trademark registration; Expanded the scope of protection, including 3-dimensional mark and mark associated with colors (three-dimensional trademark and color combination trademark); Strengthened the protection of the exclusive right to use trademarks; Added protection of "geographic mark/indication"; Strengthened protection of "well-known marks."

The third amendment of the Trademark Law was implemented in 2014, making major improvements to China's trademark system. Its overarching aims are to streamline procedures associated with acquiring trademark rights, ensure a fair market for trademark holders and clamp down on trademark infringements with a view to protecting the interests of consumers, producers and other business operators.

The amendments to the new law include, but are not limited to, measures that simplify trademark application and examination procedures, providing applicants with more user-friendly and efficient trademark registration services.

The 2019 amendment of the Trademark Law of China aims to strengthen the trademark protection, to promote a fair business environment and to effectively curb bad faith trademark registration. The revision involves a total of 6 articles (Articles 4, 19, 33, 44, 63 and 68), mainly related to the following: Adding provisions to regulate bad faith trademark registration; and increasing the compensation for infringement of trademark rights.

(2) The Relationship Between Trademark Law and Design

Trademark are protected by law after registration. Its content includes the exclusive right to use, the right to prohibit, the right to renew, the right to assign, the right to license the use, the right to inherit the trademark and the right to legal action for the trademark. The trademark right is limited to the approved registered trademark and the goods approved for use.

Compared with copyright and patent, trademark have the general characteristics of intellectual property (exclusivity, temporality and territoriality). At the same time, trademark has its own characteristics:

① Prohibition is Greater than Exclusiveness

The Prohibition Right a registered trademark relates to the illegal use of a registered trademark by others, including the use of a trademark identical or similar to a registered one on the same goods or similar goods without the license of the registrant; whereas the exclusive right to use a registered trademark relates to the registered trademark and the approved use of the trademark to the limit. Thus, the effective range of prohibition right is much greater than that of the exclusive use right.

② Relative Permanence

Trademark right have a time limit on the period of protection, but, unlike other intellectual property, this period can be renewed. The period of validity of a registered trademark shall be 10 years, counted from the day the registration or renewal registration is approved.

A trademark is but not limited to word, design, letter, numeral, three-dimensional symbol, combination of colors, and sound, as well as a combination of the above, may serve as a distinctive mark of merchandise or service to distinguish between goods or services produced or performed by different producers or operators of goods. A trademark has several functions:

① The Origin of Goods or Services: Trademark becomes a symbol of the business, representing part of the company culture and good advertising image.

② Encouraging Producers or Operators to Improve the Quality of Goods or Services: Trademark allows the products and services to be differentiated and identified.

③ Conducive to Market Competition and Advertising: Trademarks are often used as a guarantee of credit for the worth and quality of similar items carrying the same brand.

④ Intangible Assets of Reputation: Trademarks are aimed at enhancing the visibility and marketability of the products and drawing the attention of customers, typically picking one or many trademarks, or choosing a brand that is liked by the majority of people.

Trademark rights are established through registration and are protected by the law, which confers the exclusive rights to use, to disable, to renew, to transfer, to license, to inherit the registered trademark and right of trademark litigation and so on. The right to exclusively use a registered trademark shall be limited to the trademark approved for registration and the goods on which the trademark is approved to be used. Using a trademark similar to a registered trademark on identical goods or using a trademark identical with or similar to a registered trademark on similar goods, without being licensed by the trademark registrant, which may easily cause confusion shall be an infringement. Any alterations to words, graphics or other combinations of the registered trademark by the trademark owner should follow appropriate procedures according to the law.

According to Article 3, registered trademarks are trademarks approved to be registered by the Trademark Office, including goods trademarks, service trademarks, collective marks, and certification marks.

① Goods Marks

Goods marks are special marks that consist of words, graphics or a combination thereof, used on goods to distinguish the same or similar goods produced by different companies.

② Service Marks

Service marks are signs used by a service industry, for example a sign used by a person who provides a service on the item of service that he or she offers to the public. According to Nice Agreement Concerning the International Classification of Goods and Services for the Purposes of the Registration of Marks, service marks are: advertising and industry; insurance and finance; construction and repair; transportation and storage; material handling; education and entertainment, etc.

③ Collective Marks

Collective marks mean marks registered in the name of an organization (such as an association) for the members of the organization to use in commercial activities to indicate their memberships in the organization. Although the collective mark also indicates the source of the goods, it does not indicate a particular manufacturer, but represents a collective organization with a level of quality or accuracy, geographical origin, or other characteristics set by the organization (Wininger 2020).

④ Certification Marks

Certification marks are trademarks that are used to show consumers that particular goods and/or services, or their providers, have met certain standards.

(3) Protection Principles of Trademark Law

The main content of trademark rights:

① Trademark Exclusive Right

In principle, a trademark registration will confer an exclusive right to the use of the registered trademark. This implies that the trademark can be exclusively used by its owner, or licensed to another party for use in return for payment. Registration provides legal certainty and reinforces the position of the right holder, for example, in case of litigation. The owner of a registered trademark does not have the right to change the composing elements of the trademark or to expand the scope of trademark usage.

② Transfer Rights

Trademark transfer is the transfer of ownership rights for other individuals and organizations. Trademark right is a property right, so its ownership can be transferred from one entity to another. When the ownership of a registered trademark is transferred, the trademark right of the assignor disappears and the assignee becomes the owner of the registered trademark. Transfer rights is one of the most important ways for trademark owners to dispose of their registered trademarks.

③ Licensing Rights

In trademark licensing, a trademark owner (Licensor) grants permission to another (Licensee) to use that trademark on mutually agreed terms and conditions.

The trademark owner, as the licensor, signs a licensing contract with the licensee, and after paying a certain amount of royalties, the licensee can use its registered trademark within the time and territory agreed upon by the two parties, but the trademark owner needs to carry out the necessary supervision on the use of its registered trademark by the licensee.

④ Prohibition rights

Prohibition rights means that the trademark owner has the right to prohibit others from using its registered trademark without permission. According to the Trademark Law, the trademark owner is entitled to prohibit anyone from using identical or similar trademarks in respect of identical or similar goods and services without permission.

The prohibition right is applicable to "similar" and "approximate" goods, whereas the exclusive right is applicable to the approved registration of the trademark and the goods authorized for use. The applicable scope of the right to prohibit is wider than that of the right to exclusive use.

The period of validity of a registered trademark shall be 10 years, commencing from the date of approval of registration. If the registrant intends to continue to use the registered trademark upon expiry period, he shall undergo the renewal formalities within 12 months before expiry according to the relevant provisions. If failing to do so, the registrant may be granted a 6-month grace period. The period of validity of each renewal is 10 years, commencing from the day after the expiry date of the last period of validity. If the renewal formalities are not undergone within the grace period, the registration of the trademark shall be canceled.

Not every use of a trademark is infringement. Under certain circumstances, the holder of a registered trademark can be in conflict with the legitimate rights of others and the public interest. In order to strike a balance between the interests of the rights holders and the public society, necessary restrictions are set on the exercise and protection of trademark rights. Trademark right restrictions mainly include exhaustion of rights and fair use.

① Exhaustion of Trademark Rights

"Exhaustion" of trademark rights implies that once a branded product has been placed or commercialized on the market by the trademark holder or with his consent, he cannot prohibit the further commercialization of that product. His rights of a specific individual item or consignment are "exhausted" by the act of selling. The restriction of exhaustion is born out of a need to prevent trademark owners from utilizing trademark rights for more market share and obtaining unreasonable monopoly profits.

② Fair Use of Registered Trademark

Trademark law allows for third parties to refer to the trademarks of others in certain situations. Known as fair use, the overall guiding principle is that unauthorized usage of a trademark owned by someone else may be permissible if done in a way that would not create a likelihood of confusion or a false sense of affiliation, connection or association with the trademark owner.

Individuals and entities may be permitted the fair use of another's trademark under two conditions. These are known as classic fair use and nominative fair use. According to trademark law, fair use of trademark includes only directly indicating the quality, main raw materials, functions, uses, weight, quantity, or other features of goods; only bearing the generic name, design, or model of the goods; using registered trademark containing name of a place; using a three dimensional trademark for the nature or technical function of the goods; prior use of registered trademark and so on.

"Descriptive fair use" means using a descriptive mark in an ordinary, descriptive manner to describe a product or service, which would not cause confusion to relevant public.

Nominative use, also "nominative fair use", is a legal doctrine that provides an affirmative defense to trademark infringement as enunciated by the United States Ninth Circuit, by which a person may use the trademark of another as a reference to describe the other product, or to compare it to their own. Generally speaking, nominative use, if it is practiced within reasonable limits and does not cause confusion to relevant public, is regarded as a proper use of the trademark and does not constitute trademark infringement. However, if the nominative use exceeds the necessary limit or violates the agreement of the parties, there will be greater legal risks.

2.2.4 *Anti-Unfair Competition Law*

The 1967 Convention Establishing the World Intellectual Property Organization lists, under Article 2 "Intellectual Property Rights", rights arising in the field of intellectual activity such as works, inventions, marks, etc., including the protection against unfair competition.

It seems that intellectual property law and anti-unfair competition law are conflicting with each other in institutional designs, because the former aims to safeguard the "monopoly rights" of owners of intellectual property while the latter will restrict or eliminate a certain kind of "monopoly status." In fact, both share a common legislative goal, namely, to protect legitimate rights and promote social progress. The difference is that intellectual property law realizes this goal by protecting the legitimate rights and interests of intellectual property owners and encouraging knowledge innovation; while the anti-unfair competition law achieves the above goal by stopping illegal competition and maintaining the order of market competition (Wu 2013).

(1) The Development of Anti-unfair Competition Law

China's Anti-Unfair Competition Law was first adopted in 1993. For foreign businesses in China, the Anti-Unfair Competition Law has long been used to protect their intellectual property rights in China, especially in unregistered trademark and trade dress cases.

In 2017, the first amendment was made to the Anti-Unfair Competition Law as it had been in operation for 24 years since its implementation in 1993, and many of its provisions were no longer adapted to the competition activities in the new era. The Draft Revision tightens rules against commercial bribery in the following aspects:

the amendment expands the scope of commercial bribery, specifies the relationship between the employees giving bribes and their companies, increasing the responsibility of the business operator and penalties for bribery, and amplifies the means of investigation.

The amendment to the Anti-Unfair Competition Law in 2019 affirms the openness and applicability of the general provisions and improves the definition of "act of unfair competition", in particular, emphasizing the consideration of "disrupting the order of market competition" and the protection of consumer interests. The new amendment clarifies various types of acts of unfair competition. Most significantly, the Revision further specifies unfair competition acts existing in the digital economy, refining rules to regulate the acquisition and use of data and online unfair competition through the use of algorithms and technologies. The Revision strives to coordinate the rights and interests protection of public, operators and intellectual property rights holders, and manifests the emphasis on market and efficiency. Necessary but limited interventions are made to market competition in order to protect the freedom of competition.

(2) The Relationship Between Anti-Unfair Competition Law and Design

As defined in Article 2 of the Anti-Unfair Competition Law, the act that "disrupts the order of market competition and causes damage to the lawful rights and interests of the other businesses or consumers" belongs to the act of unfair competition.

It covers the "act of confusion, commercial bribery, false or misleading commercial promotion, infringement on trade secret, prize-giving sales, fabricating or disseminating false or misleading information to damage the reputation of a competitor and the online market competition." The Anti-Unfair Competition Law not only regulates the market's competition order in common areas, but also regulates the protection on commercial logos and other unregistered trademarks and business secrets that are not covered by concrete IP laws. Therefore, it is generally considered as offering supplementary protection to IP rights.

The Supreme People's Court pointed out in a notice issued in 2009 that the supplementary protection of the Anti-Unfair Competition Law does not conflict with the legislative policies of concrete IP laws. As a general principle, if concrete laws have exhaustive provisions, the Anti-Unfair Competition Law is not applied for extended protection.

On the other hand, IP rights are manifested in preventing competitors from manufacturing, using or selling their own products with IP rights. If the IP owner maliciously or inappropriately expands the scope of legal rights granted by the law in the process of exercising IP rights, the IP owner may violate the Anti-Unfair Competition Law for abuse of IP rights.

Currently, the Chinese legal profession holds two different views on the relationship between the Anti-Unfair Competition Law and the Intellectual Property Law, one claiming that the Anti-Unfair Competition Law is a supplement to the Intellectual Property Law, and that the anti-unfair competition is a kind of remedial right derived on the basis of the intellectual property rights (Kong 2017), while the other is consistent with the definition of intellectual property rights in the WIPO Convention, holding that the Anti-Unfair Competition Law and the Intellectual Property Law keep a separate and parallel relationship (Zhang 2018). However, regardless of the different views above, the Anti-Unfair Competition Law will always protect intellectual property rights and promote innovation by preventing illegal competition activities and maintaining the order of market competition.

At present, laws related to design intellectual property rights in the Anti-Unfair Competition Law are mainly Article 6, Article 9 and Article 12.

In the Article 6 of Anti-Unfair Competition Law, a business shall not commit act of confusion, which means misleading a person into believing that a commodity is one of another persons or has a particular connection with another person. It clarifies that confusion of trademark is not limited to the use of trademark in same kind of business, or the same or similar goods. In particular, when it comes to the protection of name, association confusion is especially favorable to the protection of rights. This directly reflects the characteristics of anti-unfair competition protection: in principle, acts of trademark confusion occur in the case of the same and similar goods, but if the use of non-similar goods is sufficient to mislead people into believing that there is a particular connection between two commodities, trademark rights can still be protected according to the anti-unfair competition law. For intellectual property rights holders, the Anti-Unfair Competition Law provides a very practical method for the protection of such commercial signs when they are imitated and cannot be protected by the trademark law or cannot be protected in a timely manner.

In Article 6, "a label identical or similar to the name, packaging or decoration" implies that the law can be applied to packaging, decoration, name and any distinctive signs relevant to product appearance and shape. However, application of the law requires that the relevant sign has a certain impact; in other words, as long as it is put into commercial use, it can be claimed to have a certain impact. The third paragraph of Article 6 stipulates acts of confusion such as using domain name and website with certain influence without permission. These provisions will prevent various new types of free-riding as unfair competition acts in the current social context. This kind of hitchhiking behavior, which was once in the grey area, can now be actively defended by the right holders in accordance with the law.

In addition, according to Article 9, "trade secret" means technical, operational or other commercial information unknown to the public and is of commercial value for which the right holder has taken corresponding confidentiality measures. The methods of infringing a trade secret includes theft, bribery, fraud, coercion, electronic intrusion, or any other illicit means. Furthermore, abetting a person, or tempting, or aiding a person into or in acquiring trade secret also commit acts of infringement. The employee of the right holder of a trade secret who acquires the trade secret or discloses it shall be deemed to have infringed upon the trade secret which is prohibited by law. The third party who knows such illegal act committed and still uses the trade secrets also infringes on the trade secrets. Article 9 is an effective deterrent to wrongdoers who attempt to obtain trade secrets by speculation or other improper means, which also strengthens China's protection of the rights of trade secret holders.

The provisions in Article 12 are supposed to address intellectual property disputes in online activities. Operators providing online software services may claim this article when they suffer from malicious interference by other people's products and lack sufficient evidence for copyright protection. However, not all acts of interfering or sabotaging are recognized as unfair competition, because fair competition will also inevitably bring about damage to the interests of competitors. For example, internet technology development and innovation will promote product development as well as the elimination, which are the result of normal market competition. Despite sabotaging the operation of others, the fair competition shall not be restricted by this article. The prerequisite for the application of the provisions of this Article is still to judge whether the conduct is of an unfair nature and whether it is detrimental to the order of competition and the public interest.

(3) The Protection Principle of Anti-Unfair Competition Law

According to Article 2 of the Anti-Unfair Competition Law, businesses shall, in their production and distribution activities, adhere to the free will, equality, fairness, and good faith principles, and abide by laws and business ethics.

① free will, equality, fairness and good faith principles

Free will, equality, fairness and good faith principles is also stipulated in the Civil Code and it is consistent with the principle of good faith under the fundamental principles of civil law, which requires all market participants to pursue their own interests without jeopardizing the interests of others or the public good. The principle of good faith does not have a permanent definition, but as the most important principle of civil law, its meaning cannot be simply taken on a semantic level. As general clauses, it does not have a clear concept and is often applied in a wide range of cases.

② abide by laws

This principle was added in the 2017 revision of the Anti-Unfair Competition Law to make the Anti-Unfair Competition Law coherent with other laws, and the term "law" as referred to should be specified. It should be understood as a law that regulates market behavior for the purpose of protecting competition. The Anti-Unfair Competition Law is an important part of the market regulation law, which only regulates illegal acts identified as acts of unfair competition, and thus limiting the term "law" to laws related to the regulation of market behavior is in line with the scope of application of the Anti-Unfair Competition Law.

③ abide by business ethics

With the development of emerging technologies and the increasingly diverse patterns of competitive behavior, it is difficult to develop a general understanding of business ethics in a short period of time.

According to Article 3 of Interpretation by the Supreme People's Court of Several Issues Concerning the Application of the Anti-Unfair Competition Law of the People's Republic of China, the people's court may determine a code of conduct generally followed and recognized in a specific commercial field as "business ethics" specified in Article 2 of the Anti-Unfair Competition Law, It is clear that the law is applied to regulate the behavior of "operators." Therefore, business ethics in China's Anti-Unfair Competition Law only refers to the common and universally recognized standards of conduct of transaction participants, excluding the ethical standards recognized by consumers and the public.

In terms of the determination of violation of business ethics, the second and third paragraphs of Article 3 of the Interpretation make clear the standards and considerations for the determination of violation of business ethics, stipulating that "the people's court shall, in light of the specific circumstances of a case, take into account factors such as industry rules or business usage, the subjective condition of a business, the will to choose of transaction counterparties, and the impact on the rights and interests of consumers, the order of market competition, and the public interests in judging in accordance with the law whether the business violates business ethics. When determining whether a business violates business ethics, the people's court may refer to the practice standards, technical standards, and self-regulatory conventions, among others, formulated by industry authorities, industry associations, or self-regulatory organizations."

2.3 The International Protection of Intellectual Property and Design

In the absence of any international convention in the field of intellectual property, it is quite difficult to obtain protection of intellectual property rights outside one's own country. Thus, from the 1880s, countries began to seek international protection of intellectual property rights through the signing of international agreements or conventions, which has now become a kind of legal order in the field of international economy, culture, science and technology, and trade. International treaties and agreements on intellectual property can be broadly categorized into three types, namely, institutional standards for "intellectual property protection", "global protection systems" and "registration classification" (Frankel and Gervais 2022).

The formation of the international protection of intellectual property remarks the entry of the intellectual property legislation into a new historical stage, that is, the intellectual property law formulated independently in each country, has gradually embarked on the path of integration and internationalization under the framework of international protection of intellectual property. For more than a century, countries and international organizations all over the world have successively concluded and formulated more than 30 global or regional, comprehensive or specialized international intellectual property treaties and uniform laws. On the basis of international conventions and relevant international organizations, the development of the international protection of intellectual property can be divided into three stages: the period of the Paris Union and the Berne Union, the period of the World Intellectual Property Organization and the period of the World Trade Organization (Wu 2021).

2.3.1 The Period of the Paris Union and the Berne Union

The establishment of the international protection of intellectual property goes back to 1883 and 1886 when the Paris Convention for the Protection of Industrial Property and the Berne Convention for the Protection of Literary and Artistic Works, respectively, were concluded. After the two conventions entered into force, the contracting parties of the Paris Convention formed the Paris Union and the contracting parties of the Berne Convention formed the Berne Union. Both have their own executive institutions, called International Bureaus. The two bureaus administered the above-mentioned international conventions under the supervision of the Swiss Federal Government. In 1893 the two bureaus were united under the name of the "Joint International Bureau for the Protection of Industrial and Literary and Artistic Property." Going through several changes, it was finally named the "Joint International Bureau for the Protection of Intellectual Property"(BIRPI). The BIRPI administers not only the Paris and Berne Conventions, but also the "specialized agreements" concluded under the Paris Convention. The period of the Paris and Berne Conventions witnessed the formation of the international protection of intellectual property.

The main features of this stage include: (1) The United International Bureaux for the Protection of Intellectual Property (BIRPI) focuses on global and regional multilateral negotiations between governments for enhancement of international coordination adhering to the objective of achieving integrated and comprehensive development (Zhang 1999). With the Paris Convention and the Berne Convention running effectively, a relatively unified intellectual property protection system was established within the Union. (2) The majority of industrial property conventions are led by the Paris Convention. Some conventions for substantive protection are only applicable to the Paris Union member states. For instance, the 1891 "Madrid Agreement for the Repression of False or Deceptive Indications of Source on Goods." Some are procedural treaties under the Paris Convention, such as the 1891 "Madrid Agreement Concerning the International Registration of Marks" and the 1925 "Hague Agreement Concerning the International Registration of Industrial Designs." Some are special agreements on international classification established for implementing the Paris Convention, including the 1957 "Nice Agreement Concerning the International Classification of Goods and Services for the Purposes of the Registration of Marks" and the 1958 "Lisbon Agreement for the Protection of Appellations of Origin and their International Registration." (3) UNESCO has also played an active role in promoting international protection of intellectual property rights, mainly in copyright. It has presided over the conclusion of the 1952 "Universal Copyright Convention" and the 1961 "Rome Convention." Based on the former, another copyright protection system parallel to the Berne Convention was established. Based on the latter, an international system for the protection of neighbouring rights was established.

2.3.2 *World Intellectual Property Organization Period (WIPO Convention)*

The founding of the World Intellectual Property Organization means that the international intellectual property protection system has entered a new developmental stage. In 1967, the contracting states of the Paris Convention and the Berne Convention signed the Convention Establishing the World Intellectual Property Organization (the WIPO Convention) in Stockholm, Sweden. The World Intellectual Property Organization (WIPO) was established in 1970. WIPO set the International Intellectual Property Bureau to replace the BIRPI.

The founding of the WIPO has promoted the integration of intellectual property legislation. Since 1967, with the help of the WIPO and its predecessor, the BIRPI, more than 20 international treaties have been concluded. Among them are those that provide substantive rights protection, as well as those that facilitate intellectual property protection in many countries and treaties establishing international classifications. These treaties are implemented by the domestic legislation of each contracting state, thus forming a relatively uniformed international intellectual property protection system. Meanwhile, due to the effective operation and influence of the WIPO, more countries have accepted the treaties in the Paris Convention and the Berne Convention. In 1967, 78 and 60 countries participated in these two major conventions. By 2013, the number of member states to the two conventions reached 175 and 166 respectively, which greatly expanded the scope of the international protection system for intellectual property.

The WIPO Convention made important contributions by defining the scope of "intellectual property rights" and responsibilities and institutions of WIPO. The signing of the WIPO Convention marks the establishment of the WIPO. Since then, the WIPO started to protect and manage intellectual property rights worldwide. The Convention also marked the formation of a relatively complete international intellectual property protection system.

Since the establishment of the WIPO, it has focused on assisting developing countries by providing advice, training, documentation and equipment. Specifically, the assistance includes helping developing countries establish or modernize intellectual property laws, providing group or individual training to increase the number of experts in government, industry and law enforcement and providing patent information services. The WIPO improved intellectual property laws in developing countries by enacting the "Tunis Model Law on Copyright for Developing Countries" in 1976, revising the "Model Law for Developing Countries on Inventions" in 1974, and drafting the "Model Law on Trademarks, Trade Names and Unfair Competition in Developing Countries" and "Model law for developing countries on industrial designs." This helped implement the international intellectual property protection system.

2.3.3 World Trade Organization Period

The establishment of the World Trade Organization (WTO) and the formation of the Agreement on Trade-Related Aspects of Intellectual Property Rights (TRIPS) marked a new historical period for the international intellectual property protection system, featuring high-level, integrated protection. On April 15, 1994, the final Act of the Uruguay Round initiated by the General Agreement on Tariffs and Trade (GATT) was signed in Marrakesh, Morocco. The one-package agreement in the Uruguay Round had two important outcomes: The first was announcing the establishment of the WTO, which ended the temporary application of the GATT. The second was concluding a one-package agreement including the "Intellectual Property Agreement", which was governed by the WTO.

The WTO has played a leading role in the new international intellectual property protection system. Before the Uruguay Round, although intellectual property protection systems were widely established internationally, there were obvious shortcomings: First, inadequacy of laws and relative low effectiveness of law enforcement particularly in developing countries. Second, only a few countries signed the International Intellectual Property Convention. The relevant treaties lacked effective institutions to guarantee their implementation, and there was a lack of coordination mechanism among the various conventions.

The WIPO focuses on cooperation with the WTO in international coordination of intellectual property protection. On December 22, 1995, the Directors-General of the above two international organizations signed the "Agreement Between the World Intellectual Property Organization and the World Trade Organization" in Geneva. The agreement sets rules for cooperation between the two international organizations in the exchange and use of laws and regulations. It stipulates the rules for implementing the provisions of the Paris Convention on emblems and official seals that cannot be registered as trademarks and provide for legal technical assistance and technical cooperation to developing countries, cooperation and information exchange between the International Office of Intellectual Property and the World Trade Organization secretariat. While seeking cooperation, the two international organizations have also done a great deal of work on international intellectual property protection separately. WIPO was committed to comprehensively enhancing global intellectual property protection. It administered a number of new treaties, including the "Trademark Law Treaty", "Copyright Treaty", and "Performance and Phonography Treaty", and resolved some issues not covered by the "Paris Convention" and the "Berne Convention". WTO focused on implementing the "Intellectual Property Agreement" by member states. Efforts were made by WTO to coordinate the sharing of intellectual property rights between underdeveloped countries and developed countries and to arrange multilateral negotiations about geographical indications, traditional knowledge, and biological diversity.

(1) Agreement on Trade-Related Aspects of Intellectual Property Rights (TRIPs)

In an era of knowledge economy, science and technology have become important factors driving the economic development of all countries, which play a decisive role in the world economy and trade competition. In international trade, intellectual products have become the main trading subject. Developed countries, which are major producers of intellectual property products, naturally pay more attention to the protection of intellectual property rights. The "Agreement on Trade-Related Aspects of Intellectual Property Rights" (TRIPS), which came into effect in 1995, clearly defines the scope of intellectual property protection and is the most restrictive international convention in the field of intellectual property protection. Historically, this Agreement is not only the first intellectual property convention that clearly states its link with international trade but also the first international convention to integrate the specific content and regulations of various intellectual property systems such as copyright, patent rights, and trademark rights.

The TRIPS Agreement consists of a preface and seven main parts, with 73 articles. It aims to reduce misunderstandings and obstacles in international trade, take into account the need to promote effective and adequate protection of intellectual property rights and ensure the measures and procedures for implementing intellectual property rights itself do not hinder legitimate trade.

(2) Regional Comprehensive Economic Partnership (RCEP)

The "Regional Comprehensive Economic Partnership Agreement" (RCEP) is an agreement initiated by ASEAN in 2012. It was drawn up by 15 members including China, Japan, South Korea, Australia, New Zealand, and 10 ASEAN countries over 8 years. RCEP came into effect on January 1, 2022, marking the official launch of the free trade zone, which currently has the largest population, the largest economic and trade scale, and the most promising development potential in the world. After the RCEP comes into effect, each contracting state shall protect new or original industrial designs independently. The object of protection is limited to a new or original design that is significantly different from a known design or a combination of known design features. Contracting States may ask that such protection shall not extend to designs resulting primarily from technical or functional considerations. The agreement also specifically states that each contracting state should ensure the protection of textile designs, but has the right to choose to meet this obligation through industrial design or copyright law.

RCEP consists of a preface, 20 chapters, and 4 annexes of the Market Access Commitment Form. Chapter 11 is on intellectual property, containing 14 sections, 83 clauses, and two annexes about the transition period for specific parties, and a list of technical assistance requests. It is the longest chapter with the most content in RCEP, and it is also the most comprehensive chapter on intellectual property included in the FTA signed by China so far.

Chapter 11 covers a wide range of fields including copyright, trademarks, geographical indications, patents, design, genetic resources, traditional knowledge and folk art, anti-unfair competition, intellectual property enforcement, cooperation, transparency, and technical assistance. It not only covers traditional major intellectual property issues but also reflects new trends in the development of IP protection.

Compared with the TRIPS, the intellectual property section in RCEP lays more emphasis on promoting win-win and open cooperation, building a sound system for wider protection and keeping up with new forms of business. While fully respecting the development levels of different members in the region, it provides a balanced and inclusive plan for the protection and promotion of intellectual property rights in the region. Based on the WTO's TRIPS, RCEP increased the overall level of intellectual property protection within the region comprehensively, which will help promote innovative cooperation and sustainable development within the region. The Agreement requires that each contracting party shall include a written notice of the reasons for rejection or authorization to the applicant in the industrial design registration process. The applicants should be offered an opportunity to respond by raising objections, challenging or appealing to the grant or rejection of the application, or the opportunity to challenge, appeal, revoke, invalidate or cancel registration or authorization.

(3) The Hague Agreement concerning the International Deposit of Industrial Designs

The Hague System provides a simpler and more economical system for the international registration of industrial design. With the Hague System, design owners in a contracting state can obtain design protection in all contracting states with the least formal requirements and the lowest cost. Design owners no longer need to apply for design patents one by one to obtain design protection in a contracting state, thus avoiding redundant work caused by different procedures and languages in countries.

The European Union, South Korea, Japan and the United States joined the Geneva Act of the Hague Agreement in 2008, 2014, and 2015, respectively. International design registration under the Hague Agreement has also gradually become a major path for design registration. China officially implemented the fourth revision of the Patent Law on June 1, 2021, adding design protection and extending the design protection period to 15 years. These are all preparations for joining the Hague Agreement. On February 5, 2022, China officially handed in its approval documents for joining the Hague Agreement Geneva Act, which came into effect on May 5, 2022. Since then, China become an important member of the international design registration system.

Joining the Hague Agreement will speed up the building of an innovative country, make it easier for China's innovation entities to obtain design protection abroad, strongly promote openness and economic competitiveness, and create a better environment for innovation, investment, and business. To further guarantee the implementation of the Hague Agreement, the China National Intellectual Property Administration is currently further improving the examination rules for design applied for through the Hague Agreement by amending the Patent Law Enforcement Regulations, Patent Examination Guidelines, etc. At the same time, the relevant examination procedures, information management systems, and fee systems have been adjusted and improved to provide more convenient services to domestic and foreign applicants.

References

Article 1, Copyright Law of the People's Republic of China

Article 15, International Covenant on Economic, Social and Cultural Rights

Article 18, Copyright Law of the People's Republic of China

Article 18 Paragraph 2, Copyright Law of the People's Republic of China

Article 2, Patent Law of the People's Republic of China

Article 2, Convention Establishing the World Intellectual Property Organization

Article 25 Paragraph 1, Patent Law of the People's Republic of China

Article 25 Paragraph 2, Patent Law of the People's Republic of China

Article 25 Paragraph 3, Patent Law of the People's Republic of China

Article 3, Copyright Law of the People's Republic of China

Article 39, Trademark Law of the People's Republic of China

Article 4, Paragraph 1, Article 19, Paragraph 3. Article 68. Trademark Law of the People's Republic of China

Article 5, Patent Law of the People's Republic of China

Article 75, Patent Law of the People's Republic of China

Bently L, Sherman B (2014) Intellectual property law, 4th edn. Oxford University Press, London

CCdigitallaw.ch (2022). https://ccdigitallaw.ch/index.php/english/copyright/2-what-work/21-urheberrechtlich-geschuetztes-werk/. Accessed 28 Jun 2022

Drexl J, Nérisson S, Trumpke F et al (2013) Comments of the Max Planck Institute for intellectual property and competition law on the proposal for a directive of the European Parliament and the council on collective management of copyright and related rights and multi-territorial licensing of rights in musical works for online uses in the internal market COM (2012)372. IIC Int Rev Intellect Prop Compet Law 44:322–350

Frankel S, Gervais DJ, translated by Xiao YD (2022) Advanced introduction to international intellectual property. Intellectual Property Publishing House, Beijing

Heath CG, Kamperman Sanders A (2009) Spares, repairs and intellectual property rights: IEEM international intellectual property programmes. Wolters Kluwer Law & Business, Kluwer Law International

Heller MA (1998) The tragedy of anti-commons: property in the transition from marx to markets. Harv Law Rev 1998:621–688

Kenton W (2023) What is intellectual property, and what are some types? https://www.investopedia.com/terms/i/intellectualproperty.asp. Accessed 7 Oct 2023

Kong XJ (2017) On the modernization of Anti-Unfair Competition Law. Comp Law Res 3:37–55

Lin B, Wood J, Jang S (2004) Overview of Chinese patent law. In: Paper presented at the 35th international congress of the PIPA, Toyama, 19–22

Ma N (2009) Changes in the value trends of Chinese patent legislation through three amendments to the Patent Law. Intellect Prop J 19(5):69–74

Nard CA, Madison MJ, McKenna MP (2017) The law of intellectual property. Aspen Publishing, California, p 178

Reuters (2023) Exclusive Q&A with Chinese President Xi Jinping. https://www.reuters.com/article/us-china-britain-xi-q-a-idUSKCN0SC03920151018. Accessed 7 May 2023

Wan Y, Lu HXY (2021) Copyright protection for AI-generated outputs: the experience from China. Comput Law Secur Rev 42:1–11

Wininger A (2020) Chinese trademark office issues FAQ on collective and certification trademark registration. https://www.natlawreview.com/article/chinese-trademark-office-issues-faq-collective-and-certification-trademark. Accessed 7 Nov 2023

WIPO (2015) Intellectual property handbook. https://www.doc88.com/p-0438329102844.html. Accessed 7 Aug 2022

WTO (2009) China-measures affecting the protection and enforcement of intellectual property

Wu HD (2013) Intellectual property issues concerned with unfair competition. Mod Law 35(01):37–43

Wu HD (2021) Intellectual property law. Law Press, Beijing
Xie YB, Chen Y (2014) Creative thinking and modern design. Shanghai Jiao Tong University Press, Shanghai
Xinhua (2021) China issues guideline for IPR development. http://english.www.gov.cn/policies/latestreleases/202109/22/content_WS614b1466c6d0df57f98e0aa8.html. Accessed 7 May 2023
Zhang NG (1999) Intellectual property law for international trade. Fudan University Press, Shanghai
Zhang WJ (2018) The relationship between Anti-Unfair Competition Law and intellectual property law from the case of Jin Yong v. Jiangnan. Intellect Prop Rights 10:14–23
Zhang Y, Zhao W (2021) Patent practice in China-diagnosis or treatment? https://www.iam-media.com/global-guide/global-life-sciences/2021/article/patent-practice-in-china-diagnosis-or-treatment. Accessed 7 Oct 2022

Chapter 3
Product Design and Intellectual Property

3.1 The Concept of Product Design

The International Council of Societies of Industrial Design (ICSID) adjusted the definition of product design three times at different stages. The revised goals, tasks and categories of design are as follows:

In 1970, the ICSID defined product design as a creative activity determining the appropriate characteristics of manufactured items based on industrial conditions. Appropriate characteristics of an item not only refer to the structure of an item but also take into consideration the views of both users and producers. It requires concreting abstract concepts, thus creating a unified and specific image of the item. It means focusing on the interrelationship between fundamental structure and functions, which is enabled by industrial production to expand the human environment.

In 1980, the ICSID revised the definition of product design into "a creative activity aimed at determining the exterior quality of industrial products." Although exterior quality also includes exterior features, it mainly refers to the relationship between structure and function which fits the interests of producers and users at the same time. This relationship transforms a system into a balanced whole. That is to say, it is an activity combining the function, material, structure, technology, form, colour, surface treatment, decoration and other factors of products.

In 2006, the ICSID revised the definition of product design as a creative activity whose purpose is to establish the multi dimensional quality, process, service, and entire life cycle system of a product. Therefore, design is to bring life to scientific and technological innovation. The core factor of the new concept is also a crucial factor in cultural and economic exchange. The new concept defines the task of design as "to discover and evaluate the structure, organization, function, expression, and economic relationships," which are reflected in the following aspects:

1. To strengthen global sustainable development and environmental protection (global ethics);

N. Jiang, *Design, Innovation and Intellectual Property*,
https://doi.org/10.1007/978-981-95-2042-8_3

2. To give human society as a whole, individual and collective interests and freedom to decide users, producers, and market leaders (social morality);
3. To support cultural diversity (cultural morality) in the context of globalization;
4. To give products, services and systems their identity in the expression of the (symbolic, semantic) forms and to coordinate with their (aesthetic) connotation.

As seen from the above three revisions, product design is a creative activity that organically unifies many aspects of human science, art, economy, and society. It taps into knowledge from many subjects in social science and natural science. For example, functions and materials involve Applied Physics, Materials and Material Mechanics, Mathematics, System Engineering and other disciplines. Modelling and colour involve Aesthetics, Psychology, Colour Science and other disciplines. Product application involves Sales, Value Engineering, Ergonomics (marketing) and other disciplines (Mike 1995).

WIPO (2022) pointed out in *What is an Industrial Design* that "an industrial design may consist of three-dimensional features, such as the shape of an article, or two-dimensional features, such as patterns, lines or colour." The design of a product's exterior is to combine form and function to pursue aesthetic goals. From an aesthetic point of view, product design is also a visual art, and the product is a product of visual art (Xiao 2008). But design and development, not only of the visual appearance of products but also design for manufacture, design to meet market needs, design for cost reduction, design for reliability and design for environmental friendliness. Therefore, product design refers to the visual characteristics or the form of an item, which leaves the viewer with a strong visual impression. It is also a creative activity that can meet the functional needs of human beings.

3.2 Features of Product Design

3.2.1 Product Design Includes Both Functional Design and Formal Design

These were the specialists working to improve the appearance and functionality of ubiquitous goods such as furniture and kitchen appliances.

Designers still face the task of making goods for unknown consumers, which must work well and look good but also cope with additional challenges that were less prevalent to our design forbears. They must work within a massively complex world, gathering, processing, and synthesizing vast quantities of information within a dynamic and changing environment (Morris 2009).

The economic success of most firms depends on their ability to identify the needs of customers and to quickly create products that meet these needs and can be produced at low cost. Achieving these goals is not solely a marketing problem, nor is it solely a design problem or a manufacturing problem; it is a product development problem involving all of these functions (Ma 2019).

The formal design of products can be analyzed from different dimensions. Based on the research and discussion of relevant scholars, there are three popular opinions about product aesthetics in design: The first is a one-dimensional aesthetic design concept which believes that product aesthetics is the beauty of external form, and that product design aesthetics is reflected in materials, form, colour, and texture. This is the most traditional and widely supported view nowadays. The second is a two-dimensional aesthetic design concept which believes that product aesthetics includes formal beauty(in shape) and functional beauty(in technology), that is, "external" beauty and "internal" beauty. The third is a multi-dimensional aesthetic design concept represented by the three levels of formal beauty, functional beauty, and social beauty. Don Norman, an American author, proposes the emotional system consists of three levels: visceral, behavioural, and reflective. His model is playing an increasingly important influence in modern design. Aesthetics itself is inseparable from emotional factors. Norman's design concept also fundamentally influences the aesthetic design of products.

3.2.2 Human: The Core of Product Design

At the heart of product design are people, also known as consumers or users. Products are an integral part of people's lives, and the value of products is for people to use, both in material and spiritual ways. This determines that the core of product design is people. In people-oriented innovative product design, the service quality of the product should not be compromised for function. Moreover, the structure should be designed to reduce the difficulty in use. Therefore, it is necessary to ensure that design services centre on the needs and desires of consumers (Jiang and Cheng 2013).

The core technologies for product design are product design positioning, confirmation of principle structure, and selection of styling design ideas. The technology of product design refers to the skills used in the design activities. Designing involves four basic procedures, namely, analysis, conception, design, and production (Liu 2005). Many skills are used in the process. Among the many skills, design positioning skills in analysis, confirmation of principles and structures in conception, and selection skills for shaping design ideas in design are particularly critical. These are soft skills (Jin 2002) with ideas, thoughts, and strong personalities, creating room and providing material for innovation. It is these soft skills that bring innovation to the application that have created the individuality and characteristics of the product, making them welcomed by users, and formed, at the same time, Intellectual property.

3.2.3 Product Design Motivated by Innovation

Design is a creative activity where humans conceive and plan to transform nature and society and implement such ideas and plans through certain specific means. The essence of design is innovation. Functional innovation is the soul of formal design and brings life to design. Without innovation, design is left with nothing. The form of functional innovation in transportation products can be achieved through design semantics. It is also a creative activity on "how can product design meet the efficiency requirements of functional development." It is the deepening and development of transportation product design, an inevitable result of technological progress, and an objective need for market competition and an intrinsic requirement for enterprise survival and development.

Product functions generally include practical functions, aesthetic functions and cognitive functions. Among them, practical functions are the basis of aesthetic functions and cognitive functions. It determines the structure, materials and other factors of the product, while the aesthetic functions are determined by the various forms and colours of the product that people can perceive to meet people's aesthetic needs. For modern products, people not only ask for excellent functions but also pay more attention to the aesthetic function and man-machine characteristics of the product. Functional innovation is based on innovative ways of thinking rather than fixed thinking. Functional innovation is highly original. The process is unique. The evaluation standards highlight the innovative, revolutionary results that bring social benefits. The research methods focus more on the role of imagination, intuition, inspiration, and subconsciousness in thinking (Harper 2017).

3.2.4 The Aesthetic Value of Product Design

From the concept of product aesthetic value, its main features are as follows.

(1) Aesthetic pleasure. Bringing "pleasure" is the experience of ordinary beautiful things. If a product cannot provide people with the enjoyment of beauty, it will lose its aesthetic value. This is the primary feature that distinguishes the aesthetic value of a product from other values of the product. The aesthetic pleasure of product aesthetic value is not only reflected in the stimulation of sensory perception, but also in spiritual pleasure such as emotional resonance and reflective awareness.
(2) Relational dependencies. The intangible attributes of aesthetic value and the relationship between subject and object value determine the degree of product dependence on aesthetic value. Whether a product is beautiful or not, how much value it has is determined by the consumer. Different consumers will give different processing results to the same value object due to factors such as concepts and preferences (Zhang 2018). At the same time, as a value in product value, in products with practical functions as the premise, if the product func-

tions are designed unreasonably, the aesthetic value of the product will not have any practical effect.

(3) Sensor observation. The mental process of quickly grasping the essence of rationality through perceptual perception is contemplation. Whether the product is beautiful or not, or whether it has aesthetic value, consumers will make a judgment within a short period of time after contact, while the use value requires feedback after a longer period of operation. Not only that, the spiritual attribute of aesthetic value can also play a role in promising quality for the use value of the product (Xu 2006).

(4) Diversity of performance. Clive Bell believes that beauty is a meaningful form. For the product, the general form constitutes the required material, shape, color, pattern and its combination, so that the design of the product's aesthetic value can be realized in a variety of forms, with "free development space (Huang 2005)." Because of this, in product design and marketing with mature technology, product aesthetics and its value become the competitive advantage of enterprises.

(5) Value dynamics. The relationship between subject and object determines the size of the aesthetic value of the product, and the aesthetic marginal effect makes the aesthetic value of the product change dynamically with the changes of the market and time. Because of this, while continuously improving the function of the product, the enterprise will innovate the aesthetic design of the product. And "planned abolition" accelerates this dynamic.

3.3 Types of Product Design

3.3.1 Industrial Design

The concept of industrial design originated after the Industrial Revolution in the 1860s. The founding of the Bauhaus Academy in 1919, led by Walter Gropius from Germany, marks a new stage in industrial design. With the rapid development of science and technology in modern society, various human activities have become increasingly complex and fast-paced. At the same time, industrial design has increasingly taken on an important role in various human activities. In particular, after World War II, the three breakthroughs in science and technology, namely, genetic engineering, microelectronics technology, and space development, brought about rapid changes in various disciplines, continuously changing people's way of thinking, working, and lifestyle. People placed higher demands on the design of clothing, food, housing, and travel in production, work, and life. As a result, industrial design became ever more important in modern society and finally became one of the basic theories for the design of all industrial products and environmental facilities necessary for people's production, scientific research, and everyday life. However, people still have different understandings of industrial design. In March

1964, at an industrial design education seminar in Brussels, Belgium, commissioned by the Federation joined by the United Nations Organization for Scientific and Cultural Affairs (UNESCO) and the ISCID, industrial design was defined as follows: "Industrial design is a creative act. Its purpose is to determine the formal quality of the product. Formal quality is not only limited to exterior and surface characteristics, most importantly, is the relationship between the structure and function of the product, to satisfy both producers and consumers." Since then, this definition has been revised many times by the Federation. At the 11th annual conference held in Paris in 1986, the latest and most authoritative definition of industrial design was: "As far as mass-produced industrial products are concerned, designers use the training, technical knowledge, experience, and visual sense to give new qualities to materials, structure, form, colour, surface treatment, and decoration. This process is called industrial design. According to the specific situation, industrial design should be carried out in different aspects or several aspects of the above-mentioned industrial products, and when it is necessary for industrial designers to use their own technology, knowledge, experience and visual evaluation ability to solve problems such as packaging, publicity, display and market development, this also belongs to the scope of industrial design."

3.3.2 *Traditional Handicraft Design*

Traditional handicraft design is the process of imparting the emotion and design form of traditional craftsmanship to traditional handicrafts. However, in this process, there are some generally superficial, "modern" methods. The designer either simply and directly applies patterns, shapes, etc. that are representative and local in traditional handicrafts as symbols to modern objects; or arbitrarily splices the core process technology of traditional handicrafts with modern production technology. Therefore, the product culture is not unified, and there is a sense of cultural separation. For this kind of handicraft design product, the designer's "aesthetic perception only touches itself to the surface, to the appearance of things, and thus devotes himself to the appearance of things rather than their inner qualities." Therefore, this type of handicrafts only has a "superficial" modernity. It becomes difficult to arouse the emotional identification of modern urban consumer groups with traditional handicrafts. The deep, essential sense of modernity in handicrafts comes from a design concept that captures emotion and function (Wang 2021). Traditional handicraft design mentioned in this book is equivalent to traditional craftsmanship.

3.3.3 Furniture Design

Furniture design is a design activity that mainly involves different ideas in the shape, structure, colour, and function of furniture. It is an important part of interior design, which can improve the quality and aesthetic value of the home environment to varying degrees.

Furniture design in China can be broadly divided into two categories: Chinese furniture design and creative furniture design.

Traditional Chinese furniture is not only distributed as a commercial product in the international market but also has a high status in the art market because of its prominent structural design characteristics and high practical value (Li and Yu 2021).

It has been more than 20 years since the introduction of domestic creative furniture design (Zhou and Wu 2020). Creative design gradually changes the "furniture design"from the past single, rigid, rough ones to those with distinctive features in the market. Furniture production became more tailored and thus favoured by consumers.

3.3.4 Apparels Design

Apparel design means using various fabrics as raw materials, the human body as the object, to design and plan structurally and then make the plan into reality through the processing of the raw materials. Apparel includes clothing, footwear, hats, gloves, bags, etc., which are designed to coordinate with each other and reach unique effects.

Apparel design prioritizes the function of the garment, the effect of wearing, the wearer's hobbies social recognition and the possibility of becoming a trend. Raw material and colour are chosen with the above priorities in mind. The designers then apply the basic principles and methods to produce clothing, making plans into reality. Apparel design is the creation of objects to meet people's own needs.

Apparel design can be generally divided into two types according to different objects: one is to design for a specific object, seek suitable and proportionate styles, and tailor clothing according to conditions such as age, gender, body shape, occupation, etc. Finally, design and produce clothing that can meet the needs and preferences of the specific object. The other is clothing for a large number of people, including a specific age group of one gender, or a specific occupation and a specific occasion. The latter one has a single typical object. The designer measures and investigates extensively various factors related to clothing, determines the applicable age, range of occupation, body shape, wearing time, etc. according to the model standards set by the authority, and at the same time, fits the requirements of mass production and designs related to the production.

3.4 Legal Protection of Intellectual Property

3.4.1 Problems and Countermeasures of Intellectual Property Protection of Industrial Design

(1) Content of Intellectual Property Protection for Industrial Designs

Firstly, a design is under intellectual property protection from the very beginning, and this stage is often the most vulnerable to intellectual property infringement. This stage mainly starts with ideas, drawings, instructions, and models. Generally, "ideas" belong to trade secrets, while product design drawings, instructions, and models are protected by copyright. Trade secrets can be protected by contracts, while copyright is automatically generated and can also be registered. Therefore, the focus of protection at this stage should be copyright and trade secrets.

Secondly, from planning to production, intellectual property protection should focus on registration. At this stage, enterprises that stress intellectual property protection usually apply for patents, register trademarks for designs. The main problem at this stage is that patent applications take too long, and the process is complicated, burying seeds for later infringement that may occur after the design is introduced to the market. Therefore, how to improve the patent application system is the focus at this stage.

Finally, when the product is in the market, it is also highly vulnerable to infringement. We can see rampant infringement in the forms of imitation, plagiarism, and counterfeiting. This is particularly common in the field of design and is very rampant in some fields, such as furniture design and daily necessities design. These products have a short development cycle and are being updated quickly. China's current design application takes a long time and has little protection on these products, so some enterprises will not apply for patents, even those that have applied for patents will be copied. Therefore, this stage should mainly focus on severely cracking down on intellectual property infringement.

(2) Industrial Design and Design Protection

The World Intellectual Property Organization's "Intellectual Property Law Tutorial" points out that "industrial designs belong to aesthetics, but at the same time, they are used as styles of industrial or handicraft manufactured products. Generally, industrial designs have a decorative or aesthetic value that must be visually appealing." However, the EU Design Protection Directive stipulates that "design refers to the appearance determined, in particular, by the characteristics of the line, outline, colour, shape, texture, and materials of the product itself or its decoration." China's Patent Law (2020 Amendment) stipulates that a design refers to a new design that is beautiful and suitable for industrial application by combining the overall or partial shape, pattern, or combination of colour, shape, or pattern of a product. The purpose of legal protection of design is mainly to encourage innovation in the form of the product, so as to enrich the variety of products and provide alternatives to competitive commercial products. In this way, it is possible to meet the needs of different consumers for product shapes, patterns, and colours. Therefore, the design system is very important for the development of industrial design. Both the Paris Convention for the Protection of Industrial Property and the TRIPs Agreement have put forward straightforward requirements for the protection of designs. Currently, most countries have established design protection systems. Generally, design protection is divided into two types. One is protection through patent law, and the other is protection with specific design legislation.

China and the US protect designs as part of the subject of patent law. As early as 1842, the US established a model for protecting designs as part of patent law. At the same time, the US Copyright Act also mentioned design protection.

However, most countries now have specific design legislation, such as Germany, Japan, the European Union, and South Korea (Deacons 2016). The classified design systems of the European Union and South Korea are worth-mentioning. There are two types of EU design systems: (1) Non-registered designs, that is, designs automatically enjoy a 3-year protection period from the date they are first disclosed in the EU, and there is no need to submit an application or fee. This system does not require registration, and the protection period is relatively short, making it more suitable for popular product designs. (2) For designs under a registration system, an application must be submitted to the EU Market Coordinating Authority or the Industrial Property Office of a member State, and can only be registered after passing a formal examination. The protection period is 5 years from the date of application, and it can be renewed 4 times for 5 years after the protection period expires. The maximum protection is up to 25 years. To a certain extent, the achievements of European countries, Germany, and Japan in industrial design show the importance of the design system. Design has something in common with inventions and works of art, but it also has unique characteristics. Now people are gradually reaching a consensus on design, regarding it as an intellectual achievement independent of the invention and work that embodies the decoration or aesthetic of a practical object.

(3) Industrial Design and Copyright Protection

Some of the objects protected by copyright law are closely linked to industrial design, but their protection methods and focus are different from those of patent law. The copyright law mainly protects industrial design drawings and practical art works.

① Industrial design sketches, descriptions and models

Although copyright does not protect mass-produced industrial products, it does provide protection for industrial design sketches, descriptions, and models. In other words, for a product design, copyright is first and foremost granted as long as it meets the requirements, regardless of whether a patent is applied for or mass production is carried out. And although product design sketches have been included in the scope of copyright protection from the beginning, they seem to be less valued in Chinese copyright law compared to literary, artistic, musical works, etc. This situation has not been taken seriously until the emergence of a number of cases of copyright infringement on works of design drawings nowadays. It is particularly common in design trade. For example, infringement occurs in the process of commissioned design, where the client takes possession of the product without compensation; or enterprises publicly solicit design proposals, but use the works of authors without their permission or any remuneration after the authors have been disqualified from the bidding process, etc.

② Applied Art

Art is an important component of human culture, as human beings have created culture and art along with material civilization. Art has different categories, which is also manifested legally. Works of applied art refer to intellectual creations that feature practical applicability, artistry, originality, replicability, and conform to the definition of a work. In the "Legal Terminology of Copyright and Neighboring Rights" compiled by the World Intellectual Property Organization, a work of applied art is defined as "an artistic creation with utilitarian functions, whether made by hand or produced on an industrial scale, such as small toys, jewelry, silverware, furniture, wallpaper, decorations, clothing, etc." Works of applied art are different from general industrial products as they not only serve a practical function in people's lives but also exhibit a certain level of artistic expression.

(4) Industrial Design and Trademark Protection

Trademark is an important part of intellectual property and plays a crucial role in brand establishment. There are different types of trademarks, such as word trademarks, graphic trademarks, combination trademarks, three-dimensional trademarks, etc. These trademarks are widely used in various industries. Three-dimensional trademarks are composed of three-dimensional texts and graphics. For example, the common streamlined bottle of Coca-Cola is a world-famous three-dimensional trademark. In Europe, three-dimensional trademarks are highly valued and there is a trend to replace the appearance design for product packaging. This is because the protection of appearance design has a limited duration, while the protection of trademarks is indefinite (Ma 2001). China's Trademark Law holds the principle of "combining voluntary registration and mandatory registration," which means that it is entirely up to the enterprise to decide whether to register their trademarks. Unregistered trademarks can be used, but only registered trademarks enjoy trademark rights and are protected by law. Therefore, timely trademark registration is crucial for businesses to avoid malicious trademark squatting.

(5) Industrial Design and Trade Secret Protection

The origin of "trade secrets" dates back to ancient times, and the "ancestral secret formulas" in ancient Chinese society are a reflection of ancient people's awareness of trade secrets. With the expanding scope of intellectual property rights, WIPO had already included the rights against unfair competition in intellectual property protection several years ago. Western countries attach great importance to the protection of trade secrets, and China also has relevant regulations. According to the Anti-Unfair Competition Law of China, a trade secret means "any commercial information unknown to the public, including but not limited to technology or business information, with commercial value and for which its lawful holder has taken proper confidentiality measures." Therefore, the conditions for constituting a trade secret are novelty, practicality, and confidentiality. In many cases, copyright law, patent law, etc. cannot provide comprehensive protection for design achievements. For example, copyright protection only extends to the expression of "creativity" but does not protect the "creativity" itself, patent protection covers complete designs and technical solutions, but does not protect design concepts, etc. As a result, people can protect the content of "creativity" through the avenue of trade secrets, by combining trade secret protection with copyright and patent rights, thereby enhancing the level of protection. The protection of trade secrets is generally achieved through the Anti-Unfair Competition Law and Contract Law. The Anti-Unfair Competition Law has clear provisions on the content of trade secrets, and relevant clauses can also be included in contracts regarding trade secrets.

3.4.2 Intellectual Property Protection of Traditional Handicraft Designs

(1) The Concept of Traditional Handicraft Designs

In the 2003 Convention for the Safeguarding of the Intangible Cultural Heritage, traditional handicrafts are included in the definition of "intangible cultural heritage." Literally, traditional handicrafts consist of three parts: "traditional," "hand" and "craft." The term "traditional" emphasizes the passing down from generation to generation, a historical continuity. "Craft" emphasizes the processing of various materials in creation. And "hand" stresses the participation of people in the production process, which distinguishes it from the industrial production of modern art. The word also responses to the term "tradition" and represents a production technique that has been passed down through generations. However, in today's linguistic context, traditional handicraft cannot simply be interpreted literally, but carries a deeper significance.

Many scholars define traditional handicrafts from different perspectives, because various disciplines vary in emphasis during the definition process. For example, scholar Zhang Fuchang (2005) believes that "traditional handicrafts primarily require manual labor, and they are expressed through artistic works or products with unique art styles." Traditional handicraft is a reference changing with the time. For modern times, it mainly refers to traditional forms of production, which are intricately crafted and cannot be replaced by machines, serving as decorative and appreciative crafts (Xi 2009). In recent times, the scope of the term "craft" has gradually been broadened and can be defined as the methods or techniques used in various labor-involved processing (Zhao 2012). Among relevant research, although there are different degrees of emphasis on attributes such as time, artistry, and functionality, traditional handicrafts are primarily seen as a skill mainly displayed in manufacturing processes. In current China, traditional handicrafts often include the products created, and even extend to the methods of using these products. The reason for this may be the strong correspondence between the production and the method, unlike modern crafts that can be applied to many different craft products and can also be applied elsewhere. Therefore, when traditional handicraft is mentioned, traditional handicraft products often come first to people's mind, which also makes traditional handicraft products a manifestation of traditional handicrafts.

(2) Copyright Protect for Traditional Handicraft Designs

① Determination of originality of traditional handicraft design

Although China's Copyright Law clearly states that originality is a prerequisite for the protection of works under copyright law, neither the legislation nor the judicial interpretations have provided a clear determination or criteria for originality (Tian 2010). When the definition of originality has not been legislatively clarified, there will be inconsistencies in determining originality in the judicial practice.

For example, Shaanxi folk paper-cutting artist Bai Xiu'e sued the State Post Bureau and Postage Stamp Printing Bureau for copyright infringement (Bai Xiu'e v. the State Post Bureau and the Stamp Printing Bureau of State Post Bureau 2001; Bai Xiu'e v. the State Post Bureau and the Stamp Printing Bureau of State Post Bureau 2002; Bai Xiu'e v. the State Post Bureau and the Stamp Printing Bureau of State Post Bureau 2003), which exposed the inadequacy of the copyright law. In the case of Bai Xiu'e v. State Post Bureau, the plaintiff Bai Xiu'e was a folk artist of paper cutting. She was born in a rural family in Yan'an, Shaanxi Province, in northwestern China. In 1996 she came to Beijing, where she published art books containing her paper cutting and earned an outstanding reputation for her exquisite designs and fresh rural themes. The China Post Office copied some designs from her book on its stamps. Bai sued the Post Office for copyright infringement. The Post Office claimed that paper cutting is a traditional folk art in China. Many designs have existed for hundreds and thousands of years. Bai's skills and designs of paper cutting were learned from the artists of older generations. Therefore, claimed the Post Office, the designs, as folklore works, should not be protected under the Copyright Law. The dispute between her and China Post Office is whether she is the copyright owner of her paper-cuts which are derivative from the traditional folk paper-cut design in local area. After three trials (from the intermediate people's court to the Supreme Judicial Court) she has won the case finally. The Chinese court from this case conveys a basic principle that the copyright law protects the TCEs (Traditional cultural expressions) derivative works so long as it involves creativities. However, the court doesn't illustrate explicitly that the TCEs itself should be protected or not and how to protect it with law. After three trials (from the intermediate people's court to the Supreme Judicial Court) she has won the case finally. The Chinese court from this case conveys a basic principle that the copyright law protects the TCEs derivative works so long as it involves creativities. However, the court doesn't illustrate explicitly that the TCEs itself should be protected or not and how to protect it with law.

Another example is the copyright infringement case between Chongqing Meiduo Food Co., Ltd. and Chongqing Carrefour Commercial Co., Ltd. The plaintiff, Zhao Menglin, is the copyright owner of the album "Chinese Peking Opera Facial Masks." The album contains 568 Peking Opera masks and 21 Peking Opera character paintings, all independently created by Zhao, who enjoys a high level of authority in this field. Without permission, the two defendants used 12 mask artworks from this album and part of the album's preface text on the packaging of their "Bingdianqing" mineral water products. Moreover, Meiduo had already applied for a design patent for this packaging. The defendants argued that Peking Opera masks are a form of folk art, and the intellectual property should belong to the community as a whole. The first-instance court held that Peking Opera mask art is a form of folk art that has gradually developed along with Chinese opera. Anyone drawing a specific Peking Opera mask must use certain fixed styles, colors, and patterns, which are considered folk art elements. However, the expression of Peking Opera masks is not unique. Zhao Menglin's book, "Chinese Peking Opera Facial Masks," includes 568 masks drawn in a frontal style, selecting distinctive masks and expressing them through his own artistic skills and understanding, thereby distinguishing his work from others. This constitutes a creative reworking of Peking Opera mask folk art, reflecting intellectual and creative effort and creativities, thus warranting copyright protection. The Chongqing High People's Court, in the second instance, supported this view and upheld the original judgment in favor of the plaintiff (Zhao Menglin v. Chongqing Meiduo Food Co., Ltd. and Chongqing Carrefour Commercial Co., Ltd. 2010; Zhao Menglin v. Chongqing Meiduo Food Co., Ltd. and Chongqing Carrefour Commercial Co., Ltd 2011).

At present, China has not made clear provisions on the protection of folk literature and art. However, the new art works created with folk elements and individual creative thinking have a positive impact on the inheritance and development of folk literature and art. Copyright law should also play a protective role, which is also in line with the basic concept of copyright law "to encourage innovation." The case is a successful practice of applying the copyright law to protect traditional handicrafts. In essence, it is a result of weighing the pros and cons, and also provides a reference for the application of the copyright law to the protection of traditional handicrafts.

② The fixity of traditional handicraft design

With regard to the fixity, that is, the work can be reproduced in some form by means of a tangible instrument. It must be permanent and stable instead of temporary, so that it can be perceived and reproduced. In fact, due to the living nature of handicrafts, most of them cannot be fixed in certain forms to realize complete reproduction, nor can they be fixed to some kind of tangible objects. They are usually presented through works featured by unique aesthetics and creative thinking. Thus, the identification of works is difficult. For paper-cutting, those exquisite patterns are not our only focus. Instead, we are more interested in the superb craftsmanship of the paper-cutters and inheritors, especially their individualized creativity and the thoughts, feelings and beliefs embedded in them. Therefore, the pattern created by paper-cutting is a work. The activity of paper-cutting itself is a creative process, not a work, and is therefore outside the scope of copyright protection. However, designs made by traditional handicrafts can be protected by copyright as works, i.e., traditional handicraft designs can be the object of copyright protection.

③ Types of copyright objects for traditional handicraft designs

Generally, traditional handicraft designs can be roughly divided into two-dimensional and three-dimensional. Some art forms rely on traditional craftsmanship to beautify material carriers that have a certain function, such as wallpaper and cloth. This type belongs to two-dimensional graphic design. Throughout the beautification process, wallpaper and cloth are carriers, and thus have no correlation with and do not interact with artistic expression forms. Take wallpaper printed with patterns as an example. The artistic expression embodied in the pattern beautifies the wallpaper, but does not change or affect the practicality of the wallpaper. From the perspective of copyright law, it doesn't make any difference whether the expression of a pattern is on wallpaper or on ordinary paper. Therefore, the wallpaper and the pattern are completely separated. The copyright law only protects the artistic pattern but not the wallpaper as a carrier. Thus, the traditional handicraft design can be protected as the work of fine art in this case. The three-dimensional handicraft design, such as some traditional jewelry, porcelain, etc., can be protected by the copyright law as works of applied art because of its functional and aesthetic significance, which can generally be conceptually and physically separated.

④ Copyright subject for traditional handicraft designs

Generally, traditional handicrafts belong to a certain ethnic group or community and the subject of rights should also be the relevant group, according to its group nature. However, due to the decentralized nature of the group, it will be difficult to determine the size and identity of the group as a whole, and subjects of rights will be hampered in applying for and claiming their rights. Meanwhile, some traditional handicrafts are of individual creation. This is because once a traditional handicraft has been developed and inherited for a long period of time and is still mastered by a certain person, then the sole subject of the rights of that traditional handicraft can only be that person. In addition, it is also feasible for the State to become the subject of rights in traditional handicrafts. First, when the subject of the rights of a certain traditional handicraft cannot be identified, it will be difficult to proceed with its subsequent issues of rights and obligations, fulfillment and inheritance. In order to protect this traditional handicraft, the State can become the subject of its rights, exercising regulatory rights and assuming obligations. Secondly, when the State becomes the subject of the rights, it can play an effective role in protecting traditional handicrafts that haven't exhibited their economic values but are gradually becoming extinct.

⑤ The contradiction between traditional handicraft design and copyright protection

As the spiritual and cultural wealth of mankind, traditional handicrafts show a certain degree of compatibility with copyright law. Because of this, many scholars believe that "intangible cultural heritage is the carrier of intellectual property rights" (Qi 2007) and that the legal protection of traditional handicrafts can be realized through copyright law. However, I believe that there is an inherent connection between seemingly traditional craftsmanship and the applicable objects of copyright law. Nevertheless, there are many deep-seated contradictions between copyright law and the fundamental goals pursued by traditional craftsmanship protection in terms of target legal interests and protection methods.

Traditional handicraft focuses on "original" traditional culture, while copyright attach more importance to protecting new works. The word "original" emphasizes those traditional cultures that have been handed down from ancient times to the present day and have not been altered, especially those that have not been destroyed in commercial development activities. The "new cultures," on the contrary, have been influenced by modern society and have evolved over time from their original state. This kind of culture is highly susceptible to the impact of foreign cultures and may, to a certain extent, be dependent on them, which will gradually lead to cultural "mutation." It is for the purpose of protecting the originality of this traditional culture that the call for protecting handicrafts has never stopped. However, the basic principle of "encourage innovation" of the copyright law seems to be totally contrary to the aim of traditional handicraft protection.

There is a contradiction between the group nature of traditional handicrafts and the private nature of copyright law, and a contradiction between the perpetual nature of traditional handicrafts and the limited-term protection of copyright law. Since traditional handicrafts are the crystallization of human cultural wisdom created by the entire ethnic group or even the whole society, their rights are not owned by individuals, but by a certain group. In a community, traditional culture is shared by the members of that community. Even if it is not, the owner cannot rely on it for private gains. Copyright, on the other hand, protects the author's creative intellectual work by encouraging individual innovation, providing protection for individual's rights. As a result, it seems difficult to reconcile the values between the two, which in practice also impedes protection of traditional handicrafts through copyrights.

(3) Patent Protection for Traditional Handicraft Designs

The "Didi stitch" initiated by Zou Yingzi, the embroideress of the Su Embroidery in Zhenhu, officially has got the National invention patent certificate. According to reports, it is the first invention patent on stitch in the field of embroidery arts in New China, which is 80 years away from the last stitch invention of the Su Embroidery, "random stitch embroidery."

However, the granting of this patent gave rise to a great deal of controversies as to whether or not the "Didi stitch" was inventive or original. Suzhou embroiderers questioned that "Didi stitch" is the same kind of stitch as "Diancai embroidery," which was invented half a century ago with no substantial difference. But Zou Yingzi reckoned that "Didi stitch" had its originality in terms of both its stitching variations and patterns. During the interview, no one reported the issue to relevant authorities, although it had aroused a great deal of controversy. Local people said that they knew what happened, but they would not engage in "the dispute" for the sake of relationship. What's more important is that even if Zou Yingzi obtains the patent, it will not harm the interests of local embroiderers. Even if other people use this stitch, Zou Yingzi can hardly defend his rights, because this skill itself belongs to public knowledge. As for why the government granted the patent, they believe that Suzhou embroidery infringement cases have occurred frequently in recent years, which has added certain external pressure on Suzhou embroidery circle and local government. Acknowledging the Didi stitch as "innovative achievements" can alleviate the negative impact of these cases to a certain extent. But theoretically speaking, granting a patent right of a traditional handicraft to an individual will definitely hinder the spread and exchanges of traditional handicrafts. In addition, the "Didi stitch" itself derives from the traditional Di stitch. Obviously, granting this patent is a contradictory move for the government. Despite the challenges in recognizing this patent, the government still acknowledged the creativity and novelty of this skill out of the encouragement and promotion of Suzhou embroidery. In my opinion, a certain degree of innovation can be identified in Didi stitch's expression. This stitch is suitable for a wider range of creation subjects. However, another question is brought up: whether the handicraft innovation can be patented as technology? Is it more appropriate to apply for design patent?

Article 2 of China's Patent Law stipulates inventions and creations. As technical solutions rather than concepts, inventions must possess certain values and can solve certain problems. Utility models must be products in material form, not technologies or solutions. The examination of material products normally focuses on both the internal structure and external characteristics. Therefore, products without fixed external characteristics cannot be protected by patent law. For embroidery handicrafts, distinctions of external characteristics are often subject to spatial factors. For instance, it will be challenging to discern the differences from a considerable distance when observing two embroidery pieces—one crafted with Didi stitch and the other employing a different embroidery method. In addition, utility models must be artificially created, which may pose some obstacles for traditional handicrafts that rely on natural "masterpieces." For instance, many forms of root carving draw inspiration from nature, but also require meticulous craftsmanship to enhance their aesthetic value. Due to the unique characteristics of these artworks, they are unable to receive effective design protection, which is also a dilemma in the implementation of appearance protection. Some argue that design protection is mainly suitable for mass-produced industrial products rather than for traditional handicrafts with scarcity. Personally speaking, from the physical aspect, general works in material forms can be replicated in massive quantity, while those with unique craftsmanship aesthetics and unable be replicated cannot receive design protection.

3.4.3 Intellectual Property Protection of Furniture Design and Countermeasures

(1) The Scope of Furniture Design Intellectual Property Protection

It is evident that the current furniture industry faces significant infringement problems in both design and manufacturing after a comprehensive analysis of several cases. Furthermore, some parties engaging in clear acts of infringement establish their production and processing facilities abroad, which poses significant obstacles to evidence preservation and compensation (He et al. 2020).

① Structure of furniture

Chinese furniture designers should have a clear understanding that some elements in the structural design of Chinese-style furniture are borrowed from traditional furniture. However, for complete furniture sets, the overall design involves a reconfiguration and modification by designers in response to the demands of the end consumer market. This is totally different from simply replicating traditional furniture designs. However, some individuals attempt to blur the line between inspiration drawing and infringement for their improper gains (Shao et al. 2021).

② Color and style of furniture

Furniture structure design infringement occurs in compositional details while infringement in color style of furniture is manifested on a more superficial level. Some infringers will take high-resolution video and imaging equipment when they visit Chinese furniture expositions in different regions to collect visual data about popular furniture in the market. Then they copy the design of this furniture including structure, size and color. However, the furniture, if made with cheap raw materials of poor quality, are simply counterfeits that look roughly similar to the original ones with a potential risk of reduced service life (Wei et al. 2021).

(2) Copyright Protection of Furniture Design

① Furniture as a work of art needs to be detached from practicality and artistry

In recent years, China's courts have tended to adopt the "separability standard" that an object should be granted copyright protection of applied art only if the artistry of the object can be completely separable from the practicality. But there are many criteria to judge the separability of practical artworks (Fu and Zhang 2020).

In the case of Crosplus Home Furnishing (Shanghai) Co., Ltd. v. Beijing Zhongrong Hengsheng Wood Industry Co. and Nanjing Mengyang Furniture Sales Center (2018), the Supreme Court opined that the Copyright Law protects the originality in the artistic shape or pattern of the work, i.e. its structure or form. In addition to its general and special constituent elements, the practicality and aesthetics of a work of applied art must also be separable from each other in order to be protected by the Copyright Law. This interpretation of "separability standard" is put forward by Professor WANG Qian that with the original and artistic elements removed, if the functionality of product will not be impaired, it can be judged that its artistry can be separated from functionality.

The patterns and colors of the wooden board of the Tang-style Cloakroom Combination Wardrobe were independently designed and completed by Crosplus on its own, and they reflect the creativity of Crosplus through the selection, choice, design and layout. The work possesses aesthetic significance, and shows a level of artistic creation seen in works of fine art. As to whether the practical function of the Tang-style Cloakroom Combination Wardrobe can be separated from its artistic beauty, since its practical function of placing and displaying clothes as cloakroom furniture will not be affected by changing the patterns, colors and texture of the wooden board, the arrangement of metal accessories, and the Chinese-style symmetrical design, the practical function and artistic beauty of the Tang-style

Cloakroom Combination Wardrobe can be separated from each other and exist independently. In summary, the Tang-style Cloakroom Combination Wardrobe is a three-dimensional work of plastic arts combining both practical function and aesthetic significance, thus it is a work of fine art protected by the Copyright Law.

In this case, the Supreme Court considered the practical function of Tang-style Cloakroom Combination Wardrobe was placing and displaying clothes with L-shaped structure fitting with household environment. The artistry of the furniture lays in the patterns, colors and texture of the wooden board, the arrangement of metal accessories, and the Chinese-style symmetrical design, creating an aesthetic effect that harmoniously combines Chinese classic and modern style.

Obviously, change on the artistic level will not impair the practical function of the furniture. Thus, the Supreme Court held that Tang-style Cloakroom Combination Wardrobe should be granted the copyright protection of applied art. From this judicial practice, it can be seen that the "separability standard" is not difficult to meet so that most of technical designs will be excluded from copyright protection. Currently, lots of furniture meets the "separability standard"; however, furniture should have an aesthetic value as artworks before they are granted copyright protection.

Another representative case is the judgment rendered by the Chancheng District People's Court of Foshan in July 2024. The plaintiff has been engaged in the design and sale of stylish and creative home décor clocks and decorative items since its establishment. The plaintiff's clock designs, known for their minimalist and elegant appearance and high-end aesthetic, have gained wide popularity among consumers. With significant creative effort, the plaintiff created original clock designs, including the MAC0138 Clock and Mabdelda (TYOS147) Decorative Art Clock, giving home clocks a distinctive artistic appeal. The plaintiff discovered that the defendant, through its Tmall store, was selling multiple products that were substantially similar in composition, elements, color schemes, and overall design to the plaintiff's artworks. The plaintiff claimed that, as a business peer in the clock industry, the defendant should have been aware of the plaintiff's reputation and designs, yet still chose to imitate and copy several of the plaintiff's works without authorization. This constituted a serious infringement of the plaintiff's reproduction right, distribution right, and information network dissemination right under copyright law.

The Chancheng District People's Court held that for the clock products in question to be protected as works of fine art under copyright law, two criteria must be met: (1) The utilitarian function and artistic expression must be relatively independent. (2) The independent artistic expression must possess originality that meets the minimum threshold for artistic merit required of fine art works. Regarding the first point, the court explained that the functional aspect of the clock—measuring time through powered hands—can be separated physically or conceptually from its artistic features, such as the design of the dial, hands, and scale marks, including their shapes and colors. Changing these artistic elements would not affect the timekeeping function. Therefore, the utilitarian function and artistic expression of the clock can be separated and exist independently. As such, the clocks qualify as fine art works protected under copyright law (Huizhou XX Industrial Co., Ltd. v. Foshan XX Trading Co., Ltd. 2024).

② Furniture as a work of art needs to have a certain aesthetic height

The "small coin theory" known as the general rule of copyright law puts forward a basic requirement of the personality of the author, according to which even a small amount of originality will be recognized as long as it surpasses the originality of a small coin. However, in the case of artworks, Copyright Law comes up with further requirement of an aesthetic value. That is, a higher level of originality.

In the case of Tang-style Cloakroom Combination Wardrobe, the court elaborated on designer's original creation on patterns, colors, texture of the wooden board, accessories design, purfle and style, which finally produced the furniture artworks with aesthetic value.

But the Court still has not made clear to what extent the originality needs to be satisfied for a work of applied art, and whether it is higher than the aesthetic height of an ordinary artwork. As a matter of fact, the measure of aesthetic value varies from person to person. A German scholar once said: "A judge will be incompetent if he or she is blind to literary or aesthetic value in a copyright case." Given that aesthetic value has a great subjective color, it is difficult to accurately measure aesthetic elements, and it is not appropriate for the Supreme Court to make a certain definite standard of measurement in a hasty manner. However, the measure standard can be found by reviewing past domestic court judgments.

The "Mini Beetle Bag" is independently created by Urban Forest, and its overall design is based on the shape of beetle, with the front of the bag sewn together by four pieces of pike-shaped cut-outs. In the case of Shenzhen Urban Forest Co, Ltd. v. Guangzhou Jiading Trade Co., Ltd., the Guangzhou Intellectual Property Court held that the "Mini Beetle Bag" had an aesthetic appeal mainly because of the three stitching lines on the front of the bag, and the back of the bag bulging outwards similar to the shape of the back of a beetle. Besides, the practical function of the backpack was realized when it bulged outwards for storing items, so as to achieve the purpose of expanding the storage. The design above did not meet the minimum creative requirements on the artistic level. Therefore, it did not belong to the the category of applied artwork and was not protected by China's copyright law.

The case of Fanhua Furniture v. Shanghai Meixuan and other companies is listed in the "Top 10 Intellectual Property Cases in Chinese Courts in 2019." In this case, the judgment of People's Court of the Pudong New Area of Shanghai Municipality and the Shanghai Intellectual Property Court provides a clearer idea of the judgment in deciding whether 15 furniture designs belong to works of art.

The Court held that the furniture designs shown above, such as the FRACTAL series, the PLEC dining table and the GEODA entrance cabinet, reflected the designers' unique creativity and artistic concepts in the field of aesthetics, and that their aesthetics had reached a high level of artistic creation. Therefore, they belonged to works of art.

Of the 15 furniture designs, the remaining 10 designs, although somewhat different from common furniture, were relatively simple in their modeling designs and did not reflect a certain level of artistic creation required for a practical artwork. In terms of overall appearance, the above furniture was even less different from its counterparts. Therefore, neither its overall shape nor the artistic design claimed by the plaintiff's constitute works of art.

Another representative case is the dispute over the exhibition right of a work between Fujian Hengyi Terminal Showcase Co., Ltd., Shandong Yijin Food Co., Ltd., and others. The court held that in determining whether the work in question qualifies as a work of fine art under copyright law, the following factors must be considered: (1) Whether the utilitarian and artistic aspects of the work can be separated. (2) Whether the expression, excluding the utilitarian function, is original. (3) Whether the expression, excluding the utilitarian function, reaches a sufficiently high level of artistic merit.

The court found that the triangular base, two rotating wheels, and edge-distributed hanging baskets in the Ferris wheel design of the work were essential structural components necessary for its practical function. Altering these design features would affect the Ferris wheel's ability to rotate the baskets and display products. Therefore, the artistic elements of this part of the Ferris wheel could not be separated from its utilitarian function and lacked originality. In contrast, after excluding the functional aspects, the expression involving the upper double rows of poles and spotlight arrangements, as well as the central pointer design, could be considered separately. According to the copyright registration certificate submitted in the first instance by Hengyi, these parts were independently created by its legal representative, Lin Jianhua, and possess originality.

However, the basis for granting copyright protection lies in the designer's emotional expression embodied in the external form, and such protection targets the pure artistic value of the work. Given that the protection scope and duration of fine art under copyright law far exceed those of design patents, the work must reach a relatively high standard of artistic merit—such that the general public can appreciate it as an artistic creation. In this case, the double-row poles and spotlight arrangement on the upper part of the Ferris wheel and the central pointer, while showing some degree of design novelty and aesthetic appeal, were composed of commonly used lighting arrangements and pointer shapes. Thus, despite some uniqueness, they did not reach the required level of artistic merit. The court therefore concluded that the work in question does not qualify as a work of fine art under copyright law (Fujian Hengyi Terminal Showcase Co., Ltd. v. Shandong Yijin Food Co., Ltd. et al. 2021).

As can be seen from the above cases and some of the court judgments on copyright disputes over practical works of art in recent years, the court's requirement of originality for practical works of art is remarkably higher than that for ordinary works of art. Artworks are supposed to have aesthetic effect, but even the handwriting of a 6-year-old child can reflect the author's personal choice and original expression, whereas in the field of practical artworks, an ordinary furniture design, although it may have cost a great deal of efforts, is likely to be a common creation by the designer simply to achieve practicality. If such a design is protected by copyright law, on the one hand, it is difficult to encourage innovation, and on the other hand, it may lead to a prolonged monopolization by the author of an ordinary design in the public domain.

Thus, a high aesthetic value of applied art is an essential prerequisite for recognition of originality and art in China's courts. A high aesthetic value may be proved by objective factors, such as the reputation of the designer, awards, comments of non-commercial experts, and the collection of museums. Meanwhile, it is also influenced by the judge's subjective cognition. Although the courts of various countries would like to weaken the judge's personal judgment in the trial of copyright cases, art itself has a subjective color, so a piece of furniture with relatively complicated decoration, accessories, patterns, and structures is more likely to reflect a high artistic value, while a piece of minimalist furniture of absolute beauty is difficult to be considered a "work of art" in the legal sense considering it is difficult to express verbally its originality and artistic value.

3.4.4 Problems of Intellectual Property Protection of Apparel Design and Countermeasures

Apparel often go through design, production and launch before entering the market. In different phases such as designing, developing the sample and manufacturing, apparel design appears in different forms. Generally speaking, the following products will be produced in the above processes: apparel design drawing, illustration, samples and ready-to-wear costume. Therefore, in order to clarify the current situation of copyright protection of apparel design, it is necessary to analyze each of the above carriers (Wang 2019).

1. Apparel Design Drawing

① Concept and legal attribute

Apparel design drawings are clothing design patterns drawn by designers to guide the production of costume, which are made up of points, lines, surfaces and various geometric shapes, containing the information of the direction of clothing stitches, outline proportions, sizes, angles and so on. Generally speaking, design drawings reflect the designer's aesthetic comprehension of rigor, precision and simplicity. According to Article 3 of the Copyright Law, the works referred to in this law include works of literature, art, natural science, social science, engineering technology and the like which are created in the following forms. Apparel design drawings should be protected by the Copyright Law as they embody the beauty of science. According to Article 4(12) of the Regulations for the Implementation of the Copyright Law, the apparel design conforms to the definition of "graphic work." Therefore, apparel designs in China's judicial practice are often recognized as "graphic works" for intellectual property protection.

② Infringement for apparel design drawings

Unauthorized reproduce of an apparel design drawing is undoubtedly violating the original creators' copyrights. For example, in the case of Wu Xi Seven Star Girin Uniform Co., Ltd. v. Beijing Yaku Haina Clothing Co., Ltd. (2017), the latter company reproduced the apparel design drawings created by Wuxi Seven Star Girin without permission and tendered them to a third party company, which was ultimately judged by the court to be an infringement of copyright right.

The production of apparel referred to the design drawings is generally not considered to be a "two-dimensional to three-dimensional" reproduction, and therefore will not constitute an infringement of copyright. For example, in the case of Zhang Xinyi and Nasier Reyimu (2021), the court held that the artistry of this artwork could not exist independently from its functionality which should be referred to the industrial property law. Consequently, the production of apparel based on the design drawings does not constitute the act of reproduction or distribution in the sense of the copyright law. In the case of Shanghai Comme MOI Fashion Co., Ltd. v. Guangzhou Trendiano Co., Ltd. (2021), the court also made a similar statement: "In view of the fact that the design drawings of jumpsuit in this case are categorized as product design drawings, and the jumpsuit made according to the design drawings does not constitute a work of art. Therefore, the act of producing jumpsuits based on the design drawings is an act of production, and should not be claimed as reproduction in the Copyright Law."

2. Apparel Design Illustration

① Concept and legal attribute

Apparel design illustration generally refers to the artistic technique to express the final presentation of clothing, including display of fitting, color, fabric, texture, style and so on, generally in the form of watercolor paintings. Such apparel design illustration reflects the original art than just the beauty of science, which is in line with Article 4(8) of the Regulations for the Implementation of the Copyright Law on the definition of "works of fine art": two-dimensional works of arts created in lines, colors, or other media which impart aesthetic effect.

② Infringement for apparel design illustration

Firstly, a "two-dimensional to two-dimensional" reproduction constitutes infringement for apparel design illustration.

Secondly, does the production of apparel based on the design drawing constitute infringement? Apparel design illustration (works of art) has more artistry and aesthetic effect than the apparel design drawings (graphic works) in (1).① above. The production of apparel based on the apparel design illustration can be regarded as a reproduction from "two-dimensional to three-dimensional" if it can completely reproduce the artistry and aesthetic effect thereof, for example, all kinds of dolls made according to the cartoon art works is a typical example of "from two-dimensional to three-dimensional" reproduction. However, as a special kind of industrial products, apparel is unique in its practical function, which is difficult to be separated from artistry. Therefore, in judicial practice, it is still difficult to decide whether the act of making clothes according to the design drawings infringes on the right of reproduction.

3. Apparel Sample

① Concept and legal attribute

Apparel sample refers to a series of different items produced and combined by designer according to the design drawing and other requirements during the development process, such as the collar, sleeves and pockets. The sample implies the designer's understanding of apparel design and production. It is generally recognized as a work for it represents the outcome of the designer's intellectual work. At the same time, apparel samples are necessary preparation to guide the production of clothing, so apparel samples should also be considered as graphic works.

② Infringement for apparel sample.

In the case of Beijing LINC chic Ltd. (LINC) v. Beijing Bosideng Ltd. (2020), the Court of First Instance (CFI) opined that: In essence, except for costumes specially designed for, e.g., stage performances, costume design competitions or other special occasions, that are of outstanding artistic quality and meanwhile taking no account of the functional attributes of ordinary costumes, the ordinary clothes are designed and produced for people's daily wear and aesthetic style. Incorporating ordinary garments into copyright protection is detrimental to not only the development of the garment industry, but also the public interest of society.

4. Ready-to-wear

① Concept and legal attribute

Ready-to-wear, as the name suggests, is finished apparel. In judicial practice, the plaintiffs tend to register ready-to-wear as applied art to court for protection, and the court usually judges based on the definition of applied artworks.

China's current Copyright Law and the Regulations for the Implementation of the Copyright Law do not explicitly provide for the concept of applied artworks, but Article 5(9) of the Copyright Law of the People's Republic of China (Draft Revision) published in 2014, made it clear that "applied art refers to two- or three-dimensional works of arts with practical functions and aesthetic effect, such as toys, furniture, ornaments, etc." From this concept, it can be seen that applied artworks have both practical functions and aesthetic value. Under the current copyright law, the judicial practice generally separates the practical function from the aesthetic value of an applied artwork. The copyright law does not protect the practical function, but categorizes the aesthetic value under the protection of works of fine art as long as it reaches a certain aesthetic height.

② Infringement for ready-to-wear

Since the clothing was produced, it has provided functions to keep people warm and cover the human body. Obviously, such product cannot be recognized as work under the copyright law. However, nowadays as clothing is attributed with design, aesthetics and artistry, is it possible for apparent to be protected as works? After searching for relevant cases, it can be found that apparel is scarcely recognized as works to be protected. The reason for this is the aesthetic design of apparent is difficult to be separated from its practical function. In this regard, the clothing cannot be protected by the copyright law. For example, in the case of Xi'an Eurasian University v. Hunan Benedict Clothing Company Limited (2022), the court held that "the fabric of the apparel in this case is polyester which is a commonly used fabric for this type of clothing; the design of the T-shirt includes color stitching of white and camouflage, print of the logo of the Xi'an Eurasian University. In spite of some creativity, the practicality of the T-shirt as a military training uniform weighs more. Therefore, the artistry and originality of the apparel has not yet reached the high level required for a work of art, and it will not be protected by the Copyright Law."

In another case, the plaintiff Yunchuang Clothing Design Co., Ltd. claimed that its 11 MAXRIENY brand garments constituted works of art protected by the Copyright Law, 8 of which had completed the registration or filing of works. It requested Vias Clothing Co., Ltd., Vias Clothing Co., Ltd. Guangzhou Branch, Meet Clothing Store, Peishan Clothing Store, Liwangcai Clothing Store and Kola Clothing Store to immediately stop the unfair competition and infringement of Yunchuang's copyright. Before determining whether the defendants' behavior in this case infringes on Yunchuang's copyright, it should be primarily judged whether the clothing designed and produced by Yunchuang constitutes a work of art in the Copyright Law.

The court of first instance held that the clothing in this case had a practical function, but the artistic components contained therein could exist independently of its practical function in conception. Take the black lace blouse in question as an example, even if the special design of transparent netting on the upper part of the two sleeves and fluffy modeling in the middle were removed, and the entire clothing was made in black fabric, the fulfillment of its function as a piece of clothing would not be affected in the slightest. Thus it was an artistic work protected by the Copyright Law. However, in terms of the three garments not registered for copyright, they would not be granted copyright protection due to insufficient evidence of the source and originality (Shenzhen Yunchuang Clothing Design Co., Ltd. v. Vias Clothing Co., Ltd. et al. 2019).

The court of second instance also opined that the copyrighted work of art had a practical function, and its artistic component mainly embodied in the appearance could be conceptually separated from the practical function. Therefore, the determination of the court of first instance was appropriate the court of first instance was appropriate (Shenzhen Yunchuang Clothing Design Co., Ltd. v. Vias Clothing Co., Ltd. et al. 2020).

Another representative case is the judgment rendered in April 2024 by the Gongshu District People's Court of Hangzhou, Zhejiang Province. The court held that two-dimensional or three-dimensional visual art created using lines, colors, or other methods and possessing aesthetic value falls within the scope of fine art works protected under China's Copyright Law. For a clothing design to be protected as a fine art work, its originality and artistic merit must reach the standard required of three-dimensional fine art. In this case, the clothing item at issue could not be protected as a fine art work under copyright law for the following reasons: The disputed design was a fitted black-and-white contrast color POLO dress with a knit collar. Elements such as the dress style, collar design, body-con fit, and color blocking are all commonly seen in women's fashion. Whether considered individually or in combination, these design elements are standard in ordinary womenswear and do not produce a visual effect that differs significantly from typical clothing styles. The main fabric used was also a commonly available commercial material. Therefore, the clothing in question should be classified as an industrial product rather than a copyrightable fine art work. Although the design reflects a degree of creativity on the part of the designer, its overall form does not demonstrate the level of originality and artistic value required for fine art works. The artistic expression of the dress does not surpass its utilitarian function; it remains a garment that primarily serves a practical purpose and thus falls outside the protection of copyright law (Hangzhou Inasou Fashion Co., Ltd. v. Zhejiang Hongxiu Industrial Co., Ltd. et al. 2023).

From the above analysis, it can be seen that the court usually adopts an affirmative attitude in the determination of whether apparel design drawing, design illustration and apparel samples belongs to the work in the Copyright Law. Any reproductions of these graphic works or works of art will be recognized as infringement. But it is difficult to determine whether ready-to-wear constitutes a work.

On the other hand, even if it is recognized as a work protected by the Copyright Law, the difficulties of determining infringement lie in the determination of the separation of the practicality from the artistry of ready-to-wear (in determining whether it constitutes a work or whether it constitutes a reproduction of "from two-dimensional to three-dimensional").

In conclusion, there are many deficiencies under the current laws and regulations. Chances are that the intellectual property of apparel design may not be effectively protected through the single legal approach of Copyright Law. Clothing enterprises are encouraged to seek protection through various paths, such as design patent, trademark right, anti-unfair competition and so on. They also can select more appropriate and economical way to protect the intellectual property by taking into consideration the stage of business development, enterprise scale as well as different personal demands.

References

Beijing First Intermediate People's Court (20 Nov 2001) The Case of Bai Xiu'e v. State Post Bureau, Stamp Printing Bureau of State Post Bureau, Copyright Infringement Dispute [2001] No. 185;

Beijing High People's Court (6 Nov 2002) The Case of Bai Xiu'e v. State Post Bureau, Stamp Printing Bureau of State Post Bureau, Copyright Infringement Dispute [2002] No. 252

Beijing High People's Court (15 Dec 2003) Dispute over Copyright Infringement in the Case of Bai Xiu'e v. the State Post Bureau and the Stamp Printing Bureau of the State Post Bureau for Not Entering into a Contract with Her, Modifying and Using Her Work without Her Consent [2003] No. 823

Beijing Intellectual Property Court (2017) The Case of Wu Xi Seven Star Girin Uniform Co.,Ltd v. Beijing Yaku Haina Clothing Co., Ltd. [2017] No. 1214

Beijing Intellectual Property Court (2020) The Case of Beijing LINC chic Ltd. (LINC) v. Beijing Bosideng Ltd [2020] No.87

Chongqing First Intermediate People's Court (8 Mar 2011) The Case of Zhao Menglin v. Chongqing Meiduo Food Co., Ltd. and Chongqing Carrefour Commercial Co., Ltd., Copyright Infringement Dispute [2010] No.460

Chongqing High People's Court (19 Jul 2011) Zhao Menglin v. Chongqing Meiduo Food Co., Ltd. and Chongqing Carrefour Commercial Co., Ltd., Copyright Infringement Dispute [2011] No.188

Co., Ltd. v. Zhejiang Hongxiu Industrial Co., Ltd. et al., Copyright Ownership and Infringement Dispute [2023] Zhe 0105 Minchu No. 10000

Design protection in the European Union (2016). https://www.deacons.com/tc/2016/03/07/design-protection-in-the-european-union/. Accessed 7 Nov 2022

Foshan Chancheng District People's Court (4 Jul 2024) The Case of Huizhou XX Industrial Co., Ltd. v. Foshan XX Trading Co., Ltd., Copyright Ownership and Infringement Dispute [2023] Yue 0604 Minchu No. 8075

Fu L, Zhang M (2020) Discussion on copyright protection of furniture design as applied art. https://mp.weixin.qq.com/s/2-IknVtyGcRK2AdV8tF58A. Accessed 4 Sep 2022

Guangzhou Haizhu District People's Court (2019) The Case of Shenzhen Yunchuang Clothing Design Co., Ltd. v. Vias Clothing Co., Ltd., Vias Clothing Co., Ltd. Guangzhou Branch, Meet Clothing Store, Peishan Clothing Store, Liwangcai Clothing Store and Kola Clothing Store [2019] No. 8655

Guangzhou Intellectual Property Court (2020) The Case of Shenzhen Yunchuang Clothing Design Co., Ltd. v. Vias Clothing Co., Ltd., Vias Clothing Co., Ltd. Guangzhou Branch, Meet Clothing Store, Peishan Clothing Store, Liwangcai Clothing Store and Kola Clothing Store [2020] No. 4408

Hangzhou Gongshu District People's Court (15 Apr 2024) The Case of Hangzhou Inasou Fashion

Harper KH (2017) Aesthetic sustainability: product design and sustainable usage. Routledge, London

He YM, Zhao B, Xiao JH (2020) The influence of drying methods on the dimensional stability of solid wood flooring for ground heating. For Prod Ind 1:25–28

Huang KF (2005) Aesthetic value theory. Yunnan People's Publishing House, Kunming

Jiang B, Cheng X (2013) Research on the way of creating intellectual property in the product design. Packag Eng 18:88–91

Jin ZY (2002) Soft technology: the space and substance of innovation. Xinhua Publishing House, Beijing

Li CH, Yu SJ (2021) Analysis on the key points of intellectual property protection in the design and manufacture of Chinese style furniture. China For Prod Ind 12:94–96

Liu GZ (2005) Follow path of Chinese contemporary industrial design. Decoration 1:6–9

Ma XS (2001) Innovation and protection-a patent management insight. Science Press, Beijing

Ma HY (2019) Product aesthetic value and its design innovation dimension. Packag Eng 40:102–106

Mike B (1995) Product design. CRC Press LLC, Florida

Morris R (2009) The fundamentals of product design. Bloomsbury Publishing, London

Ningbo Intermediate People's Court (7 Jan 2022) The Case of Fujian Hengyi Terminal Showcase Co., Ltd. v. Shandong Yijin Food Co., Ltd. et al., Dispute over Exhibition Right of a Work [2021] Zhe 02 Minzhong No. 4782

Qi AM (2007) Comprehensive intellectual property protection of intangible cultural heritage. Electron Intell Prop 6:19–22

Shaanxi High People's Court (2022) Xi'an Eurasian University v. Hunan Benedict Clothing Company Limited [2022] No. 115

Shanghai Intellectual Property Court (2021) The Case of Shanghai Comme MOI Fashion Co., Ltd. v. Guangzhou Trendiano Co., Ltd. [2021] No.879

Shao XD, Zhang JJ, Du Y et al (2021) Parametric design method of hardwood furniture components based on NX. For Prod Ind 2:48–51

Supreme People's Court (2018) The Case of Crosplus Home Furnishing (Shanghai) Co., Ltd. v. Beijing Zhongrong Hengsheng Wood Industry Co. and Nanjing Mengyang Furniture Sales Center [2018] No. 6061

Tian Y (2010) A brief discussion on the constituent standards of work originality. Sci Educ Guide (Mid-month Ed) 2:122

Wang J (2019) Apparel design copyright protection study. https://mp.weixin.qq.com/s/QP-1BiGw-3Wwc91hir9JDw. Accessed 7 Sep 2022

Wang WN (2021) Design to give a sense of modernity: the path of returning traditional handicrafts to modern everyday life. Art Des Res 3:7

Wei LS, Zhang JH, Su RZ (2021) Study on the relationship between surface morphology and color of decorative materials. China For Prod Ind 58(06):13–20

WIPO (2022) What is an industrial design. http://www.wipo.int/designs/en/. Accessed 7 Oct 2022

Xi RY (2009) Will 'Chinese handicrafts' truly become a 'masterpiece'? - A brief discussion on the current situation and revival of traditional Chinese handicrafts. Sci Technol Inf 13:184

Xiao ZQ (2008) Expression of emotion symbols in product design. Packag Eng 29(9):149–156

Xinjiang Uygur Autonomous Region Higher People's Court (2021) The Case of Zhang Xinyi and Nasier Reyimu [2021] No. 318

Xu HC (2006) Design aesthetics. Tsinghua University Press, Beijing

Zhang FC (2005) Discussion on the revitalization of China's traditional handicraft industry. Art Life 4:62–63

Zhang YH (2018) Design aesthetics. China Textile Press, Beijing

Zhao Y (2012) Analysis of the concept of 'handicrafts'. J Nanjing Art Inst 3:85–88

Zhou PP, Wu Q (2020) Research on intellectual property protection in creative furniture design in China. For Prod Ind 10:80–81

Chapter 4
Environment Design and Intellectual Property

4.1 The Concept of Environment Design

4.1.1 The Definition of Environment Design

Environment design incorporates a series of techniques, principles and methodology in different disciplines. It usually refers to a comprehensive design and planning in environmental space and art, including environment and facility, space and decoration, form and structure, materials and color, light, practical function and aesthetic function (Hu and Lu 2018). Environment design (2022) is a new approach in planning consumer products and industrial processes that are ecologically intelligent, sustainable, and healthy for both humans and our environment. Environment design is the process of addressing surrounding environmental parameters when devising plans, programs, policies, buildings, or products. It seeks to create spaces that will enhance the natural, social, cultural and physical environment of particular areas (Caves 2004).

Environment design became independent from planning design, which is equally important with planning design and residential design (Han and Yang 2001). In environment design, the natural ecological environment is explored to achieve a harmonious symbiosis between people and the environment (Han and Yang 2001). The "environment" mainly refers to the various spaces and places where people live in real life from the perspective of design. Broadly speaking, space and place is expected to cover the whole world we live in. From the viewpoint of design method, exterior environment design is "public" where architects, urban planners, landscape designers and sculptors have all been involved in this field (Ren 2004).

N. Jiang, *Design, Innovation and Intellectual Property*,
https://doi.org/10.1007/978-981-95-2042-8_4

4.1.2 Aim of Environment Design

Environment design, design for environment, eco-design, green design, sustainable design, design for sustainability, cradle to cradle—all these terms refer to integration of environmental requirements in all stages of the product development process, with the aim of reducing the environmental impact of all life cycle steps and maximizing sustainability.

At its root, environmental design is not necessarily about new technology, although recent advances have furthered the field considerably. It is about using what is already there, instead of demolishing and leveling a building site, for example. Working with the imperfections and unique aspects of each individual site ultimately makes the end product operate more smoothly, at a lower cost (Brady 2022). The need to understand the patterns of interaction between the forces of nature and buildings has produced a demand for computing power large enough to perform the analysis. It is only through our ability to import the real complexities of the natural world into cyberspace that we can test the environmental performance of not-yet-constructed buildings (Hagan 2008). With the application of intelligent technologies such as big data and cloud computing, some scholars have proposed to integrate interactive environmental design into the construction of smart cities. To enhance the vitality of smart cities' environment is not just rely on the advanced science and technology, also needs the involvement of interaction design, thus, interactive environment design become the new horizon of smart city construction, we should extend the vision of smart city construction from the development and application of urban technology to the interactive environment design, and building a smart interactive environment with more intelligent, more convenient, and more attention to the human living experience (Deng et al. 2017).

4.2 Features and Values of Environment Design

4.2.1 Features of Environment Design

Lawrence Halprin is a master of human environment design and one of the leading architects among the third generation of the U.S. architects. He worked in urban planning, city design, landscape design, architectural design and methodology. In brief, the core of Halprin's ideas in environment design mainly lies in three aspects: First, environment design serves people having activities in real environment. Human beings interact with the environment and the two are interdependent. Secondly, design is an integrated issue, in which the process is as important as the result. A proper design is recommended to be come up with collective intelligence of users. Thirdly, environment problems should be solved on the basis of, or in accordance with, ecological principles (Zhang and Cheng 1992).

(1) Integrity (Hu and Lu 2018)

From the point of view of the behavioral characteristics of the design, environment design is a kind of art that emphasizes the overall effect, in which the creation of physical elements (including a variety of outdoor architectural components, decorative landscapes, etc.) is very important. But the primary thing is to grasp the overall design of the outdoor environment. A complete environment design is required not only to fully reflect the nature of the various substances that constitute the environment, but also manifest a unified and perfect overall effect.

(2) Human-Environment Interaction

For a long time, the relationship between people and the environment has been a prominent issue in architectural design, and no matter in what type of environment design, people and nature, and their relationship are important considerations. In order to meet a wide range of social needs, architecture must reflect the cultural characteristics of the times, regions, nationalities and the general public to keep pace with social life and social development. Environment design will combine the landscape with cultural elements such as humanities, history, customs, regions and so on. The architectural landscape in the urban residence may embrace local customs or exotic styles. The interaction between people and environment is mostly manifested in the psychological activities and external performance after stimulus and the transfer of activity space, so the two complement and constrain each other at the same time (Hu and Lu 2018).

(3) Integration of Architecture with Environment

Environment and architecture are not independent of each other, but interrelated and integrated. In the process of design, we must pay attention to the matching and integration of architecture with environment. An organic and unified integration of architecture and environment will achieve a high degree of consistency in style, culture and form. Designers show environmental concern and value for sustainability, indigenous plants, utility, quality and safety (Breed 2022). They hope natural environment factors would be more considered in future environmental design and better utilize natural environment to improve human artistic sensibilities by enhancing design environment (Chen et al. 2013).

(4) Principles of Environment Design

When carrying out environment design, the designer's ideas and methods are crucial. The corresponding design principles should be followed: First, the environment design should make full use of environmental elements, such as space layout and landscape design which are important parts of environment design. The designer should fully express the characteristics of the environmental elements through appropriate planning, so that the environmental space presents an artistic effect. Secondly, designers should respect human feelings in environment design. One of the important purposes of environment design is to make users feel comfortable. Therefore, the environment design must take into account the behavioral habits and mental state of people. The value of the architecture will be realized only if the environment and the users are in harmony with each other (Qiu 2022).

In the artistic design of the environment, the design approach and expression of innovation should also consider the following two aspects: First, the environment design should focus on its practical function because human serves as the subject of architectural design. If a building shows more artistry than the functionality, its practical value will be severely reduced. Therefore, in terms of the environment design, designers should pay attention to the functionality of the built environment, such as the building's walls, floors, and other scenic views, etc. The demands of the the residents should be considered so that the building can not only present the artistic value but also enrich people's daily life by rendering comfort and convenience. Secondly, the innovative expression of environment design should be reflected in the emotional satisfaction and cultural connotation of the building. Environment design is the visualization of art, so the cultural connotation of the building and the emotional needs of the user is an important embodiment of its artistic value. The designcr can influence the emotions and mental state of the users through color, space form design, etc., so that they can get along with the architectural environment more harmoniously. The expression of cultural connotation can be realized in landscape design, furniture design style and other scenes, such as typical patterns, symbols and other cultural elements (Qiu 2022).

4.2.2 Value and Necessity of Environmental Design and Protection

Values are the ideals or principles we consider important in our lives, the ideas that give purpose and meaning to our thoughts and actions (Rokeach 1973). They are qualities that society considers worthwhile as ends in themselves—such as liberty, truth, and justice—that form the basis of our customs and institutions. Judgments about ethical behavior are a manifestation of values (Snow et al. 2000). Values are based on the comparative worth we ascribe to things, whether tangible or intangible (Murphy 2016). Aesthetic values refer to the quality of the human experience and the extent to which that experience brings sensual and emotional pleasure and satisfaction (Murphy 2016).

Environment design can be subdivided into indoor environment design, built environment design, virtual environment design, landscape architecture design, the public art design and so on. Different types of environment design carry different design purposes and values. The purpose of the indoor environment design is to improve the living environment of the human, to experience a comfortable and warm feeling, in further to transform the nature. In another word, indoor design is a move to modify the natural, which will extremely lay important impact on the human living environment (Wen and Shu 2013). For Built environment design, once a building has been built, it could last more than hundred years, and the society's general assumptions at the time of its building decide the requirement level of functionality, whether safety, usability, accessibility, and provisions of building services (such as elevators and air conditioning) (Kose 2016). While the public art design is the embodiment of the ideal and passion of modern urban culture and urban life, which is a unique way to shape, memorize and enjoy the city and is the symbol of the geographical location and geographical features of the urban cultural spirit (Jiang 2019).

(1) Value of Architectural Design

Architectural design is crucial to the development of the construction industry, for good design ideas can effectively guide the construction of the architecture to be both practical and artistic, highlighting the economic value and social value of the building. Architectural design is an important part in the whole construction process, where designers have to reasonably divide the spatial layout of the building, and consider the environment design of the building through scheme of color, layout, landscape and interior decorations to create an artistic effect and value. It can be seen that the architectural design is a highly comprehensive work, serving as a guidance to the subsequent construction of the building.

Architectural design is considered the basis and the first phase before bringing the idea to reality. Under these lines, you will discover more about what architectural design is, its different types and some helpful examples. The reason for architects' interests in design is clear. They usually tried to design more than the enclosed space and be responsible for at least a part of the interior as well and so extended their practice to design furnishings and to commission tradesmen to realize these ambitions. As architecture had existed long before the other design fields, craftwork and trade skills had for a long period been architecture's only true competitors (Lieke 2008).

(2) Value of Landscape Architecture

Landscape design deals with form and meaning and is concerned with the organization of a physical, functional and aesthetic arrangement of a variety of structural elements to achieve desired social, cultural and ecological outcomes.

In general, the values of landscape architecture lie in three broad areas: aesthetic, ecological, and social. Landscape architecture is committed to enhancing human experience, sustaining environmental quality, and establishing social equity. Just as importantly, landscape architecture values the spiritually satisfying and psychologically health-giving benefits of people's harmonious relationships with one another and with their environment. More than anything else, landscape architecture values a holistic approach to addressing utility, beauty, and health as complementary, not competing interests.

Landscape architecture is not simply for creating a landscape effect, but also to further improve the ecological environment of urban waters, enhance the economic value of the land surrounded, improve water quality, air quality and so on. The combination of natural landscape improvement and cultural landscape protection can not only reflect the historical and cultural heritage and landscape characteristics of gardens, but also highlight the cultural connotation and local landscape characteristics of the modern urban landscape (Yu 2022).

(3) Value of public art design

Public art has gained a prominent role in urban design in many contemporary Western countries, and it can also play an important role in the creation of a recognizable identity of a city. Apart from the fact that art per se increases the level of visual quality in any urban space, it also promotes the strategies of a society in terms of enhancing the level of art education for its citizens, while also being a part of certain strategic goals (Arandelovic 2018).

Numerous forms of visual art, such as performances, public shows, installations, actions, and mutual cooperation through art with local communities constitute an important part of urban city space nowadays (Miles 1997). Conventional art presentations have been left in order to make a closer coherence between artists and viewers, thus laying a new approach to art with a less elitist artistic approach (Miles 1997).

"The contribution of public art is often deliberately symbolic," often turned into a tourist landmark as "a positive development in bringing visitors to a part of the city otherwise off the tourist map and for encouraging awareness of the ethnic diversity of the city." Also, the aim of public art can be to engage the public in the community or provoke unending polemics. Both can be seen in Berlin. Berlin has become one of the most attractive global cities, and public art can help it to keep that role in the future and further attract tourists as an inherent part of the public space in the city. Thus, public art can have an even bigger role in the identity and branding of Berlin and might become a relevant factor for the city's development in the future.

4.3 Types of Environment Design

4.3.1 Architectural Design

(1) The Concept of Architectural Design

As a creative product of human beings, architecture aims to satisfy people's needs both physically and psychologically, to provide people with places for various activities. On the material level, architecture and natural environment constitute the physical space on which human beings rely for survival; on the spiritual level, it symbolizes social culture and makes up an important part of human civilization (Hu and Lu 2018). Architectural design is a discipline that focuses on covering and meeting the needs and demands, to create living spaces, using certain tools and especially, creativity. Therefore, the aim is to combine the technological and the aesthetic, despite the general belief that architecture is only a technological task (Architectural design 2020). The model of the architectural design illustrates the use, site, technology and form. "Use" refers to how people use space which includes learning about human body dimensions, movement and perception. "Site" refers to how a building relates to a site and its surroundings, such as the knowledge about site, topography, orientation, transportation, and so on. "Technology" refers to the construction of a building and includes knowledge of materials, structure and construction. "Form" means the form and perception of a building, which includes basic knowledge and perception of form, space, material, light and color. Design is the integration of different design issues and the practice of transforming a design idea into physical architecture (Gu and Bo 2013). However, the concept of architecture is not the simple sum of these four aspects, and the extra quality is contributed by design.

It mixes design, understood as the creative process, and architecture, which is based on the creation and presentation of solutions at a technical level. By mixing both disciplines, architectural design seeks the values and formal qualities of the works, through spatial experiences. In general, we associate it with drawings, sketches or outlines of a project, and it is one of its fundamental bases. In this aspect of architectural design, there are also other factors involved, that are related to geometry, space or aesthetics, among others. After all, architecture, and therefore architectural design, is made up of many elements and processes or phases.

(2) Architectural Design

Drawings Architectural drawings serve for architectural design, so different design drawings are required in different stages of architectural design, such as preliminary design drawings in the initial schematic stage, followed by technical design drawings and construction drawings. The art of architectural drawing serves both as a kind of how-to book about the techniques of architectural drawing and as an examination of the creative impulse which that technique intimately serves. "Architectural artwork" should be distinguished from design or process drawing in architecture. The latter is about architecture as structure and object, and its various goals are to envision, propose, document and guide the production of building. It is limited by the goals of the actual design and making of a building. Architectural artwork, in contrast, may have nothing to do with architecture as a structure. Rather, it seeks to represent building or ideas about building and is defined by the self-imposed limits set by the artist. It is more concerned with the visual experience of the drawing than with the object that it represents (Robbins 1997).

(3) Architectural Models

Architectural model is a three-dimensional model that organically combines design drawings with the three-dimensional space, which is helpful for the creation of design because it can present a visualized form of the design and make up for the limitations of the architectural drawings for illustration. It is part of the designer's design process, but also an expressive way to present the design. An architecture model is a partial abstraction of a system. It is an approximation, and it captures the different properties of the system. It is a scaled-down version and is built with all the essential details of the system. Architecture modeling involves identifying the characteristics of the system and expressing it as models so that the system can be understood. Architecture models allow visualization of information about the system represented by the model (Kumar et al. 2014).

(4) Architecture

Architecture is a general term for buildings and structures. It is the artificial environment built with utilization of materials, techniques and application of scientific law, principles of "feng shui" and aesthetic theory in order to meet the needs of social life. For clarification of the usage, buildings will be distinguished from non-architectural structures which are not occupied by people in long term. And some architectural scholars, for the purpose of avoiding confusion, will name buildings as "architecture" if its exterior appearance is specially designed by people. Human beings have built various kinds of buildings to provide space and support for the functioning of society. Those buildings as the major creations in artificial environment often guarantee a stable space for people's residence and other activities like religion, business and production.

The word *architecture* can have many meanings. Architecture can be both an art and a science, a process and a result, and both an idea and a reality. People often use the words "architecture" and "design" interchangeably, which naturally broadens the definition of architecture (Craven 2021). From the Latin word *architectura*, the word we use describes the job of an architect. The ancient Greek *arkhitekton* was the chief builder or master technician of all craftsmen and artisans. In the dictionary, "architecture" has two meanings: (1) The art and science of designing and building structures, or large groups of structures, in keeping with aesthetic and functional criteria. (2) Structures built in accordance with such principles (Cyril ed al. 1975).

4.3.2 *Landscape and Garden Design*

(1) The Concept of Landscape and Garden Design

Landscape architecture as an English term appeared for the first time in the title of the book 'On the Landscape Architecture of the Great Painters of Italy' by Scott in 1828. Subsequently it was used by Frederic Law Olmstead and Calvert Vaux at the design competition for the Central Park in New York in 1858. The profession became official, when in 1863 the title 'landscape architect' was first used by the state appointed Board of Central Park Commissioners in New York City (Evert ed al. 2010; Steiner 2001).

The definition of landscape architecture according to the International Federation of Landscape Architecture (IFLA) is: "A profession and academic discipline that employs principles of art and the physical and social sciences to the processes of environmental planning, design and conservation, which serve to ensure the long-lasting improvement, sustainability and harmony of natural and cultural systems or landscape parts thereof, as well as the design of outdoor spaces with consideration of their aesthetic, functional and ecological aspects (Evert ed al. 2010; Steiner 2001)."

(2) Principles of Landscape and Garden Design

The development of gardens is closely related to the life of mankind as different environmental factors and national habits in different countries around the world will give rise to different garden styles. In the contemporary era, landscape architectural practice exists in an international market of planning and design services. History shows that international practice in landscape architecture has occurred for many hundreds of years (Zhang Y 2021). The landscape and garden design is different from that of visual art and painting creation, because it requires rational thinking, subjective cognition and creativity to establish varied associations between the representation of landscape and garden and the physical object. In the design process, designers should deal with site problems featuring multi-dimension and multi-location; focus on the long-term impact and benefits of landscape evolution and development; and reveal social, political, environmental, and aesthetic values, making it adaptable, flexible, and inspiring. "With an artistic mood to build a garden, then the garden becomes a new source of artistic mood" delivers a wonderful message in Qi Biaojia's "Mountain Note." An intelligent gardener and visitor must be able to understand the "garden" means more than a spatial form, but a process of mutual elaboration and formation of the "artistic mood" (Li X 2020). The natural landscape has its own harmonious and stable structure and function, so the artificial design must be adapted to the original "design" of the natural landscape to minimize the negative effects of the landscape elements created by human, and to ensure the integrity of the overall landscape structure and function. As a discipline, landscape architecture is situated at the interface of the arts, the sciences, and the humanities. This unique position provides many perspectives from which to assess design success or failure. It also provides access to many opportunities for design innovation (Murphy 2016).

(3) Landscape/Garden Design Drawings

Landscape/Garden design drawing is a tool for designers to express their ideas and communicate with each other, a direct visual product for clients to understand the final effect of the design. The professional drawing of landscape design involves the drawing specifications of three majors: architecture, landscape architecture and urban planning, which is determined by the characteristics of the landscape design. In the design process, in order to accurately and vividly express each design detail, it is necessary to draw a variety of drawings with artistic expression, such as using plan, elevation, section and perspective drawings to provide illustrations.

The construction drawing of landscape and garden actually puts various indicators and construction elements in a visualized form, which will guide the landscape construction and serve as the reference for construction. The drawing is divided into five parts, including catalogs, notes, detail drawings, general drawings and several professional drawings (Wu 2021).

(4) Landscape/Garden Design Models

The model is an abstraction or simplification of an entity or phenomenon in the real world, an object or concept that represents an objective matter consciously with the help of entities or virtual method, and an expression of the most important components of an entity or phenomenon and their interrelationships with each other. Its purpose is for describing, explaining, predicting or designing the entity or phenomenon (Yuan and Cheng 2018).

Similar to architectural models, landscape/garden design models can also play a role in visualizing the design. Landscape as three-dimensional construction, it elaborates on the visual manifestation of open spaces, surfaces, screens and volumes and their relationships in terms of structural organisation (e.g., balance, tension, rhythm, proportion, scale) and ordering principles (e.g., axis, symmetry, hierarchy, datum, transformation) (Bell 1993).

4.3.3 *Public Art Design*

(1) The Concept of Public Art Design

Public sphere is one of the concepts commonly adopted by academics in English-speaking countries in recent years, which refers to the space with open and public features, freely visited and recognized by the public. And public art refers to the art creation and corresponding environment design in this public space. Simply put public art is art in public spaces. The term "public art" may conjure images of historic bronze statues of a soldier on horseback in a park. Today, public art can take a wide range of forms, sizes, and scales—and can be temporary or permanent. It often interprets the history of the place, its people, and perhaps addresses a social or environmental issue. Public art can include murals, sculpture, memorials, integrated architectural or landscape architectural work, community art, digital new media, and even performances and festivals (What is public art 2022).

The public art abroad originated in the United States in the 1960s and it gradually developed into a prevailing art concept (Dong and Dai 2011). Early practices focused on creating urban characteristics, attracting investment and boosting tourism, and later developed to enhance and activate urban public space, and to reflect community values and identity through the application of of urban public art (Jia and Xu 2014). Especially the creation of war and disaster memorial space has successfully constructed a collective memory, such as the Memorial Site for the Murdered Jews of Europe in Berlin, Germany, the Vietnam War Memorial and other war memorial spaces; the 9/11 National Memorial Park, the Oklahoma City Bombing Memorial Park and other disaster memorial spaces; the Japanese American Historical Plaza, Civil Rights Movement Monument and other political memorial spaces.

(2) Forms and Features of Public Art Design

① Two-dimensional public art design

Two-dimensional public art refers to the art creation in public space attached to the wall, ground or flat space. Its material only occupies a very small volume of space or it is just a two-dimensional design mainly relying on visual effects to convey the information. It is divided into traditional mural creation and contemporary mural creation in terms of painting style, into drawing and processing categories in terms of creation method, and into static and dynamic forms in terms of forms of expression.

② Two-point-five dimensional public art design

Two-point-five-dimensional, also known as semi-three-dimensional, is a form between two-dimensional form and three-dimensional form in terms of the categorization of spatial forms. It is often placed on the surface of walls or buildings because it just occupies a small amount of space. As for the function, two-point-five-dimensional public art designs can be used for spacial decoration and thematic creations. When it comes to the form, two-point-five dimensional form can express both flat space and deep space, so it is widely used in public art creation.

③ Three-dimensional public art design

Three-dimensional public art design is most widely used in real life; it is the most common form of public art, which includes urban sculpture, urban art installations, practical art facilities and other public art designs with three-dimensional physical characteristics. This kind of art design occupies three-dimensional space; meanwhile, it also requires a certain amount of space to be placed and a certain viewing distance to be appreciated.

④ Four-dimensional public art design

Four-dimensional public art design is added with the concept of time based on the three-dimensional design, so that viewers can appreciate the artistic effect of different forms through the change of time, such as the kinetic sculpture. Besides, there are also some works static in the original state, but conveying a psychological dynamic change through artistic form changes or comparisons.

⑤ Sensory experiential public art design

Due to the rapid development of contemporary technology, new technologies and new energy has paved for new forms of art creation. Contemporary public art is not limited to the construction of one or a group of artistic forms, but can use a certain form of art as a medium to create a multi-sensory experience to satisfy the spiritual needs of the viewer and stimulate the audience's emotions. Multi-sensory experiential art designs often create a new way of experience through changes of form, space and time. It does not only stay in the visual and tactile level, but also includes the auditory, olfactory, gustatory, physical and other multi-sensory experience, focused more on the interaction between the works and the viewer to stimulate the viewer.

Public art not only reminds people of local history, but also makes this history precious in the hearts of the people and preserves a good memory for the city. Public art embodies an understanding of the town itself and an attitude towards the people, with a significance to maximize the benefits for citizens such as bringing confidence, happiness, outlook as well as spiritual comfort. What distinguishes public art is the unique association of how it is made, where it is, and what it means. Public art can express community values, enhance our environment, transform a landscape, heighten our awareness, or question our assumptions. Placed in public sites, this art is there for everyone, a form of collective community expression. Public art is a reflection of how we see the world—the artist's response to our time and place combined with our own sense of who we are.

Public art can sometimes be purely an accessory and just one more marketing trick. We have examples from history of when public art and architecture in Rome or Florence during the time of the Reformation was included in city celebrations while in the nineteenth century it was used in fabricating the "City Beautiful".

4.4 Intellectual Property Protection in Environment Design

4.4.1 The Way of Protecting Environment Design Through Intellectual Property

In 1988, the United Kingdom enacted the Copyright Act, which stipulated that design drawings and buildings were considered part of architectural creations under the protection of copyright. In 1990 the United States made amendments to Architectural Works Copyright Protection Act to protect the copyright of architectural design, and stipulated that protection would be granted to "general drawings and blueprints, plans, sections, elevations, floor plans, structural drawings, study models, working models, representational models, collages of architectural photographs with scenes, computer-generated architectural images, and constructed buildings". The AWCPA defines an architectural work as "the design of a building as embodied in any tangible medium of overall form as well as the arrangement and composition of spaces and elements in the design, but does not include individual standard features" such as common windows, doors, and other staple building components (Lewis 2020). France also passed copyright law that protected copyright of architecture in 1992. It also stipulates that if photographs of completed buildings are taken for commercial use or if a movie or television is shot in a building, the designer must be paid. Article 3 of China's copyright law separately provides for architectural works, and stipulates that the types of works related to architectural design also include works of art, architectural works, graphic works, model works, and some special forms of public art design such as musical fountains may also constitute other types of works.

In addition to protection through copyright, some of the equipment, design, and construction methods in architectural design can also be protected through design, utility model, and patent. In 2008, Singaporean designers applied to the Intellectual Property Office of Singapore to grant a design patent to their design concept of installing "sky gardens" in residential buildings. In 2019, the JPO amended its Design Law and Design Examination Guidelines, which came into effect on April 1, 2020, by Cabinet Decree of November 1, 2019. The revision involves the inclusion of indoor and outdoor building designs as objects of protection, the enhancement of associated design protection, and the extension of the term of protection, etc. In July 2001, China's Patent Examination Guidelines clarified the granting of design patent protection to stationary buildings that do not depend on geographic conditions in construction and that can be reproduced. There is also a case of architectural design protection in China. Red Star Macalline Group applied for a design patent (CN201030194914.9) with the name of "Commercial Building (Zhenbei Store)" on June 8, 2010, and obtained authorization on March 9, 2011. In the case of the Red Star Macalline Zhenbei Road Branch design patent invalidation, the claimant argued that the design patent was for a real estate building and not a product. They also claimed that a construction or design drawing was necessary to implement the design patent, and without it, the building could not be constructed. Therefore, the design patent could not be put into mass production. Additionally, the name of the design patent indicated that the building must be built in a specific location and environment, making it unsuitable for industrial production. This goes against the provisions of Article 4 in Section 2 of the Patent Law. The Patent Reexamination Board holds that "suitable for industrial application" means that the design can be applied to industrial use and put into mass production. The design involved in the case is for buildings, which means it can be applied to industry use and put into mass production. For architectural construction drawings and design plans, as long as they are only needed for real production, the drawings and whether there is a bird's eye view have nothing to do with "fit for industrial application" as stipulated in the Patent Law. Some restoration methods of the ancient buildings and gardens left to this day have been applied as patents. Enterprises protect technical indicators unsuitable for patent application or disclosure through trade secrets, such as design drawings, patented technology, data calculation formulas, structural calculation methods, design procedures, etc. The unique decorative design of certain stores can also be protected through trademarks and anti-unfair competition laws. For example, Apple's store design and construction have already been applied as a trademark.

4.4.2 Scope of Protection for Architectural Design

In the general process of architectural design and construction, architectural works grow from an idea to a real object. Various forms of intellectual property are generated at different stages, such as sketches, design drawings, construction drawings, design instructions, and architectural models. These all reflect the unique aesthetics of architectural designers and can be protected by copyright as works. Although architectural works are clearly stipulated in copyright law. "Works of fine arts" means two- or three-dimensional works of the plastic arts created in lines, colours or other media which impart aesthetic effect, such as paintings, works of calligraphy and sculptures. However, this does not mean that all buildings, construction drawings, and architectural models can be protected as architectural works. The Architectural Works Copyright Protection Act of 1990 explicitly extends copyright protection to the embodiment of architectural works in a tangible medium of expression, including the arrangement and composition of spaces as well as the overall form but not including individual standard features nor the making, distributing, or public display of pictorial representations of a building in which an architectural work is embodied which is ordinarily visible from a public place. The WIPO defines an architectural work as "the creation of a building in aesthetics. This type of creation normally includes designs, sketches, models, established buildings and other architectural structures." Section 2 of the current Berne Convention stipulates that *sketches and three-dimensional works are relative to geography, topography, architecture or science.* Article 4 of China's "Regulation for the Implementation of the Copyright Law" refers to works of "architecture" means works with aesthetic effect which are expressed in form of buildings or structures. The thin scope of protection for architectural works is due to several related factors: most buildings are functional; individual standard features cannot be protected; an architect's arrangement and composition of design features is often treated as analogous to a compilation; and the idea/expression dichotomy and the scenes a faire doctrine both operate to restrict the protectable elements in architectural works (Shipley 2010).

(1) Determination of Originality

The sine qua non of copyright is originality. To qualify for copyright protection, a work must be original to the author. See Harper & Row. Original, as the term is used in copyright, means only that the work was independently created by the author (as opposed to copied from other works), and that it possesses at least some minimal degree of creativity. To be sure, the requisite level of creativity is extremely low; even a slight amount will suffice. "Originality" means that a work must be created independently, rather than copied (Wang 2015). In response, Professor Liu Chuntian (2014) pointed out that a work should be the result of the author's own choices, trade-offs, arrangements, design, integration, and description. It should not be a copy of an existing work, nor deduced according to an established program or procedure (method)."

The 1990 US Architectural Works Copyright Protection Act states that the originality of architectural works is shown through the selection, adjustment, and arrangement of elements that are not protected by copyright. Architects are allowed to add new design elements to the standard buildings that are not protected. In this case, the building is still protected by copyright. Internal architectural elements can also be protected (H.R. Rep. No. 735, at 6949 1990). According to Judge Stanley Birch of the U.S. Court of Appeals for the Eleventh Circuit, the requisite creativity for architecture to be copyrightable is analogous to that required for a compilation; the architect's selection, coordination, or arrangement of the standard features may, together, constitute a protectable whole (Intervest Constr., Inc. v. Canterbury Estate Homes, Inc., 554 F.3d 914). The Copyright Law Implementing Regulations stipulates that architectural works must have "aesthetic effect" and belong to the same category as artworks. Therefore, some scholars believe that standards for the identification of architectural works should be as high as that of fine art. However, there are some scholars who hold the opposite view and believe the standard should not be too high. In copyright infringement and unfair competition disputes between Guangzhou Aimei Network Technology Co., Ltd. and Guangzhou Weigou Information Technology Co., Ltd., etc. (2018), the plaintiff claimed to be the exclusive licensor of the product design work, architectural work, and artwork for the

"Mida Minik" small karaoke room. The defendant's "Lingda Minik Jukebox" resembles the plaintiff's karaoke room. The plaintiff believed that the defendant's product infringed on the copyright of its "Mida Minik" small karaoke room, and, at the same time, infringed on its decoration, thus constituting unfair competition. The court held that to define the copyright of an architectural work, its artistic rather than practical function should be focused on. More importantly, the designer or builder's original artistic elements of the building or structure are of great significance. Practical features in buildings should be excluded from the copyright. The protection of architectural works can only extend to the building itself, excluding construction materials and technical solutions. The protection involves only the exterior, including lines, decoration, color, etc., and does not involve the internal features or decoration of the building. Therefore, the karaoke rooms involved in the case should not be protected as architectual works. Different types of works have varying judging criteria for originality in copyright law. To determine the originality of an architectural work, it is necessary to consider the design space of functional design. When the functional design is not only practical but also has a large design space, that is, having various forms, the functional design is still original. In April 2025, the Chaoyang District People's Court of Beijing rendered a judgment in a case involving copyright infringement. The court found that the defendant's liquor bottle design, which imitated the architectural appearance of CITIC Tower (also known as China Zun), infringed upon the plaintiff's copyright in the architectural work. The court held that although the design of CITIC Tower was inspired by the form of the ancient Chinese bronze ritual vessel known as "Zun", its overall appearance and detailed design features presented a distinct artistic expression with unique aesthetic appeal. This expression demonstrated originality and thus qualified as an architectural work protected under copyright law (Chao Yang Fa Yuan WeChat Official Account 2025).

(2) Determination of Non-functional

The construction is closely related to science such as mathematics and physics. The building also has its proper functions and uses. The aesthetic effect referred to in the definition of an architectural work is generally interpreted as a building that gives people a visual sense of beauty. The aesthetic effect distinguishes an architectural work from an ordinary building. Besides being practical and useful, most importantly, an architectural work should have its unique architectural design and artistic beauty independent of practical function.

For works of applied art, architectural drawings, plans, and models registered under the US Copyright Act 102 (a) (5) are not protected by copyright if their functional elements cannot be separated from the aesthetic elements and exist independently (Oravec v. Sunny Isles Luxury Ventures L.C., 469 F. Supp. 2d 1148). The House Report on the AWCPA envisions a two-step process for determining functionality: first, determine whether there are any original design elements, including the overall shape and interior design; second, if there are original elements, then it is necessary to determine whether those elements are functionally required (H.R. Rep. No. 735, at 6951 1990). Functional considerations may, for example, determine only particular design elements. Protection would be denied for the functionally determined elements, but would be available for the nonfunctional determined elements. In each case, the courts must be free to decide the issue upon the facts presented, free of the separability conundrum presented by the useful articles doctrine applicable for pictorial, graphic, and sculptural works (Shipley 2010). And it does not matter whether a building depicted in plans has been constructed or can be constructed in order for the plans to be protected as an architectural work (Hunt v. Pasternack, 192 F.3d 877). In the case of Shine v. Childs, the court said it was irrelevant whether a skyscraper for the World Trade Center site could be constructed from the plaintiff's highly-acclaimed designs, renderings, and models (Shine v. Childs, 382 F. Supp. 2d 602). The court said that the Second Circuit "[had] twice noted that plans or designs not sufficiently detailed to allow for construction still may be protected."

In the first instance of a copyright ownership and infringement dispute between Shenzhen Broadwell Environmental Technology Co., Ltd. and Shenzhen Zhongde Membrane Structure Co., Ltd., the plaintiff discovered that the defendant had misappropriated the plaintiff's photography on its website. The architecture on the image was designed and constructed by the plaintiff. The plaintiff enjoys the copyright of the architecture, but the defendant pretended to be his product. The plaintiff believed this was an infringement on the copyright of their construction work and sued the defendant. The court held that an architectural work refers to an aesthetically significant work in the form of a building or structure. The building in the case was not an architectural work. Therefore, the plaintiff's claimed copyright over the architectural work was not established. The plaintiff provided seven images as evidence to assert the copyright of the architecture/construction work, but the images only show the exterior design and practical function of the building. As the copyright law does not protect practical factors such as technical solutions and practical functions, the case was dismissed.

The "dichotomy of idea/expression" is the basic principle for identifying copyright objects in copyright law. Together with "originality", it defines the rights of copyright owners. Combined with "substantial similarity", it defines the freedom to act for the public to use works (Feng and Diao 2021). In Oravec v. Sunny Isles Luxury Ventures case, the court found that the building design was original, and that "PBS (pictoral, graphic or sculptural work) derivative copyright of an earlier registered architectural work did not invest the PGS work with the same copyright status as the earlier registered architectural work; the prior copyrights did not extend their architectural work protections forward to encompass future derivative designs. Copyright does not protect ideas, only the tangible expressions of ideas; thus, copying ideas is not infringement, so long as one does not trench on the particular expressions of the idea."(Oravec v. Sunny Isles Luxury Ventures L.C., 469 F. Supp. 2d 1148). In Ale House Management v. Raleigh Ale House, Inc., the court noted that the closest similarity between the plans was the "concept of using an island-or peninsula-shaped bar to bisect a seating area which has booths on one side and stool seating on the other. But at this level of generality, the AHM design is nothing more than a concept, as distinct from an original form of expression, and is not copyrightable." According to the court, this similarity was nothing more than an unprotectable idea (Ale House Mgmt. v. Raleigh Ale House, 205 F.3d 137).

When original expression in architectural design can hardly be separated from design idea or design function, it will cause confusion between idea and expression, function and expression. This type of original expression cannot be protected by copyright law. Otherwise, it will not only harm the public rights and interests but may also blur the boundary between patent law and copyright law. Architectural designs with practical functions can possibly get protection after being incorporated into designs or utility models.

4.4.3 Types of Architecture, Architectural Design Drawings and Architectural Models

In the general process of architectural design and construction, architectural works grow from an idea to a real object. Various forms of intellectual property are generated at different stages, such as sketches, design drawings, construction drawings, design instructions, and architectural models. These all reflect the unique aesthetics of architectural designers and can be protected by copyright as works. Different countries and regions divide buildings, architectural plans, and architectural models into different categories. The major categorization includes three types: in the broadest sense, in the broad sense, and in the narrow sense:

In the broadest sense, architectural works include buildings, architectural plans, and architectural models. For example, section 101 of the Copyright Law of the United States defines an "architectural work" as the design of a building as embodied in any tangible medium of expression, including a building, architectural plans, or drawings. The work includes the overall form as well as the arrangement and composition of spaces and elements in the design but does not include individual standard features (17 U.S.C. §101). While revising the "Copyright Law", the definition of "architectural works" was revised to "an aesthetically significant work in the form of a building or structure, including plans, designs, sketches, and models that serve as the basis for its construction". This definition includes architectural plans and architectural models.

In a broad sense, an architectural work includes buildings and architectural models. A two-dimensional architectural plan is classified as a graphic work. The differentiation is made according to forms, whether it is three-dimensional or two-dimentional. For example, section 4 of the UK Copyright Act stipulates that an "architectural work" is in the form of a building or a model of a building, excluding design drawings or other drawings. Architectural plans or other drawings are "graphic works", as stipulated in this section, and "graphic works" is a type of work listed alongside "architectural works". Copyright laws in Australia, New Zealand, Canada, Ireland, India, and Israel all have similar provisions. Furthermore, Article 2 (1) of the Berne Convention also distinguishes between "architectural works" and "works related to architecture" when defining types of works with architectural design plans fall into the latter category.

In a narrow sense, an architectural work includes only the building itself. For example, Japan's Copyright Law stipulates architectural works in section 10 (5). Drawings, diagrams, models, and other academic graphic works are included in section 6. The current Copyright Law in China also adapts this narrow sense. Architectural works include only three-dimensional buildings. Architectural designs and architectural models are protected as works of art, graphic works, and model works.

(1) Graphic Works and Model Works

"Graphic works" means such works as drawings of engineering designs and product designs for the purpose of actual construction and manufacturing, and as maps and sketches showing geographical phenomena and demonstrating the fundamentals or the structure of a thing or an object. Construction drawings include plans, elevations, sections, supporting facility plans, etc., which show the logical relationships between the internal and external structures of the building. It clarified the scientific and regular nature of architectural design and construction. Featuring the beauty of science, construction drawings are graphic works under the protection of copyright law. There are various types of architectural design plans. Some only depict the internal structure of the building, such as the room layout and pipeline arrangement (internal structure plan). Some outline the exterior of the building (exterior design plan) with meticulous and accurate scientific drawing methods. Others depict the exterior shape of the building (exterior renderings) with artistic techniques, such as the night view in the "Bird's Nest Fireworks Case"(Wang 2014).

"Model works" means three-dimensional works made on the basis of the shape and the structure of an object to a certain scale, for the purpose of display, test or observation. The architectural model includes a construction model before the building is completed and a miniature model after the building is completed.

According to the definition in the Regulation for the Implementation of the Copyright Law of the People's Republic of China (2013 Revision), "model works" means three-dimensional works made on the basis of the shape and the structure of an object to a certain scale, for the purpose of display, test or observation. Architecture works can be regarded as three-dimensional works and protected by copyright law. For example, Beijing AVIC Zhicheng Co., Ltd. v. Shenzhen Feippengda Manufacturing Co., Ltd. is a typical explanation for this. "J-10 Aircraft (single-seat)" (referred to as "J-10") is a new type of aircraft. In November 2007, AVIC Zhicheng was authorised to manufacture "J-10" model and advocate the intellectual property rights on their own behalf. With authorisation obtained, AVIC Zhicheng started to manufacture scaled-down "J-10" models, based on "J-10" original blueprint and current design. Feipengda started to manufacture and sell "J-10" models since June, 2011. AVIC Zhicheng believed that the alleged infringing product caused infringements on AVIC Zhicheng's right to reproduce and distribute of the graphic work, artwork or model works of "J-10" design blueprint and model. This case is a typical one involving the question of whether a military aircraft's designs and its model constitute an artwork and model work in the sense of China's Copyright Law. First, the court did not rule out the eligibility of "J-10's" design to be protected by Copyright Law as an artwork. However, the court held that it can be regarded as an artwork and protected if it did bear ingenious artistic expression besides designs determined by its utility. However, in the verdict of Court of Second Instance, a model has better ingenuity as it has higher resemblance to the original article or can better satisfy the practical need. The "J-10" model is a scaled down from the "J-10" aircraft, but that's where its ingenuity is according to the implement regulations of Copyright Law. It is a model work and shall be protected (Ten innovation intellectual property cases in Beijing during 2015, 2016). However, in the retrial, the court held that the model involved in the case was scaled down in proportion to the original blueprint and current design. The model is not the result of choices, trade-offs, arrangements, design, integration, or description. No new points, lines, surfaces, geometric structures, or expressions were created. The "J-10" model is a scaled-down copy which only went through a technical process, so it is not protected by China's copyright law. Therefore, an architectural model protected by copyright law should be original. It should not be an accurate scaled-down copy. The creator must make choices and trade-offs to bring originality to the building.

In the copyright and unfair competition dispute between Fisher Technology Co., Ltd. and Shanghai Dongfang Teaching Aids Co., Ltd. and Shanghai Yaxun Intelligent Robot Technology Co., Ltd. (2019), the Shanghai Intellectual Property Court examined whether the 30 three-dimensional designs in question qualified as model works under China's Copyright Law. The court held that, based on the legislative intent of China's Copyright Law, a model work must meet three criteria: 1. It must serve purposes such as demonstration, experimentation, or observation—typically involving intellectual creations related to geography, topography, architecture, or science; 2. It must possess originality. A three-dimensional model that simply enlarges, reduces, or reproduces an object to scale is merely a copy of the object. A model work must be based on the shape and structure of a real object and made to scale, but its design must demonstrate originality; 3. It must be fixed in a tangible three-dimensional form.

First, the 30 three-dimensional designs are abstracted from real-world mechanical and engineering structures. Although corresponding objects or structures exist in reality, the designs are not mere replicas—they reveal the underlying mechanical principles and physical structures of those real-world entities. Second, the designers selected and refined elements from existing machinery and engineering structures, abstracting and simplifying them. During the creative process, they made choices regarding the form and structure, resulting in designs that showcase the beauty of science and technology. The layout, structural arrangement, and component combinations reflect the designer's original thought and planning, demonstrating originality. Finally, the use of components following the instruction manual allows the construction of tangible three-dimensional forms identical to the diagrams provided. This satisfies the requirement of fixation in a physical form. In conclusion, the court found that all 30 three-dimensional designs met the criteria for model works under China's Copyright Law. Each constitutes an independent model work, separate from any graphic works, and is entitled to copyright protection.

(2) Fine Art and Architectural Works

Artworks have certain similarities with architectural works. Both are works with "aesthetic effect" and give people a sense of beauty. As Professor Zheng Chengsi said, in the Copyright Law, architectural works can be called marginal objects between scientific works and works of art. In Germany, architectural works are classified as works of art (Zheng 2007). The 1990 China Copyright Law did not list architectural works as an object of copyright. The 1991 Copyright Law Implementing Regulations classified architectural works as artworks for protection but did not define architectural works. In the current copyright law, architectural works are no longer one of the fine arts. It is now parallel to artworks under copyright protection.

"Works of fine arts" means two- or three-dimensional works of the plastic arts created in lines, colours or other media which impart aesthetic effects, such as paintings, works of calligraphy and sculptures. When designing a building, the designer will draw sketches and renderings in the initial planning stage. The drawings can generally show the exterior of the architectural work. They are graphic artworks with aesthetic effect composed of lines, colors, etc. They have some originality and fit the definition of artwork. Therefore, they can be protected by copyright law as artworks. Section 2.7 (3) of the Beijing High People's Court Guidelines for the Trial of Copyright Infringement Cases (hereinafter referred to as the "Trial Guidelines") stipulates: "Architectural designs reflecting the aesthetic appearance of architectural works may be protected as works of art." Section 2.8 (2) of the Trial Guidelines stipulates: "A building design drawing used only for construction is an engineering design plan." Therefore, in a wide variety of architectural design drawings, design drawings belong to the works of art and engineering drawings, thus protected by copyright law. However, section 2.8 (1) of the "Trial Guidelines" also states that technical solutions, practical functions, operation methods, etc. contained in engineering designs, objective geographical elements and facts contained in maps and diagrams, are not protected by copyright law. Therefore, the copyright of an engineering design drawing should exclude objective elements and facts such as technical solutions and operation plans.

"Works of architecture" means works with aesthetic effects which are expressed in the form of buildings or structures. Two points can be inferred from the definition of an architectural work: First, only a building or structure can be protected as an architectural work. Second, to be viewed as an architectural work, the building must also have aesthetic effect. Architectural work is a comprehensive form of art which combines various orderly spaces and integrates the surrounding cultural and natural environment. It not only has practical functions but also meets aesthetic requirements. Furthermore, architectural work is designed and constructed according to building codes and standards under scientific calculation. Therefore, an architectural work is a special type of work that is both artistic, practical, and scientific.

According to China Copyright Law, architectural design drawings are classified as engineering design drawings, and architectural models are classified as model works. Therefore, architectural works should not include architectural plans and architectural models. In other words, architectural works, engineering designs, and architectural models are protected as independent forms of work. The Copyright Law only protects the exterior of architectural works. Drawings, architectural models, and buildings are different in form. They represent different states or levels of architectural work. This is why China's copyright law protects the drawings and models in one way and the buildings in another.

4.4.4 *Infringement and Liability in Environment Design*

(1) Reproduction of Architectural Works

The copyright of architectural works includes the reproduction right among copyright property rights. Reproduction includes various types: "from two-dimensional to two-dimensional," "from two-dimensional to three-dimensional," "from three-dimensional to two-dimensional," "from three-dimensional to three-dimensional," and "from with a carrier to without a carrier." Whether from a design drawing to an architectural work is a two-dimensional to three-dimensional reproduction, there has always been much controversy in practice. The French Intellectual Property Code states that the reproduction of an architectural work means that construction is once again carried out according to a drawing or standard plan. The Japanese Copyright Law stipulates that the reproduction of an architectural work includes the act of constructing an architectural work based on its architectural drawings, while the Italian Copyright Law holds that the right to change an engineering design "from two-dimensional to three-dimensional" belongs to neighboring rights. China's Copyright Law has no stipulation on this. But if it does not follow the same principles in the judicial field, it does not comply with the basic principles of copyright law.

① Reproduction from "three-dimensional" to "three-dimensional"

For instance, in the case of The Olympic National Stadium v. Beijing Panda Fireworks (Group) Holding Co Ltd., the defendant has developed a Bird's Nest-named fireworks product, which looks very much like the unique figure of the stadium in discharge. Six months later, a lawsuit seeking four million yuan in compensation woke up the Beijing company, which is now accused of violating copyright law by the Olympic National Stadium Co Ltd. The court holds that the "Bird's Nest" fireworks product displayed the characteristics of the intertwined, bowl-shaped structure of the steel trusses used in the National Stadium architecture to a large extent. It highly imitates the National Stadium. Therefore, it is considered a reproduction of the original intellectual achievements of the National Stadium's architectural works by being substantially similar to the structure of the National Stadium. Without evidence of permission, the manufacture and sale of "Bird's Nest" fireworks products infringed on the plaintiff's rights to reproduce and distribute the National Stadium architectural work. Therefore, as long as the product copies the original characteristics of an architectural work, even if the carrier for originality is different, it is still a reproduction in copyright law.

② Reproduction from "two-dimensional" to "three-dimensional"

The copyright law protects the original artistic expression of the building, not the construction method and construction technology used to build the building. Moreover, the architectural design is protected as an architectural work because of the creative expression in it. Therefore, from two-dimensional to three-dimensional, if a building reproduces the original artistic expression of the architectural design, then it is a copy. The performer transformed the architectural design into a building, changing only the form without changing the original part that is protected by copyright law (Yin 2009). For architectural works, if constructing a three-dimensional building based on a design drawing only uses construction methods on the drawing rather than the aesthetic components, then it is not a two-dimensional to three-dimensional reproduction. However, if the construction results in the expression of the aesthetic concept contained in the architectural design drawings, it can be regarded as a two-dimensional to three-dimensional reproduction.

③ Reproduction from "three-dimensional" to "two-dimensional"

The reproduction from three-dimensional to two-dimensional in architectural works is usually by painting, photoing, and filming. Section 22 of China's Copyright Law stipulates that it is proper to copy, paint, photo, and film works of art set up or displayed in outdoor public places. According to the provisions of section 9 (2) of the Berne Convention relating to the "Exception" of the "reproduction right", that is, the "three-step test method." First, it shall be a matter for legislation in the countries of the Union to permit the reproduction of such works in certain special cases. Second, does not conflict with the normal use of the work. Third, does not unreasonably harm the author's legitimate interests. Normally, the creator incorporates their own judgment and choices to create new works such as photography and paintings when transforming an architectural work from three-dimensional to two-dimensional. At the same time, there is no conflict between the use of graphic works and three-dimensional works. The transformation does not harm the legitimate rights and interests of the original author.

(2) Determination of Substantial Similarity

"Contact + substantial similarity" is the basic rule for determining whether a work is infringed in judicial practice. Access requirement can be fulfilled by proving that the defendant had an opportunity to access the copyrighted material. Most courts recognize that an opportunity to access can be demonstrated by proving widespread dissemination of a work or that a "chain of events exists" from which access can be inferred (4 Nimmer & Nimmer, supra note 71, § 13.02(A)). If two works or techniques are identified as substantially similar, it means the work or technique that is created later is identical in the ideas and forms to another one (Wu 2015). "Substantial similarity" means the alleged infringing work or technology copies or comes from previous works or technology with intellectual property rights. The former does not count as a creative new work or technology. Whether determined by the lay juror or intended audience, the basic test for illicit copying is whether there is substantial similarity between protectable elements in the plaintiff's and defendant's works. The legal standards vary from Circuit to Circuit, and have changed over time. They also vary medium to medium: assessing similarities becomes very different depending on whether one is considering music (melody, harmony, rhythm, instrumentation, etc.), or novels (plot, dialogue, setting, sequence, characters, etc.), or computer programs (as you saw in Computer Associates). For architectural design, the "abstraction-filtration- comparison test" method can be applied to determine whether there is substantial similarity between the works. Firstly, abstract the conceptual content of architectural design works, including design indicators, design concepts, design performance, design specifications, construction plans, technical plans, etc. Secondly, filter out the conceptual elements that do not belong to the protected objects of copyright law, the parts that belong to the public intellectual domain, and even the elements under copyright protection but do not constitute intrinsic content. Once all of the unprotected aspects of the architectural work are excluded, the second step in the subtractive approach is to determine whether the remaining elements of the allegedly infringing work are substantially similar to the protected elements in the plaintiff's work (Sturdza v. U.A.E., 281 F.3d 1287). As mentioned earlier, the protection of architectural works is similar to the protection of compilation works. Even if certain elements in the architectural design lack originality or belong to the public intellectual domain, they should still be protected by copyright law as long as the combination or arrangement constitute originality of the overall or part of the building appearance. Providing architectural works with only thin protection does not fulfil the constitutional goal of providing an incentive for architects to create useful and original works. Therefore, the US courts have adopted the intrinsic similarity test in the analysis of architectural works infringement cases. The plaintiff must prove intrinsic similarity by showing that the expression of the ideas is substantially similar from the perspective of the ordinary observer or "the intended audience of the work"(Universal Furniture Int'l, Inc. v. Collezione Europa USA, Inc., 618 F.3d 417). During the substantial similarity comparison, it is also necessary to consider the core content of the architectural design, such as architectural positioning, structure, layout, and appearance.

In the copyright infringement case of the Martyrs' Cemetery relief sculptures (2019), Hebei Shanren Sculpture Co., Ltd. (hereinafter referred to as the "Shanren Sculpture Company") and Hebei Zhongding Garden Sculpture Co., Ltd. (hereinafter referred to as the "Zhongding Sculpture Company") were professional institutions engaged in sculpture design, production, and installation. In December 2017, Shanren Sculpture Company and the People's Government of Sanhe Town, Bozhou District of Zunyi City, Guizhou Province (hereinafter referred to as the "Sanhe Town Government") negotiated cooperation in the sculpture project for Sanhe Town Daoba Martyrs' Cemetery. Shanren Sculpture Company delivered the completed design drawing and exhibition board of the case-related work, "Great Victory of Daoba", to Sanhe Town Government for review and made changes several times as required by Sanhe Town Government, but the two parties failed to reach an agreement. Later, Zunyi Branch of Guizhou Huilong Construction Engineering Co., Ltd. made slight modifications to the works of Shanren Sculpture Company without the permission of the copyright owner, and reproduced the infringing sculpture from two-dimensional to three-dimensional. The sculpture was then produced and installed in the Cemetery. In this case, the court used overall comparison and main part comparison in making judgments on substantial similarity. Although the first parts of the two works differ in their artistic techniques, the "Great Victory of Daoba" relief is composed of three parts, and the second part, the "Daoba Victory" campaign, is the main body of the entire work. The second part of the alleged infringing work (i.e. the main part of the entire relief) is essentially identical to the copyrighted work in question. Judging on the entire architectural work can avoid the problem of deviating from the architectural work itself when discussing similarity or degree of similarity. If only the extracted elements are compared, without considering the position and status of these elements in the architectural works, it is easy to make wrong judgment and cognitive errors. When comparing the specific structures of architectural works, it is necessary to consider the specific style, craftsmanship, and the position and importance of creative elements within the architectural works. If they are core elements of high originality and distinctive recognition, they should be subject to a higher level of protection. The Higher People's Court of Guizhou Province found at second instance that the infringement was established, but held that as Daoba Martyrs' Cemetery was an important venue for revolutionary tradition education and patriotism education, it was inappropriate to enter an judgment in favor of the demolition of the alleged infringing sculpture, taking into account the principle of interest balance and the effective use of resources, and the claim of Shanren Sculpture Company for stopping the infringement and demolishing the infringing sculpture was not required to be supported, if the infringement compensation standard was appropriately raised to sufficiently remedy the rights of Shanren Sculpture Company. While one test may not fit every situation, it is important to analyze which current test or combination thereof will best suit the constitutional intent of the copyright clause and the legislative intent of the Copyright Act (Morgan v. Hawthorne Homes, Inc., 2009 U.S. Dist. LEXIS 31456).

(3) Tort Liability

Due to the large investment and long construction period of architecture, the remedy for infringement is different from general situations. Some judgments require the infringing building to be modified until it is no longer the same or similar to the protected architectural work. For those unsuitable for demolition, the court changes the liability from "demolition of the sculpture" to payment of fair usage fees.

In the case of Porsche AG v. Beijing Techart Auto Sales Co., Ltd (2008). regarding architectural work infringement, specific measures were taken to cease the infringement. The court, taking into account the defendant's infringement methods, scope, degree of subjective fault, and the design cost of relevant architectural works, requires the defendant to make alterations, only removing those exterior designs that are the same or similar to the main features of the plaintiff's architectural works, rather than demolishing or rebuilding the entire structure directly. This not only protects the plaintiff's legal rights but also reduces the defendant's losses, making it a valuable attempt to explore new forms of ceasing infringement in civil liability. In the case of Institute of Oceanology of the Chinese Academy of Sciences and Zheng Shouyi v. Liu Junxian, Laizhou City Wanlida Stone Co., Ltd., and Yantai Environmental Art Management Office (2012), the court found that the defendant, Yantai Environmental Art Management Office, was not subjectively at fault. The Office had paid a corresponding price to obtain the infringing sculpture, which was used for public welfare purposes. Removing the sculpture would incur significant waste of social resources. Therefore, the court changed the responsibility of Yantai Environmental Office from stopping the infringement and removing the sculpture to eliminating the impact and paying fair usage fees. Taking Hebei Shanren Sculpture Co., Ltd. v. Hebei Zhongding Garden Sculpture Co., Ltd. as an example, people's courts have actively incorporated the core socialist values into intellectual property justice throughout the process and underpinned the core socialist values in legal interpretation and application of the law in the whole process. The proper trial of copyright cases involving red classic works is an important part of spreading the positive energy of judicial protection of intellectual property. This case is a copyright dispute related to a red classic piece. The second-instance judgment upheld the principles of respecting the law, rights, and classics, gave remedies to the right holder by increasing the infringement compensation and royalties while deciding against the cessation of infringement, and gave full consideration to the effective protection of rights with effective regard for passing on classics, enabled the judgment results to conform to the law, social conditions, and public will, and achieved the organic integration of legal, political, and social effects.

4.4.5 Fair Use of Outdoor Artwork

Article 24 of China's Copyright Law stipulates specific cases for fair use: "In the following cases, a work may be used without permission of, and without payment of remuneration to the copyright owner, provided that the name or appellation of the author and the title of the work are indicated, the normal use of the work is not affected and the legitimate rights and interests enjoyed by the copyright owner are not unreasonably prejudiced." The tenth case on the list is "copying, drawing, photographing or video-recording of a work of art put up or displayed in public places". Generally speaking, architectural works are usually located in outdoor public spaces, so transforming architectural works from three-dimensional to two-dimensional through copying, painting, photographing or video-recording is considered fair use under copyright law. The problem arising here is whether it is a copyright infringement to commercially use the results of copying, painting, photographing, or recording architectural works, such as selling photographs of architectural works or using images of architectural works in film and television works.

(1) Fair Use of Outdoor Artwork: Specific Situations

Outdoor artworks not only possess the general characteristics of art pieces, but as a form of public art, they also exhibit the publicness of theme and space. Outdoor artworks are supposed to be displayed for a long period, and their representativeness and symbolism will be strengthened over time. Eventually, the author's intellectual property rights become blurred and integrated into the public, which is the main reason for establishing terms for fair use of outdoor artworks. Intellectual property right is an absolute right, so the restrictions imposed on the rights of the copyright holder should be handled with caution to specify the circumstances of rights limitation. Therefore, it is particularly important to define the meanings of "outdoor" and "public artwork".

The Taiwan scholar Yang Zhijie (2012) has his views on "art or architectural works": artistic works or architectural works displayed on a long-term basis on streets, in parks, on outside walls of buildings, or other outdoor locales open to the public, may be exploited by any means except under the following circumstances: reproduction of a building by construction of another building; reproduction of a work of sculpture by production of another sculpture; reproduction for the purpose of long-term public display in locales specified in Article 58 of Copyright Act; reproduction of artistic works solely for the purpose of selling copies. According to Article 18 of the Interpretation of the Supreme People's Court on the Application of Law in the Trial of Civil Disputes over Copyright, "The artistic work located or on display in an outdoor public place as specified by Article 22 (10) of the Copyright Law refers to sculptures, paintings, calligraphies and other artistic works that are displayed or located in an outdoor public place. For the copy, painting, photographs or video figures of the above-mentioned artistic works, the results may be used in reasonable form and within reasonable scope, which does not constitute any infringement." The interpretation of "artistic work in public place" and "paintings" by the Legislative Affairs Commission of the National People's Congress is as follows: "artistic work displayed or located in an outdoor public place mainly refer to paintings, sculptures, calligraphies, etc. that are located in squares, streets, intersections, parks, tourist attractions, and buildings. For example, the inscriptions and reliefs around the Monument to the People's Heroes; the paintings, sculptures, calligraphies, and statues of people around the Beijing Workers Stadium; murals on the walls of music academy teaching building, etc".

(2) Ways of Using the Work

Professor Wu Handong (2013) believes that any commercial use is definitely not fair use, but non-profit use may not necessarily be fair use. In his view, fair use is a non-profit use, and others are not allowed to use copyrighted works for profit. Professor Wang Qian (2019) holds a different view. He believes that outdoor art works can be reproduced from three-dimensional to two-dimensional, and if the resulting copies are commercially utilized without conflicting with the normal use of the original art works or unreasonably damaging the interests of the authors, it can be considered as a profit-oriented reuse.

"In the case of Mr. Sun vs Shanghai Education Publishing Co., Ltd., involving attribution, reproduction, and distribution of works rights infringement (2020), Sun created the poem "Western Fantasies" and the article "I Applaud and Call for Western Development". Education Publishing Co. published the book "Chinese

Language Teaching Reference Materials", which provides a detailed analysis and introduction of the artistic conception, meaning, and related ancient poems corresponding to each stanza of the poem "Western Fantasies", as well as introductions to the Dunhuang Flying Apsaras and the Wild Goose Pagoda mentioned in the poem. In the "Related Links" section of the book, there is a brief introduction of the author Sun, and the full text of the article "I Applaud and Call for Western Development" written by Sun is quoted. Sun believes that the publishing house has infringed upon his copyright. The court trial found that the accused infringement of the book "Western Fantasies" was for the purpose of providing teaching reference materials and post-class exercises supplementary to the Chinese language textbook. The book analyzed and commented on the artistic conception and meaning of the poem "Western Fantasies" in the Chinese language textbook, and introduced related ancient poetry, cultural and natural landscapes that are in line with the poem's content. Therefore, this section is intended to introduce, comment on, and analyze the poem "Western Fantasies" in the Chinese language textbook. Although it quotes parts the poem, the purpose of the quotation is for poem analysis and introduction to background information mentioned in the poem in order to facilitate teaching or students' understanding. Such usage is within a fair range. Relevant content does not constitute any other harm to Mr. Sun's interests, and the author's name and title have been indicated. Therefore, the use of "Western Fantasies" by the Publishing House in the accused infringing books complies with the fair use conditions stipulated in China's Copyright Law and does not constitute an infringement of Sun's copyright.

The legislative intention of the Copyright Law is not to grant creators absolute monopoly over the dissemination of their works, but rather to provide creators with limited monopoly rights to ensure they receive reasonable economic income from their works, in order to encourage more people to engage in creative activities. "Fair use" is a right limitation on copyright holders. Since outdoor public artistic works have a special public nature, copyright law must restrict the rights of corresponding copyright holders. The use of the work includes direct use and potential use. Direct use refers to copyright owner's using their existing exclusive rights, such as granting permission for others to make copies. Potential use refers to a type of use that does not immediately affect the exercise of the rights of the owner, but the intangible economic effects may indirectly impact the market share of the work, ultimately reducing the tangible income of the rights holder (Zhang 2012). Therefore, to identify how works are used is needed for determining the fair use of architectural works. The two-dimensional reproduction and commercial use of flat outdoor art works will inevitably conflict with the interests of the copyright owner, making it difficult to constitute fair use. However, for three-dimensional outdoor art works such as the sculpture in question, even if the flat reproduction of the work constitutes commercial use, it will not conflict with the owner's use, reducing the tangible benefits of the rights holder. Although the law does not explicitly define what constitutes fair use of architectural works, basic principles for determining fair use can be applied, such as "three-step test" in the Berne Convention and the four key factors of fair use in the United States. In determining whether the use made of a work in any particular case is a fair use the factors to be considered shall include: (1) the purpose and character of the use, including whether such use is of a commercial nature or is for nonprofit educational purposes; (2) the nature of the copyrighted work; (3) the amount and substantiality of the portion used in relation to the copyrighted work as a whole; and (4) the effect of the use upon the potential market for or value of the copyrighted work.

The best-known case discussing this limitation on architectural copyright is Leicester v. Warner Brothers. Andrew Leicester, an artist known for large scale public art, was retained by R&T Development Corporation to create a substantial artistic work that would become part of a new office building in downtown Los Angeles, a twenty-four-story architectural work called the 801 Tower. Leicester's contract with R&T gave it a license to make reproductions of Zanja Madre in brochures, advertisements, catalogs, and similar publications, and Leicester promised not to make any duplicate, three-dimensional reproductions of the work. In 1994, Warner Brothers obtained permission from R&T to use the 801 Tower in filming "Batman Forever." Leicester and the building's architect were not consulted. The building, serving as the Gotham City Bank, is shown in the movie. Four of the distinctive towers in the street wall portion of Leicester's work appear in several scenes in the movie, but the rest of the Zanja Madre was not in the film. The major point of contention was whether the AWCPA should be construed to eliminate separate protection for sculptural works attached to buildings. Judge Fisher have remanded the case for a thorough determination of conceptual separability. If Leicester's towers were determined to be separable, then Warner's pictorial reproductions of them would not be exempt under Section 120(a) but instead would be infringing.

4.4.6 Ownership of Copyright in Environment Design

In environment design, be it architectural, landscaping, or public art, it all involves multiple creative stages from design to completion and the participation of multiple parties. Therefore, it is specific and complex. The AWCPA does not address copyright ownership, but the standard American Institute of Architecture (AIA) contract provides that "the architect shall be deemed the author of the documents and drawings prepared with respect to [a particular] project and shall retain all rights to said documents including copyrights (Johnson v. Jones, 149 F.3d 494)." When it comes to graphic works, model works, and architectural works, it is also necessary to consider whether they are commissioned works, collaborative works, works made in the course of employment, or legal entity works, and determine the ownership of copyright based on specific situations.

(1) Commissioned Work

For the current construction industry in China, commonly it is the construction party that commissions the design party to complete the construction works. According to the Copyright Law of China, "The ownership of copyright in a commissioned work shall be agreed upon in a contract between the commissioning and the commissioned parties. In the absence of such a contract or of an explicit agreement in the contract, the copyright in such a work shall belong to the commissioned party." By signing contracts and terms, the rights related to the architectural design belong to the construction party or the design party.

In the copyright dispute case between Wuhan Xinjianye Advertising Decoration Co., Ltd. (Wuhan Xinjianye) and Dongfeng Honda Automobile Co., Ltd. (Honda) etc. (2019), Wuhan Xinjianye claims that it was commissioned by Honda to provide architectural renderings and CAD drawings of the Honda 4S store. Honda authorized various local dealerships, including Beijing Guoji Longsheng Automobile Co., Ltd. (Beijing Guoji), to use the aforementioned drawings to construct the Honda 4S store without obtaining the copyright for the architectural works. Beijing Decheng Zhidi Real Estate Development Co., Ltd. and Beijing Guoji were the actual builders of the 4S store. Therefore Wuhan Xinjianye claims that the actions of the three defendants collectively infringed upon its copyright of the architectural work of Honda 4S store. For the renderings, the court believes that since Wuhan Xinjianye is unable to submit the original "Design Contract" or other relevant evidence, and Honda does not acknowledge the existence of this contract, it cannot be determined that there is a commission relationship between the two parties regarding the exterior design of the Honda 4S store. It also cannot be determined that whether Wuhan Xinjianye actually created the disputed renderings or obtained the copyright from others. Therefore, their claim of copyright ownership over the disputed renderings lacks factual basis. For CAD drawings, the court believes that although the "Architectural Structural Design Contract" signed between Wuhan Xinjianye and Wugang Design Institute does not explicitly specify the ownership of the copyright of the CAD drawings with the term "copyright", given the provision in the contract that 'The ownership and modification rights of the CAD drawings designed by Party B shall be owned by Party A', the fact that both parties are not legal professionals, and the factors such as the fees specified in the contract far exceeding the design fees paid by Honda to Wuhan Xinjianye, it would be reasonable that the term "ownership" in the aforementioned provision encompass "copyright".

Therefore, to ensure clear ownership of architectural works, both parties should clearly stipulate the ownership of copyright at the time of contract formation to prevent future ownership disputes. It is worth noting that for the winning design party, the rights ownership can be determined according to the contract signed. If there is no agreement, the copyright of the architectural design belongs to the design party. For the design party that did not win the bid, the copyright should belong to the original design party. The construction party or other third parties cannot use these architectural designs without permission, otherwise it will constitute copyright infringement. For complex and challenging architectural works, it is common for two or more design parties to form a joint party to participate in the design bidding. The results created by the joint unit should be collaborative works.

(2) Service Works

In China, service works are typically divided into ordinary and special ones, and the Copyright Law of China has made corresponding provisions for each. According to Article 18 of the Copyright Law, a work created by a natural person when fulfilling the tasks assigned to him by a legal entity or another unincorporated organization shall be deemed to be a service work. The copyright of such a work shall be claimed by the author, but the legal entity or unincorporated organization shall have a priority right to exploit the work within the scope of its professional activities. In the next 2 years after the completion of the work, the author shall not, without the consent of the legal entity or organization, authorize a third party to exploit the work in the same way as the legal entity or organization does." For certain special service works, the author only has the right of authorship, while other rights of copyright are enjoyed by a legal entity or unincorporated organization, who can reward the author. Architectural design mainly involves the creation of design drawings with material and technical support from the legal entity or unincorporated organization that bear legal responsibility. For general architectural works, according to the professional practice system of architects in China, the creative activities of architects are based on design parties. Architects, as employees of design parties, are expected to fulfill their duty to utilize the material and technical conditions of the party, such as background information and site data, to complete the work of the design party. Generally, they need to sign the design drawings and be responsible for the design documents, which aligns with the requirements for relevant professional works. Architectural works are similar to engineering projects in respect of large investments and high technical requirements, and generally belong to special service works. On the one hand, this protects the interests of investors, and on the other hand, once it involves construction quality issues, design parties can share the significant financial responsibilities since it is difficult for architects to bear the all.

In the case of East China Architectural Design & Research Institute Co., Ltd. (ECADI) v. Ling Kege et al. (2020), ECADI (designer) and Wuhan Country Garden Company (employer) signed the "Construction Project Design Contract (I)" for the "Wuhan B Hotel" project, stipulating that the employer entrusted the designer to undertake the design of Wuhan XX Center Hotel project, and deliver construction drawing design documents, etc. Ling Kege and Xu Qiyuan are former employees of ECADI. After leaving their jobs, Ling Kege and Xu Qiyuan co-authored an article titled "Spatial Experience Design: Hubei A Hotel Design", which was published in the second issue of "Times Architecture" in 2014. The article includes a project overview, and the accompanying images are actual photos and floor plans of Wuhan B Hotel. The ECADI claims that the "Wuhan B Hotel" project design drawings are the works of a legal entity rather than special service works. The court believes that the "List of Key Design Personnel" in Annex 1 of the "Construction Project Design Contract (I)" clearly states that Ling Kege is the chief designer. The drawings involved in the case also contain information such as "Chief Designer Ling Kege". Therefore, in the absence of evidence from ECADI to prove that the originality of the design drawings involved, as graphic works, are based on the legal person's will, it should be determined that the creation was completed by specific designers. Therefore, ECADI's claim lacks factual and legal basis. This court does not support it.

In order to achieve the creative purpose and realize the expected social significance, there exists a situation where a construction party is in charge of a certain building project, and completes the creation and construction by fully utilizing its own resources and material conditions, with the design party assuming legal responsibility. In this case, the architectural work is very likely to be a legal entity's work. The difference between legal entity's works and service works lies in whether the design and expression of architectural works fully represent the will of the organization. For service works, the freedom of thought for architects is limited, and they are not allowed to sign their names. All rights, including the right to sign, belong to the design organization.

References

17 U.S.C. §101

4 Nimmer & Nimmer, supra note 71, § 13.02(A)

Ale House Mgmt. v. Raleigh Ale House, 205 F.3d 137

Arandelovic B (2018) Introduction to public art. In: Public art and urban memorials in Berlin, pp 27–38

Architectural design: Definition, types and examples (2020). https://www.mchmaster.com/news/architectural-design-definition-types-and-examples/. Accessed 10 Sep 2022

Beijing Intellectual Property Court (2019) Wuhan Xinjianye Advertising and Decoration Co., Ltd. and Dongfeng Honda Automobile Co., Ltd. and Other Copyright Ownership and Infringement Disputes Civil Judgement of the Second Instance [2019] No. 2758

Bell S (1993) Elements of visual design in the landscape. E & FN Spon, London

Brady A (2022) What is environmental design? https://www.allthingsnature.org/what-is-environmental-design.htm. Accessed 22 Jun 2022

Breed CA (2022) Value negotiation and professional self-regulation environmental concern in the design of the built environment. Urban For Urban Green 74:1–13

Caves RW (2004) Encyclopedia of the city. Routledge, London, p 225

Chao Yang Fa Yuan WeChat Official Account (2025). https://mp.weixin.qq.com/s/qzj7wGVQET-pBjX7KsWwfxQ. Accessed 23 Jul 2025

Chen S, Chen FH, Tan T (2013) Artistic conception expression of water spray pattern in environment design: a case study of Chinese Meishan Cultural Eco-Garden. Appl Mech Mater 409:742–745

Craven J (2021) Defining architecture and design. thoughtco.com/what-is-architecture-178087. Accessed 27 Jun 2022

Cyril MH (ed) (1975) Dictionary of architecture and construction. McGraw-Hill, New York, p 24

Deng DX et al (2017) Interactive environment design in smart city. IOP Conf Ser Earth Environ Sci 81:1–4

Dong Q, Dai XL (2011) Urban public art planning: a new research field. J Shenzhen Univ Human Soc Sci Ed 3:147–152

Environmental design (2022). https://www.encyclopedia.com/environment/encyclopedias-almanacs-transcripts-and-maps/environmental-design. Accessed 28 Jun 2022

Evert KJ (ed) (2010) Encyclopedic dictionary of landscape and urban planning. Springer, London, p 509

Feng XQ, Diao JX (2021) From value orientation to subsumtion purpose: conceptual clarification of idea/expression dichotomy. J Shanghai Jiaotong Univ Philos Soc Sci 29(02):27–39
Gu DQ, Bo TW (2013) An introduction to architectural design. China Building Industry Press, Beijing, p 34
Guangzhou Intellectual Property Court (2018) Copyright Infringement and Unfair Competition Dispute between Guangzhou Aimee Network Technology Co., Ltd. and Guangzhou Microdog Information Technology Co., Ltd. and Others—Judicial Determination of Architectural Works under the Copyright Law [2018] No.2162
Guizhou High People's Court (2019) Hebei Shanren Sculpture Co., Ltd. v. Hebei Zhongding Garden Sculpture Co., Ltd., People's Government of Sanhe Town, Bozhou District of Zunyi City, Zunyi Zhonghecheng Agricultural Development Co., Ltd., Guizhou Huilong Construction Engineering Co., Ltd., and Zunyi Branch of Guizhou Huilong Construction Engineering Co., Ltd. [2019] No.449
H.R. Rep. No. 735, at 6949 (1990)
H.R. Rep. No. 735, at 6951 (1990)
Hagan S (2008) Five reasons: To adopt environmental design. Harv Des Mag 2008:100–114
Han XQ, Yang J (2001) Several issues worth discussing in the environmental design of current residential areas. J Archit 2001(07):52–55+68
High People's Court of Beijing Municipality (2008) Beijing Techart Automobile Sales Co., Ltd. v. Porsche AG (copyright infringement dispute) [2008] No.325
High People's Court of Shandong Province (2012) Institute of Oceanology of the Chinese Academy of Sciences and Zheng Shouyi v. Liu Junqian, Laizhou City Wanlida Stone Industry Co., Ltd. and Yantai Environmental Art Administration Office (appeal of copyright infringement dispute) [2012] No.33
Hu HY, Lu HY (2018) Architectural environmental design: thinking, designing and drawing. Chemical Industry Press, Beijing, p 13+19
Hunt v. Pasternack, 192 F.3d 877
Intervest Constr., Inc. v. Canterbury Estate Homes, Inc., 554 F.3d 914
Jia XS, Xu CJ (2014) Review of the theory and practice of "urban memory" in China. Arch Res 1:22–32
Jiang T (2019) Urban public art and interaction design strategy based on digital technology. Clust Comput 22:3471–3478
Johnson v. Jones, 149 F.3d 494
Kose S (2016) Built environment design toward an inclusive society: how can we improve the existing infrastructure in cities? Advances in Design for Inclusion. Adv Intell Syst Comput 500:307–313
Kumar A, Nori KV, Natarajan S et al (2014) Value matrix: from value to quality and architecture. In: Economics-driven software architecture, pp 205–240
Lewis HL (2020) Who owns the plans: Copyright protection for architectural designs. https://www.linkedin.com/pulse/who-owns-plans-copyright-protection-architectural-designs-lewis. Accessed 28 Oct 2022
Li X (2020) Creating a garden with meaning and creating meaning with garden: a literati garden from the seventeenth episode of dream of red mansions. Landsc Archit 27(06):42–47
Lieke B (2008) Architectural design, Wörterbuch Design. Birkhäuser Basel, pp 16–17
Liu CT (ed) (2014) Intellectual property law (fifth edition). Renmin University Press, Beijing, p 54
Miles M (1997) Art, space and the city: public art and urban futures. Routledge, London
Morgan v. Hawthorne Homes, Inc., 2009 U.S. Dist. LEXIS 31456
Murphy MD (2016) Landscape architecture theory: an ecological approach. Island Press, Washington, DC, p 22
Oravec v. Sunny Isles Luxury Ventures L.C., 469 F. Supp. 2d 1148
Qiu J (2022) Methods and innovative expressions of architectural environment design. Ind Archit 52(04):238
Ren MF (2004) Modern environmental design. Chinese Garden 3:63–66

Robbins E (1997) The art of architectural drawing: imagination and technique. Urban Des Int 2:124–125

Rokeach M (1973) The nature of human values. The Free Press, New York

Shanghai High People's Court (2020) Civil Ruling on Trial Supervision of Copyright Ownership and Infringement Disputes between Sun Depin and Shanghai Education Press Co. [2020] No.2415

Shanghai Intellectual Property Court (2018, September 19) The Case of Fisher Technology Co., Ltd. v. Shanghai Dongfang Teaching Aids Co., Ltd. and Shanghai Yaxun Intelligent Robot Technology Co., Ltd., Copyright Infringement and Unfair Competition Dispute [2018] Hu 73 Minzhong No.268

Shanghai Intellectual Property Court (2020) East China Architectural Design and Research Institute Co., Ltd. and Ling Kego and other copyright ownership, infringement dispute civil second instance case civil judgement [2020] No.177

Shine v. Childs, 382 F. Supp. 2d 602

Shipley DE (2010) The architectural works copyright protection act at twenty: has full protection made a difference? J Intellect Prop Law 18(1):1–62

Snow DL, Grady K, Ewing MG (2000) A perspective in ethical issues in community psychology. In: Handbook of community psychology, pp 897–917

Steiner FR (2001) Landscape architecture. In: Smelser NJ, Baltes PB (eds) International encyclopedia of the social & behavioral sciences. Elsevier, Oxford, pp 8270–8275

Sturdza v. U.A.E., 281 F.3d 1287

Ten innovation intellectual property cases in Beijing during 2015 (2016). https://www.ciplawyer.com/html_e/ComprehensiveCases/20160414/136348.shtml. Accessed 28 Oct 2022

Universal Furniture Int'l, Inc. v. Collezione Europa USA, Inc., 618 F.3d 417

Wang Q (2014) Research on the expression of architectural works. Stud Law Bus 31(06):126–132

Wang Q (2015) On the qualification of equal proportional models in copyright law: a review of the "first aircraft model copyright infringement case". China Copyright 4:5–8

Wang Q (2019) Intellectual property law tutorial, 6th edn. People's Publishing House of China, Beijing

Wen Y, Shu J (2013) Research on indoor environment design based on ancient gardens-built environment. In: Du W (ed) Informatics and management science II, Lecture notes in electrical engineering, vol 205, pp 455–463

What is public art (2022). https://www.americansforthearts.org/by-topic/public-art. Accessed 28 Sept 2022

Wu HD (2013) Research on the system of reasonable use of copyright, 3rd edn. China University of Political Science and Law Press, Beijing, p 174

Wu HD (2015) On the infringement rules of "substantial similarity + contact". Law Sci 8:63–72

Wu KL (2021) Analysis of problems and measures of construction drawings for landscape design. Sichuan Cement 4:166–167

Yang ZJ (2012) Copyright law judgment and commentary. Xuelin Publishing Co., Ltd., Shanghai

Yin ZQ (2009) Scope of architectural works and cognizance of copy infringement. Intellect Prop 1:68–72

Yu R (2022) The use of landscape design techniques in urban landscape space—a review of urban landscape art and design. Build Struct 52(13):154–155

Yuan YY, Cheng YN (2018) Process, logic and modeling—an analysis of parametric landscape architecture planning and design. China Garden 34(10):77–82

Zhang M (2012) Effect of TRIPS agreement (article 13) three-step test on copyright limitation: on EU-US dispute over US copyright act 110(5). Mod Law Sci 34(03):173–177

Zhang Y (2021) Place making in international practice of landscape architecture: a study of Australian practices in China. Springer, Berlin, pp 1–8

Zhang C, Cheng L (1992) Lawrence Haplin's environmental design thought. New Archit 3:36–39

Chapter 5
Visual Communication Design and Intellectual Property

5.1 The Concept of Visual Communication Design and Intellectual Property

Visual communication design is the process of creating effective visual content for digital and print media. Professionals in this field use their creativity and knowledge of layout, typography, image editing, and graphic design to create designs that help tell stories, convey information, and create a positive impact on audiences.

Visual communication design is the process of transmitting a message from a sender to a receiver using visuals. The visuals can be anything from text to images to symbols. The goal of visual communication design is to create visuals that are effective in transmitting the message and that are easy for the receiver to understand. Visual communication design involves understanding the principles of design, as well as the psychology of colour and perception. Good visual communication design makes information easy to understand and engaging to look at. Visual communication design includes display design, logo design, type design, packaging design and many others (Xie 2022).

The term became popular after the 1960 World Design Congress in Tokyo, Japan, which included the design of newspapers, magazines, posters, and other printed materials, as well as media such as movies, television, and electronic billboards. They transmit relevant information through visuals and thus complete the expression of style. This process is called visual communication design. In short, visual communication design is "the design for people to see and the design to inform."

Visual communication design derived from Graphic Design, which originated in Europe and America in the middle of the nineteenth century. Visual communication has evolved over time. Early man communicated with symbols and drawings on cave walls. These drawings were used to convey messages and ideas. As time passed, new technologies were developed that allowed for more visual communication. The printing press allowed for the spread of images and information, and the development of photography and film allowed for the capture and distribution of

N. Jiang, *Design, Innovation and Intellectual Property*,
https://doi.org/10.1007/978-981-95-2042-8_5

images around the world. Today, we use digital technologies to communicate visually through social media, video conferencing, and virtual reality. The ways in which we can communicate visually continue to evolve, providing new opportunities for us to share our ideas and experiences.

Visual communication design is an active process of communicating specific content through visuals. It relies mostly or partly on vision and uses two-dimensional image representations such as signage, typography, painting, graphic design, illustration, color, and electronic devices. In visual communication design cases, it would be more influential to integrate the text into communication, education, and persuasion of the audience. That is, visual communication design is goal-oriented, which means it conveys certain information to the target audience with effective visual content and exerts some impact on the target.

Visual communication design mainly uses visuals to convey all kinds of information to audiences. The designer is the sender of the information, and the audience is the receiver. Visual communication includes two basic concepts: "visual symbols" and "communication". A "visual symbol" is something that humans can see with their eyes. "Communication" means the sender conveys the message to the receiver through symbols. The sender and receiver can be either human beings or non-human beings, such as communication between all living creatures, between humankind and nature, between humankind and the environment, and between people. There are four basic elements for successful communication, namely, the sender, the message, the medium, and the receiver. Communication cannot be achieved without any of these.

5.2 The Features of Visual Communication Design

5.2.1 Timeless

In an age of rapid development, visual symbols are used in all art forms, such as costume design, graphic advertising design, environmental art design, commercial photography, and corporate design. The symbols can be concrete or abstract, a shape or an image, serious or relaxed, with human expressions or showing the harmony between man and nature.

5.2.2 Commercial

Visual communication design is an art that serves modern businesses. It includes logo, advertising, packaging, and environment design, as well as corporate design. They are called "visual communication design" because these designs use visuals to deliver messages to consumers. It bridges between businesses, products, and consumers.

5.2.3 *No Borders*

Visual image has the unique advantage of transcending national borders and language barriers. It is a special form of language that can deliver messages and exchange ideas visually. Besides, universal visual expressions should be adopted in purpose in some designs. For example, the design of tourist traffic maps, guide maps, and public signs must be in line with international general visual standards. In the information age when cultural exchanges between various ethnic groups are becoming more and more frequent, designers use visual images and international general visual symbols to help eliminate language barriers between humans so that messages and thoughts can be quickly identified and disseminated through visual communication. In the field of culture and ethics, visual communication influences people's ideas, feelings, and thoughts with its unique charm. Visual communication has played an immeasurable role in the development of modern society through the transcendence of nations, cultures, and regions.

5.2.4 *Interactivity*

In the information age, the most popular communication method is undoubtedly new media. Advanced technologies, equipment, and research methods enable designers to continuously expand and enrich their perspectives and ways of thinking. At the same time, it also opens a channel to show oneself and the value of one's existence in society. In the information age, one-way communication has become obsolete. The interaction between the sender and receiver of a message has become a new research topic for visual communication design. Visual communication designers should be able to fully consider the diverse needs of the audience to raise their awareness and encourage interactions (Chen 2016).

5.3 Types of Visual Communication Design

5.3.1 *Type Design*

As a natural product born through cultural and emotional exchanges, writing is of great importance in human culture. With the progress in human civilization, a scientific, complete, and standard writing system has gradually been formed. Writing is a visual symbol that constitutes a necessary medium for conveying thoughts and feelings in a society featuring changes. In addition, the "aesthetic visualization" of characters has become an important task for visual communication designers. The Chinese characters are not only an epitome of national culture but are also used by many designers to deliver emotions and messages. The characters thus become more practical and meaningful (LYU 2022). Type design is a crucial aspect of visual communication design. It is used in various fields like logo design, packaging design, bookbinding design, poster design, and web design. These designs can be found in multiple new media, including graphic media, online media, video media, and outdoor advertising, which are closely related to our daily lives.

A typeface is the design of lettering that can include variations in size, weight (e.g. bold), slope (e.g. italic), width (e.g. condensed), and so on. Each of these variations of the typeface is a font. There are thousands of different typefaces in existence, with new ones being developed constantly. The art and craft of designing typefaces is called type design. Designers of typefaces are called type designers and are often employed by type foundries. In desktop publishing, type designers are sometimes also called font developers or font designers.

Designers generally change the stroke, shape, and structure when designing fonts. First, a stroke can either be thick or thin, straight or twisted, but the thickness and straightness must be in harmony. A font should not be added with too many styles. The designer should ensure the integrity of the main strokes, which are crucial to the legibility of the character. Moreover, the font should not be too complicated. Second, the fonts have a square frame. In creative design, the font frame can be flattened, lengthened, tilted, curved, rounded, trapezoidal, triangular, etc. Finally, the font structure can also be transformed boldly. It can be scattered and restructured by changing its shape, integrating with word meaning and decorating with elements. With enough imagination, new fonts can be created from abstract or concrete graphics so that the fonts will be more expressive and eye-catching (Guo and Zhao 2010).

5.3.2 Logo Design

Nowadays, printing, photography, design, and image communication are becoming more and more prominent. The development of technology already empowered non-verbal communication to catch up with verbal communication. A logo, on the other hand, is a special way of communication. When people see smoke rise, they associate it with a fire underneath. Smoke is naturally a sign of fire. In an age of poor communication, people used smoke to deliver messages similar to fire (indicating emergencies, alarms, etc.). Smoke is like a signal. It rises high and melts away slowly. Besides, it has clear images and outstanding features to be seen from afar. Therefore, any language or written communication cannot reach the speed and effect of this non-verbal transmission in that era. Although current language and literal communication technology have advanced to the extreme, direct communication methods such as "signs" can get the message across at a glance. They are not restricted within one country or language, and can meet people's growing living needs. The unique advantage makes it irreplaceable by any other communication method. Nowadays, a logo is often the core of a brand image or an identification symbol indicating the characteristics of things. It uses simple, prominent, and easily identifiable images, graphics, or text symbols as intuitive language. In addition to expressing something or a substitute, it also expresses meaning, emotion, and instructions.

In terms of expression, signs can be divided into three types: graphic signs, sound signs, and touch signs. Graphic signs are the combination of special patterns and special characters, generally including special patterns, special fonts, and synthetic fonts. Sound signs, such as QQ beeps, fire alarms, and class bells. Touch signs, such as blind sidewalks.

The essential feature of a logo is its practical function. Although the logo in art design has some aesthetic value, the practicality is valued more than its beauty. Signs include public signs, traffic signs, safety signs, operation signs; national, regional, urban, ethnic and family signs; signs specific to social groups, enterprises, and events, such as emblems, logos, factory logos, association logos, etc.; signs used for specific products; those used exclusively for groups or private property, such as seals, signatures, flower prints, seals, and branding, etc., each with its unique uses. In particular, legal trademarks also shoulder the task of safeguarding their interests.

Second, the logo is recognizable and prominent. Each symbol has its own characteristics which make it easy to recognize. The symbol reflects the characteristics of the thing itself and indicates different meanings between things. The main function of symbols is to distinguish logos and signify belongings. All signs are directly related to the fundamental interests of countries, groups, and individuals. Therefore, they must not be identical or confused to avoid misunderstandings. The trademark must have distinctive characteristics so that people can recognize and remember it as soon as they see it. Prominence is another important characteristic of a logo. Other than a hidden logo, most signs are set up to attract people's attention. Logos should have strong, eye-catching colors and simple graphics.

Finally, the logo is also diverse. There are many types of signs for various uses. They are extremely diversified in use, composition, and form of expression. There are two-dimensional logos, three-dimensional logos (such as relief, garden carving, any three-dimensional object, or using a specific style of packaging, container, etc. as a mark), those directly using physical objects and words and those concrete or abstract. Logos are rich and diverse in forms of expression. With the development of technology, culture, and art, it is always constantly updating.

5.3.3 Packaging Design

Packaging design is a professional discipline that combines natural science and aesthetics to protect products and promote sales during distribution. Packaging is the general name of containers, materials and auxiliary equipment for storage according to some usage methods. It mainly includes packaging design, packaging structure design, and decorative design. Design is an important way to add value to products. The higher the added value of products, the more profit a company makes. Packaging design enables certain products that are not originally of high value to be sold at a high price. It plays an important role in production, distribution, sales and consumption. At the same time, with the commodity trade economy, modern design standards and technology developing rapidly, the development of packaging design has also entered a new era (Liu 2020).

Packaging has become a primary vehicle for communication and branding (Rettie and Brewer 2000). Packaging plays an important role on attracting the consumers' attention and creating hedonic and sensory expectations, which may affect actual product experience. The function of food and beverage packaging has gone beyond the initial purpose to control portions and preserve the product (De et al. 2020). In this sense, shape and color play a fundamental role, since consumers spot the products at a given distance and start processing the more conspicuous visual elements well before being captured by minor details or semantic information (Schifferstein et al. 2013). There are studies which have identified the functions of individual packaging design elements such as color, image, shape, material, label and typography and the perception of the consumer (Bloch 1995). The form or exterior appearance of a product is means to communicate information to consumers. Studies shows that it is feasible to manipulate the imagery and position of product by selecting and using different design elements. This will influence the perception of the product and thereby directly influence the consumer's buying decision (Meyers-Levy 1995).

Packaging products include boxes, bottles (cans), bags, etc. There is usually some text on the packaging. These words include necessary information such as brand, product name, manufacturer and location, product composition, volume, model and specifications, etc., as well as explanatory text such as product use, precautions, production date and shelf life, etc., as well as promotional text.

Take food packaging as an example. Food packaging contains many elements. Generally, it can be divided into packaging materials and packaging design. In terms of packaging materials, food is closely related to human health, so packaging materials must meet the needs for food safety. In terms of packaging design, it is necessary to comprehensively consider various factors such as food attributes, characteristics, and brands to carry out the integrated design of food packaging. Food packaging design involves two factors: graphic elements and three-dimensional elements. Graphic elements include all two-dimensional visual elements, such as characters, and patterns, while three-dimensional elements refer to structural designs such as boxes used in packaging (Wan 2021). By integrating various elements, food packaging is designed to attract consumers, thereby increasing sales.

Safety in packaging design is mainly related to two factors:

(1) Content safety, which aims to the proper preservation of the package itself and its content.
(2) Ecosystems and human health safety, when hazards are related either to dangerous packaging contents or unsafe packaging components.

Preservation is the most important function of packaging. The increasing attention to this aspect is partly due to economical motivations (such as product recalls, damage to reputation, loss of sales, etc.) and legislation requirements during the distribution process. Many authors highlight the importance of laboratory simulation to test adequacy of packaging systems.

From a marketing point of view, it is also important to recall the fact that consumers often let their moral views influence their buying decisions. Of course, designers need to take into account the fact that culture does seem to condition how consumers view specific design details56 and keep abreast with such changes.

Sustainable packaging design is a challenging topic because environmental issues have come to dominate social concerns, whereas packaging is perceived as an ancillary activity, with a strong environmental impact. Throughout their life cycle, packaging systems consume renewable and non-renewable resources and energy, create waste, generate emissions and emit pollutants. For these reasons, efforts must be made to encourage reduction (i.e. modifying or limiting the way in which packaging is manufactured or used), packaging reuse and recycling of packaging materials (Azzi et al. 2012).

5.3.4 Poster Design

A poster refers to text, images, and paintings with specific meaning posted on the street or in public places. It is a form of outdoor advertisement. Modern poster design has a history of more than 100 years. In the middle of the 19th century, due to the Industrial Revolution, there was a boom in diversified commodities. The local European market could no longer satisfy the needs of the commodity economy. This conflict led to European colonial expansion and the development of poster design. The Industrial Revolution also brought about larger printers in the printing industry, greatly improving printing efficiency, and leading the poster industry into a "golden age". Nowadays, with the continuous development of social economy, science and technology, poster design in various countries is constantly improving. It has formed unique styles and characteristics throughout a long historical period. People use posters not only for communicating but also for meeting their aesthetic needs. They pay much attention to the innovation in the forms of advertising, hoping the posters can accurately express the theme ideas. Although the forms of other advertising methods are becoming more and more diverse, poster design is still the most commonly used advertising method due to its affordable cost, wide application, and easy production. With a growing appreciation and pursuit of arts among the public, some excellent poster designs become valuable collections.

Posters can be divided into commercial and non-commercial ones in terms of purpose. A poster with a commercial purpose is a commercial poster, also known as a "commercial advertisement". In a commercial society, people generally think that commercial advertising is one of the vehicles that can bring economic value, that is, for-profit advertising. The value of commercial advertisements is immeasurable. Great commercial advertisements can help products quickly occupy the market, promote sales, and realize the value of products. A poster for a non-commercial purpose usually refers to a poster serving political and social ideology. It includes public service posters and cultural posters which are often employed by political and social ideologies to appeal to or warn the public.

Posters generally have the following characteristics:

(1) Strong visual impact. Unlike ordinary works of art, posters are for people to see, so designers pay particular attention to the visual effect of posters in distance. Living a fast-paced modern life, people spend less time reading posters. This forces designers to design posters with a stronger visual impact that can instantly attract people's attention. At the same time, the speed, effectiveness, and accuracy of the message delivered in the poster cannot be compromised.
(2) Innovative and unique. Creativity in poster design is like a soul to the human being. Whether it is a brilliant innovation has become one of the key factors in judging the success of poster advertisements. An original innovation not only highlights the purpose and theme of the poster but also underlines the visual image language. It helps amplify the power and depth of the messages in a poster, making the poster very persuasive and appealing.
(3) Cover broad content. The poster can demonstrate everything. The theme of the poster can be important issues such as the international situation, political policy, and a community with a shared future for mankind, etc., which are complex and logical. It can also be the notice of a short theatrical performance, various exhibitions, promotions, etc., which is temporary and small.
(4) Accurate message delivery. All posters are aimed at accurately delivering messages. The poster design must have a clear theme. Moreover, the message should be targeted without ambiguity and inappropriate terminology. The designer should strive to communicate with and resonate with the audience through posters. All forms of posters are also aimed at accurately delivering messages.
(5) Diverse themes and forms. Take a single-picture poster as an example. It is the most commonly used form to describe a theme by designers. It features low cost, little time consumption, less innovation, and simplicity. Take series posters as an example. It represents repetitive, proportional emphasis, which can cause even more resonance and response in the audience. Moreover, series posters bring better visual experience to the audience. However, in contrast to a single-picture poster, it is more expensive and time-consuming. It is more difficult for designers to arrange creativity.

5.4 Legal Protection of Intellectual Property

5.4.1 *Problems of Intellectual Property Protection of Type and Countermeasures*

(1) International Treaty

"Vienna Agreement for the Protection of Type Faces and their International Deposit"

This agreement was signed in 1973 by 11 countries, including France, the Federal Republic of Germany, Hungary, Italy, Liechtenstein, Luxembourg, the Netherlands, San Marino, Switzerland, the United Kingdom, and Yugoslavia. For the purposes of this Agreement and the Regulations, (i) "type faces" means sets of designs of: (a), letters and alphabets as such with their accessories such as accents and punctuation marks, (b) numerals and other figurative signs such as conventional signs, symbols and scientific signs, (c) ornaments such as borders, fleurons and vignettes, which are intended to provide means for composing texts by any graphic technique. The term "type faces" does not include type faces of a form dictated by purely technical requirements.

The Contracting States undertake, in accordance with the provisions of this Agreement, to ensure the protection of typefaces, by establishing a special national deposit, or by adapting the deposit provided for in their national industrial design laws, or by their national copyright provisions. These kinds of protection may be cumulative. The term of protection may not be less than fifteen years, and may be divided into several periods, each extension being granted only at the request of the owner of the protected type faces.

The Agreement requires the ratification of 5 countries for entering into force. However, as of January 1, 1988, only two countries had sent instruments of ratification, so the agreement has not yet entered into force. The Additional Protocol to the agreement extends the font protection period to no less than 25 years, which did not enter into force since only two countries have approved it. Despite the agreement not entering into force, it is of guiding significance as the only international agreement on intellectual property rights protection in fonts.

(2) British Protection Model

In 1988, the United Kingdom introduced the Copyright, Designs and Patents Act, which provides protection for typefaces through copyright. Section 54, paragraph 2 of this law stipulates acts that infringe typeface copyright, while paragraph 1 states situations where the infringement is not constituted. Therefore, the two judgements (whether or not an infringement) stipulated in the Section can almost determine all typeface-related infringement cases. Thus, we can infer: to determine whether a certain action infringes typeface copyright, paragraph 1 and 2 of Section 54 are the legal basis for judgement. The typeface copyright protection period is 25 years. The above provisions indicate that the primary purpose of this Section is to prevent other typeface designers from creating products that are identical or similar to the original typeface products. However, it does not impose any restrictions on the normal use of typeface products.

(3) U.S. Protection Model

The United States protects typeface through design patents. In 1996, the "Guidelines for Examination of Patent Application for Computer-Generated Icons" stated in Article 5 that "PTO personnel should not reject claims for type fonts under Section 171 for failure to comply with the 'article of manufacture' requirement on the basis that more modern methods of typesetting, including computer-generation, do not require solid printing blocks." It essentially recognizes the inclusion of computer fonts within the scope of patent protection. The protection period for design patents in the United States is 14 years from the date the patent is granted to the rights holder in accordance with the law. However, in practice, people often use contracts to protect typefaces, while the protection of design patents is rarely adopted. This is because typefaces can be used for a long time, while the protection period for design rights is relatively short. If the design patent is used to protect typefaces, it will have a detrimental impact on the long-term rights and interests of the owner.

(4) German Protection Model

Germany enacted the "Typeface Act" in 1986. According to this Act, for typefaces with originality, they can be protected not only by copyright law based on patterns, but also by design law based on models. According to the German "Typeface Act", the protection period for printed materials is 10 years. The holder can extend it for 5 years, 10 years, or 15 years, but the total period cannot exceed 25 years. This showcases that Germany has adopted the "Typeface Act" as a specific legislation to protect typeface design.

(5) China Protection Model

The legal protection of typeface design copyright is one of the highly debated issues in the field of intellectual property in China. Scholars' opinions on whether typeface possesses copyrightability are mainly divided into three. First, typefaces should have copyrightability and should be protected by the Copyright Law (Li and Zhang 2016). For example, some scholars believe that both individual Chinese characters and certain kinds of typefaces may meet the originality requirements under the Copyright Law. Secondly, typefaces have a limited degree of copyrightability. Some judgments hold that only typefaces with significant originality created with great effort are eligible for protection under the Copyright Law. Providing copyright protection to those with low originality would seriously affect the public interest (Jiangsu High People's Court 2012). Thirdly, typefaces are not copyrightable. Some scholars pointed out that, on the one hand, those computer fonts that can be reused have a low level of artistic creativity and cannot meet the general requirements of originality under the Copyright Law. On the other hand, those typefaces that are original but primarily serve practical functions should also be excluded from the protection scope of the Copyright Law. Therefore, typefaces cannot receive strong protection under China's Copyright Law (He and Yan 2012).

In the case of Beijing University Founder Electronics Co., Ltd. (Founder) vs. Blizzard Entertainment Ltd. (Blizzard) (Supreme People's Court 2010), Founder claimed that Blizzard copied and installed Founder's "Lanting" font in the online game "World of Warcraft", without authorization from Founder, and infringed Founder's rights of reproduction, distribution and remuneration, and also infringed Founder's information network communication right in its font. Beijing Municipal High People's Court held that the font was neither a program referred to in the Regulations on Protection of Computer Software, nor the documentation for the program, so Founder's claim that its "Lanting" font should be protected as computer software under the Copyright Law could not be established, and its claim that Blizzard infringed its copyright in the font computer software shall not be supported. Founder's "Lanting" font was the art of calligraphy composed of lines with a certain aesthetic significance which met the conditions of art works set forth in the Copyright. However, the Supreme Court concluded that Founder's "Lanting" font was computer software, instead of art work (MMLC Group 2022). In addition, take the case of Beijing University Founder Electronics Co., Ltd. (Founder) vs. Guangzhou Procter & Gamble Co., Ltd. (P & G) and Beijing Carrefour Commercial Co., Ltd as an example. The Court of first instance accordingly concluded that Founder's "Qianti" font had certain originality and met the requirements on art works under the Copyright Law, so it may be protected as a whole; however, for the single characters in the font shall not be protected as art works. Founder's request on identification of P & G's use of "Rejoince" (in Chinese characters), the art works in "Qianti" font as copyright infringement had no legal basis, so all Founder's requests were rejected by the Court. And the court of second instance concluded that P & G's acts would not infringe the copyright, whether or not "Rejoince" in "Qianti" font constituted art work (MMLC Group 2022). In the above two cases, the first case considered that individual characters with originality in the Chinese printed font library belong to art work defined by the Copyright Law, and ruled that the defendant constituted copyright infringement and should bear corresponding liability.

In the latter case, it is believed that it has constituted an "implied license", "the disputed words 'Rejoice' applied on the so-called infringing products were designed by NICE Company (NICE) using the legal version of Founder's "Qianti" style font library under the authorization of P&G. According to the facts in this case, NICE is deemed as having been entitled to conduct advertising designs with specific single words in the font, and permit its clients (P&G in this case) to copy and publish the design work. Therefore, the appellee's disputed conduct should be considered as permitted by the appellant." In the copyright infringement dispute case involving Guangdong Renzhiguan Food Co., Ltd., Guangdong Xiqi Food Co., Ltd., etc. (Intermediate People's Court of Rizhao City 2023), the court believes that Weifang Character Cultural Center enjoys corresponding copyright for the "Character Workshop Su Bai Ti" font, which has been registered by the National Copyright Administration as an art work. Each individual character in the registered

"Character Workshop Su Bai Ti" constitutes a unique piece of art work. The sufficient number of pieces together form a new typeface, namely the "Character Workshop Su Bai Ti". Based on this, it can be determined that Weifang Character Culture Center enjoys the copyright of all individual characters in the art work "Character Workshop Su Bai Ti", without mentioning the copyright of the entire character library. The defendant shall bear the corresponding civil liability for copyright infringement. In cases of infringement disputes over other copyrights and property rights, such as Beijing Founder Electronics Co., Ltd. v. Zanhuang County Zaoyuan Fruit Co., Ltd. (High People's Court of Hebei Province 2021), the court found that while the strokes and structure of Chinese characters indeed belong to public domain, the fonts involved in this case distribute discerning features with its horizontal, vertical, curved and hooked strokes designed with different thickness, length, and curvature variations, which clearly differs from the basic characteristics of existing public domain character strokes. Thus the typeface in question stands out from the existing ancient calligraphy typeface and common typeface in existing computer libraries, as well as common new hand-drawn art typeface. This typeface has certain originality as the outcome of artificial intelligence and it falls under the category of intellectual property. Therefore, it constitutes the art work as defined by copyright law.

Does Chinese printed typeface have originality? Does it constitute a work and what kind of work it is?

Typeface design is often envisioned by a designer in their mind, after which they draw the desired outline of the characters on a computer and establish a font library. When importing typefaces into a computer, designers also need to constantly modify the structure of the fonts to make them look more coordinated and distinctive. They are different from ordinary Chinese characters. Being more than an ideographic writing, they also demonstrate originality purely from the designer, which is a higher level of aesthetic pursuit. The multi-dimensional and complex character structure of Chinese printed fonts, compared to the simple horizontal arrangement of western alphabetic letters, is more intricate in its form and more prominent in style, making it easier to constitute art works in the sense of copyright law. Chinese printed fonts that are original, replicable, and within the statutory copyright protection period can be protected as art works under the copyright law of China. So individual fonts naturally have originality and enjoy copyright.

"Font library is a collection of many individual characters, which also share the same style." However, the lack of originality of the font library means that it does not constitute a work. Firstly, the fonts in the font library are original, but the library is simply a collection of well-designed fonts arranged for the convenience of the public use. Secondly, font library is a type of computer program that simply displays specific results after running of the program. It does not possess the aesthetic value found in art works or calligraphy; therefore, it is not protected by copyright law. Computer software is essentially a series of code that realizes font conversion in a way that can be read by computers. Therefore, computer font libraries are considered software and are protected by computer software copyright. The computer font library enjoys multiple copyrights, which exist on different copyright objects, namely font design draft copyright, font work copyright, and font library software copyright.

5.4.2 *Intellectual Property Protection of Special Symbols*

Signs include not only commercial ones used by companies, but also special symbols used by social groups, enterprises, and events, such as emblems, conference symbols, factory symbols, and association symbols for interests' protection. The Administrative Regulations for Special Symbols in China stipulate that special symbols refer to such symbols as titles and abbreviations, emblems and articles of auspiciousness, which are composed of words and designs and used in national or international cultural, sports, scientific research or other social and public welfare activities held with the approval of the State Council.

In Germany, exhibition symbols are considered as a form of commercial symbols, and listed under the protection of the Act on the Protection of Trade Marks and other Signs. Section 15 of the Act stipulates that "the acquisition of the protection of a commercial designation shall grant to its proprietor an exclusive right; third parties shall be prohibited from using the commercial designation or a similar sign in trade, without authorisation, in a manner liable to cause confusion with the protected designation; third parties shall be furthermore prohibited from using the commercial designation or a similar sign in trade if there is no likelihood of confusion mentioned above, in so far as the use of the sign without due cause takes unfair advantage of, or is detrimental to, the distinctive character or the repute of the commercial designation." Based on this Section, during the 1999 Berlin Electronics Fair (IFA), Sennheiser company unlawfully used the exhibition logo in its electronic product advertisements without permission from the organizers. Thus, the organizer Messeberlin GmbH filed a lawsuit against Sennheiser for infringement. Both the Berlin District Court and the Court of Appeals ruled that Sennheiser violated the commercial trademark rights of Messeberlin GmbH.

The United States also regulates exhibition symbols through trademark law, categorizing them as trade dress through precedents. The US courts continuously expanded the scope of trade dress through a series of cases, initially including the external shape or configuration of a product, packaging, colors, design, and the combination of color and other factors. Later it was expanded to the total image of a product. Ultimately, in the 1992 case of Two Pesos, Inc. v. Taco Cabana, (Two Pesos) the U.S. Supreme Court defined trade dress as the "overall image of a business engaged in commercial activities".

Currently, China does not have specific regulations on exhibition symbols, nor does it classify exhibition symbols under any specific laws. Instead, provisions of relevant laws will be reasonably applied, such as the Trademark Law, Patent Law, Copyright Law, and Anti-Unfair Competition Law. As for texts, graphics, letters, numbers, three-dimensional symbols, color combinations, and sounds, as well as the combination of the aforementioned elements, they can receive trademark protection. For original content such as theme songs, emblems, slogans, etc. that cannot be registered as trademarks, the Copyright Law can be applied to protect them in the form of copyright. And for three-dimensional symbols like mascots, they can also be protected by the Patent Law when meeting the requirements of appearance design. Certain acts of infringement that constitute unfair competition can also be regulated by the Anti-Unfair Competition Law.

With the continuous opening up and growth of the sports industry, the development and protection of sports event logos have become a focal point in the field of intellectual property. Regarding the Olympic symbol, the United States protects them through laws such as the Ted Stevens Olympic and Amateur Sports Act, and can also invoke domestic intellectual property laws such as the Trademark Law, Copyright Law, Patent Law, and Anti-Unfair Competition Law for comprehensive protection. For judicial practice, in the case of San Francisco Arts and Athletics Inc. (SFAA) v. U.S. Olympics Committee (USOC), (San Francisco) the US court's judgement is as follows. On certiorari, the Supreme Court, Justice Powell, held that: (1) the statute granting the United States Olympic Committee exclusive use of the word "Olympic" did not require proof that unauthorized use was confusing; (2) word "Olympic" was not a generic word for which trademark protection was unavailable; (3) First Amendment did not prohibit Congress from granting exclusive use of word "Olympic", and (4)the USOC was not a governmental actor to whom the Fifth Amendment applied. The judgement actually lowered the standard for infringement of the Olympic symbol in order to strengthen the IPR protection for sports event logos and promote the development of the sports industry and sports economy. Section 110 of the Amateur Sports Act of 1978, 36 U.S.C.S. § 380, provides that, without the consent of the United States Olympic Committee (USOC), certain commercial and promotional uses of the word "Olympic" were subject to a civil action by the USOC for the trademark infringement "remedies" as provided in the Lanham Act, 15 U.S.C.S. §§ 1051 et seq. In this case, Petitioner SFAA, a nonprofit California corporation, originally sought to incorporate under the name "Golden Gate Olympic Association," but was told by the California Department of Corporations that the word "Olympic" could not appear in a corporate title. After its incorporation in 1981, the SFAA nevertheless began to promote the "Gay Olympic Games" using those words on its letterheads and mailings and in local newspapers. The SFAA later claimed that its use of the word "Olympic" was intended to make a political statement about the status of homosexuals in society. Although the USOC requested the SFAA to discontinue the word "Olympic" in its description of the planned games, the SFAA continued to use the word, and the USOC brought suit against the SFAA and its president in the federal district court, which eventually granted the USOC summary judgment and a permanent injunction against the SFAA's use of the word "Olympic". On appeal, a panel of the United States Court of Appeals for the Ninth Circuit affirmed with respect to the grant of summary judgment and the injunction, expressing the view that § 110 granted the USOC exclusive use of the word "Olympic" without a requirement that the USOC prove that the unauthorized use was confusing, and without regard to the Lanham Act's statutory defenses for unauthorized use of a trademark. (San Francisco)

In addition, in the case of O-M Bread, Inc. v. United States Olympic Committee (O-M Bread), a prior use exception was proposed. The court believes that it should provide protection for prior users while also not infringing upon the legitimate rights of the United States Olympic Committee. Therefore, for the balance of the two interests, the court proposes that the rights of prior users, although protected, should be limited to their original scope and should not be expanded. United States Olympic Committee (USOC) filed trademark opposition against application of bakery to register mark "OLYMPIC KIDS" for bakery goods. The Trademark Trial and Appeal Board of the United States Patent and Trademark Office sustained opposition, and bakery appealed. The Court of Appeals, Pauline Newman, Circuit Judge, held that bakery's grandfathered rights under Amateur Sports Act to continue to use its "OLYMPIC" marks for bread and bakery products did not extend to its registration of "OLYMPIC KIDS" for bakery products (United States Court of Appeals).

UK enacted the Olympic Symbol (Protection) Act in 1995. It establishes the legal status of the British Olympic Association and defines the protected elements of Olympic symbols, including the Olympic name (e.g., Olympia, Olympic), symbols, emblems, and the like. The Act also regulates the infringement of Olympic symbols. It stipulates that the actions against the Olympic symbol, the Olympic motto or a protected word directly infringe the Olympics association right. For example, printing the Olympic symbol on product packaging without permission from the British Olympic Association. Indirect infringement refers to the adoption of symbols same or similar to the Olympic symbol as to be likely to create in the public mind an association with it. In addition, in cases of indirect infringement, the accused infringer can invoke fair (or legitimate) use as a defense. In addition, in 2006, the UK also enacted the "London Olympic and Paralympic Games Act", which incorporates the symbols, motto, and related words of the International Paralympic Committee, thereby expanding the scope of protection of the 1995 Act. At the same time, both acts provide broader protection for the Olympic symbol compared to a trademark.

During the Winter Olympics, the Beijing Organising Committee for the Winter Olympics submitted 315 trademark applications for protection. As a new category of intellectual property, the Winter Olympics logo is not only protected by the Intellectual Property Law of China, but also by laws specifically designed for it. On 28th June 2018, the State Council of the People's Republic of China issued Order No. 699 for revising the "Regulation on the Protection of Olympic Symbols". The revised version came into effect on 31st July 2018. The regulation takes the Olympic symbol as the protected object, expanding the scope of protection to torch design, Olympic motto, and proprietary names. It specifies the International Olympic Committee, the China Olympic Committee, and the institutions applying for hosting the Olympic Games in China and the organizations holding the Olympic Games in China as the rights holders. It also stipulates that the validity period of the Olympic symbol is 10 years and can be renewed upon expiration. The Regulation comprehensively stipulate the scenarios, methods, and restrictions for the use of the Olympic symbol in a bottom-line manner. Therefore, the user of the Winter Olympics symbol should not only comply with the provisions of the Copyright Law and the Trademark Law, but also be subject to the restrictions and constraints of the Regulation. The Regulation also stipulates that no person shall use the Olympic symbol for commercial purposes without the permission of the Olympic symbol rights holder. In some cases, attaching the Olympic symbol to products is a form of implicit commercial use. For example, custom fresh milk cakes with the image of "Bing Dwen Dwen" and coffee shop's "Bing Dwen Dwen" image latte art are all considered commercial use, which poses a risk of infringement on Winter Olympics intellectual property rights. In addition, the "Measures for the Protection of Asian Games Signs" issued by the State Administration for Industry and Commerce, and the "Beijing Olympic Intellectual Property Protection Regulations" formulated by the Beijing Municipal Government can also provide relevant references for the protection of sports event symbols. The reasonable use of the Winter Olympics logo in non-commercial contexts is protected by law, such as its use in news reporting or commentary, in academic articles or personal biographies, and in factual statements related to geography or cultural education. Non-profit organizations or entities should comply with the "Rules of the Organising Committee of the Beijing 2022 Winter Olympic and Paralympic Games Concerning the Non-commercial Use of Symbols" (Winter Olympics Organizing Committee Announcement [2019] No. 19) for usage, and should use them according to the permitted scope, signed commitments, and technical specifications established by the Beijing Winter Olympics Organizing Committee. They must not engage in any activities that infringe upon the intellectual property rights of the Committee, nor assist any third party in activities that may lead to confusion about any specific connection with the Beijing Winter Olympics Organizing Committee or the Beijing Winter Olympics.

5.4.3 *Intellectual Property Protection of Packaging Design*

(1) Copyright Law Protection

The protection object of the Copyright Law of China is works. Product packaging, as an intellectual achievement, is something that showcases creativity and ideas through a certain medium. It also possesses aesthetic appeal in order to attract consumers. For example, if the patterns, texts, colors, or their combinations on a package are original, it constitutes works of fine art under the Copyright Law, and is eligible for protection. A work enjoys copyright from the moment it is completed. Therefore, the packaging is protected by copyright law when the design is completed. Without permission, others are not allowed to copy, distribute, or engage in other similar activities. As copyright is acquired naturally, the most effective method to get strong evidence support of copyright ownership is to register copyright at the time of completion of the work. This method is particularly suitable for products with a wide variety of packaging and strong variability, such as mooncake box packaging. In addition, copyright enjoys long protection period. For works created by legal entities or other organizations, the protection period for copyright property rights is fifty years. For works created by individuals, the protection period for copyright property rights is the lifetime of the author plus fifty years after their death, which can provide long-term protection for product packaging.

However, the disadvantage of this method lies in the weak protection of copyright. When the rights holder asserts their copyright, the other party usually argues that the rights holder's work lacks originality or that the work is in the public domain, thereby opposing their copyright. In judicial practice, the protection of copyright is also weaker compared to that of patent rights.

(2) Patent Law Protection

Designs, utility models and inventions are all protected under patent law. Packaging design can be protected by the corresponding law as a form of design. The so-called design is a new design applied in industry with respect to shape, color, etc. The combinations that may constitute a design are: the shape of the product, the pattern of the product, the shape and pattern, the shape and color, the pattern and color, the shape, pattern and color of the product. The purpose of their protection is to protect the intellectual achievements of the designers and encourage originality. If the packaging design of a product has novelty, that is to say, the packaging design, as a design, is different from the design which has been openly used at home and abroad or which has been published in domestic and foreign journals before applying for a patent, then the right holder of the packaging design can apply for a patent of the relevant design, and the packaging design which has been granted a patent can be protected by the corresponding law. The biggest advantage of choosing Patent Law to protect the intellectual property rights of packaging design is its absolute exclusive right. Anyone even the creator of the design cannot use the package without the permission of the patentee.

In the case of Dongguan Heishou Shifu Washing Products Co., Ltd. vs. Wang Huaguo and Others (Guangdong High People's Court 2011) on design patent infringement dispute, the Court held that since the design in question was mainly a combination of color and pattern, the comparison should be based on the color and pattern. Accordingly, although the barcode printed on the outer carton of the allegedly infringing hand washing powder was consistent with the commodity barcode applied for registration by Heishou Shifu, the barcode was excluded from the scope of comparison because the barcode and the corresponding numbers only take up a small part of the lower right corner of the right view of the carton and did not belong to the category of color and pattern, and would not have any effect on the appearance of the carton. By comparing the allegedly infringing design and the design in question, it can be seen that in either view, the difference between the two is mainly: the allegedly infringing design is a pattern of about 4 cm × 4 cm in size in the center of the box; while the design in question is a different pattern of 4.5 cm × 4.5 cm in the center of the box.

The court of first instance held that, for the general consumer, the visual effect of the pattern was more prominent than the other parts of the box, therefore, although the allegedly infringing design and the design in question had similar design elements, the design elements in the center of the two boxes were not same or similar. Besides, for the general consumer, the pattern design in the center of the box had a more prominent visual effect. Therefore, the court of first instance held that the allegedly infringing design was neither identical nor similar to the design in question. The court of second instance agreed with the court of first instance, that the pattern in the middle of the box was different: for the allegedly infringing design, it was a hand-shaped pattern in the middle of the pattern while in terms of the patent it was a person's image. Considering that the pattern occupies a more prominent position in the middle of the box and has a significant impact on the overall visual effect, the two designs are not similar.

In the case of the administrative dispute over the invalidity of the design patent right of the "Lufeng Off-road Vehicle", (Beijing Municipal High People's Court 2018) the second-instance judgment pointed out that the weight of specific design features on the overall visual effect should be judged based on the knowledge level and cognitive ability of the general consumers. The observation of all design features should be based on the overall effect to examine the weight of each design feature on the visual effect of the design. All the factors that can affect the visual effect of the design as a whole should be considered comprehensively. When judging the weight of the specific features on the overall visual effect, the conclusion should not be hastily drawn based on the direct visual perception or the proportion of the feature in the overall design. Instead, the weight of each design feature in the overall visual effect should be determined on the basis of the general consumer's perception of the design space, taking into account the position of the corresponding design feature in the overall design, whether it is easily observed by the general consumer, and the frequency of the design feature in the existing design as well as whether the design feature is restricted by function, aesthetics, or technology.

When judging whether a packaging design infringes the rights of others, the scope of infringement shall be determined by following the rules of overall observation and comprehensive judgment. That means, the general consumers shall judge whether the visual effect of the design patent and the infringed product is obviously different from each other from the whole rather than based on the local designs only. In the judging process, the general consumers shall make a comprehensive judgment, not only consider the impact of the similarity on the overall visual effect but also pay attention to the impact of the difference on the overall visual effect. Then conclusion will be drawn whether there is a difference in the overall visual effect of the two and whether the difference constitutes a substantial difference. Whether there is a prior art defense should also be determined by comparing the design of the allegedly infringing product with a prior art design to determine whether they are identical or without difference in essence. In addition, based on the knowledge level and cognitive ability of the general consumer, a comprehensive judgment should be made in light of the overall visual effect of the design that contains all the design features.

China's Patent Law provides that after granting the design a patent, no entity or individual shall, without permission of the patentee, exploit the patent, that is to say, they shall not make, sell, or import the product incorporating its or his patented design, for production and business purposes. Without the permission of the patentee, any exploitation of its patent leads to infringement of patent rights." Thus, it is clear that infringement of a design patent should contain the following elements:

If a dispute arises as a result of exploitation of a patent without permission of the patentee, that is, the patent right of the patentee is infringed, the dispute shall be settled through consultation between the parties. If the parties are not willing to consult or if consultation fails, the patentee or interested party may take legal action before a people's court, and may also request the administration department for patent-related work to handle the dispute. If, when handling the dispute, the said department believes the infringement is established, it may order the infringer to cease the infringement immediately; if the infringer is dissatisfied with the order, he may, within 15 days from the date of receipt of the notification of the order, take legal action before a people's court in accordance with the Administrative Procedure Law of the People's Republic of China. If the infringer neither takes legal action at the expiration of the time limit nor ceases the infringement, the said department may file an application with the people's court for compulsory enforcement. The administration department for patent-related work that handles the call shall, upon request of the parties, carry out mediation concerning the amount of compensation for the patent right infringement. If mediation fails, the parties may take legal action before the people's court in accordance with the Civil Procedure Law of the People's Republic of China.

(3) Trademark Law Protection

The United States began to protect trade designs with trademark law since the enactment of the Lanham Act in 1946. Trade designs include design of labels, packaging, containers, and even the design and shape of the product itself. Section 45 of the Lanham Act provides that the term "trademark" includes any word, name, symbol, or design, or any combination thereof, to identify and distinguish his or her goods from those manufactured or sold by others. Although, to a certain extent, the U.S. Lanham Act protects trade dress by equating it with trademarks for protection, there are some differences between the two in terms of the scope of protection. Trade designs emphasize the entire design of a product or product packaging, while only a portion of trade designs can be protected as a trademark.

In Europe, the protection of trade design mainly relies on trademark law. Article 4 of the European Union Trademark Law states that a trademark includes the image of a product, the form of its packaging, and a visually expressive sign. The concept of trademark in the EU Trademark Law includes color trademarks, three-dimensional trademarks and sound trademarks, and especially includes the shape of goods and packaging.

In China, having the same function with the trademark, the packaging design of the goods also can be used to indicate the source of goods, and can be applied as the three-dimensional sign trademark. If the commodity packaging with distinctive features will indicate the source, which fully meets the standards stipulated in Article 8 of the Trademark Law, it can be applied as a trademark and protected by Trademark Law.

In the Review of No. 32315366 "Kinder" trademark, the No. 32315366 trademark for chocolate product packaging applied by Ferrero is an eggshell-shaped three-dimensional logo in red, blue and white combined with the word "Kinder", that is, the combination of an eggshell-shaped three-dimensional trademark, colors, text and other graphic elements. According to the document production of the State Intellectual Property Office, the registration of application for chocolate commodities has went through preliminary examination, but the application for sweets commodities has been rejected.

With regard to the inherent characteristics of the goods, chocolates can be made into any shape after processing, which grounds for the registrability. In terms of distinctiveness, the eggshell-shaped three-dimensional logo with specified colors has distinctive features when used on chocolate goods. Besides, the foreign word "Kinder" is also distinctive. That is, the combination of distinctive packaging and graphic signs forms a three-dimensional mark with distinctive features. At the same time, Ferrero has continued to use the one-dimensional logo on its chocolate products for nearly ten years, which has formed a stable association between the trademark and the applicant in public cognition, based on which the source of goods can be identified by the three-dimensional trademark. In terms of non-functionality, the three-dimensional eggshell-shape serves as a unique tear-open container, and this shape is not generated by the nature of the goods themselves. Instead, the shape of the trademark packaging determines the shape of the inner goods. As the eggshell-shape is not intended to achieve a certain technical effect and can be replaced by other packaging shapes, this artistic design will not significantly affect the consumers' intention to buy chocolates, thus the design is non-functional. In terms of identity and similarity, based on the judgment of distinctiveness, the three-dimensional logo in the shape of an eggshell with specified colors is not identical or similar to other three-dimensional logos, nor is it identical or similar to other flat logos when combined with the foreign word "Kinder". So the relevant public will not feel confused to the source of the chocolate products. To sum up, the three-dimensional logo trademark applied by Ferrero Company in the category of commodity packaging has registrability in chocolate goods. If the scope of use of the trademark is extended to sweets, such as rice pudding and other sweet products with spherical or ellipsoidal shape, it may violate the principle of non-functionality and be denied of registration.

(4) Anti-unfair Competition Law Protection

In 1993, China began to implement the Anti-Unfair Competition Law. For Article 6, paragraph 1, it can be understood in two ways: using packaging and decoration of another person's commodity with certain influence without permission will be regarded as unfair competition even if it does not cause confusion; using packaging and decoration similar to other commodities will be regarded as unfair competition when it indeed causes confusion. In addition, Article 18 also provides provisions on the legal responsibility. Anti-unfair competition law plays a primary role in protecting commodity packaging and decoration.

In the case of red-can herbal tea, on 16th August 2017, in Beijing, China, the Supreme People's Court issued verdicts in the two cases concerning the disputes between Guangdong JDB Beverage and Food Co., Ltd. (JDB) and Guangzhou Wanglaoji Health Industry Co. Ltd. (Wong Lo Kat), a subsidiary of Guangzhou Pharmaceutical Holdings Limited (GPHL). The court ruled that as both GPHL and JDB had made important contributions to the formation of the packaging and decoration of the "red Wong Lo Kat herbal tea cans" (the "packaging and decoration rights"), both sides may, without prejudice to the legitimate interests of others, share the use of the red can design. The two cases are central to a series of disputes between the parties relating to the ownership of the packaging and decoration rights. The cases were both separately filed on 6th July 2012, by each of the parties respectively, with each party claiming the rights to the packaging and decoration of the famous "red Wong Lo Kat herbal tea cans" and claiming that the production and sales of herbal tea by the other party using the red can design constituted infringement.

At first instance, the Guangdong High People's Court ruled that the packaging and decoration rights belonged to Wong Lo Kat. They ruled that, as JDB did not enjoy the rights and interests involved in the packaging and decoration, the production and sale of canned herbal tea with (1) "Wong Lo Kat" on one side and "JDB" on the other side of a red can; or (2) "JDB" on both sides of a red can; constituted infringement. The court of first instance then ordered JDB to stop infringement, publish a statement to eliminate the influences of their infringement and compensate Wang Lo Kat for economic losses of RMB 150 million along with reasonable expenses of RMB 260,000. Unsatisfied with the first instance verdicts, JDB appealed to the Supreme People's Court in Beijing. The court decided that the well-known trademark, in this case, was the "red Wong Lo Kat herbal tea can" comprised of the words "Wong Lo Kat in yellow text on a red background, certain patterns and their arrangement" on the canned tea products.

GPHL, as the exclusive rights holder and the Licensor of the registered trademark "Wong Lo Kat" had argued that as the "Wong Lo Kat" trademark packaging and decoration formed an integral part of and played a significant role in indicating the source of goods, consumers would certainly relate red Wong Lo Kat herbal tea cans with the rights holder of the trademark "Wong Lo Kat"—GPHL. It was also argued that recipe or taste would not affect the consumer's identification and judgment of goods. JDB, the actual party producing the Wong Lo Kat herbal tea in red cans, argued that the rights to the packaging and decoration of the red cans were independent of the trademark rights. Therefore ownerships of the trademark right to "Wong Lo Kat" should not be affected by the right to the packaging and decoration. They also claimed that, as the red can design was used by JDB in combination with a specific recipe, which consumers "loved", the relevant packaging and decorating rights should belong to JDB. The Supreme People's Court, after considering the history and development of red Wong Lo Kat herbal tea cans, the background of past cooperation between the two sides, consumer awareness and the principles of fairness, decided that both GPHL and JDB contributed to the formation, development and goodwill of the packaging and decoration rights. They considered that it would be unfair to either party if the packaging and decoration rights were solely awarded to one of them. The Court ruled that, under the principle of good faith, respect for consumer awareness and upholding the legitimate rights and interests of others, the packaging and decoration rights should be shared between GPHL and JDB. On this basis, the claims of both parties were rejected. In its judgment, the Supreme People's Court also stated that:

The legal framework for intellectual property law was created to protect and encourage innovation. The act of creating and contributing intellectual creations to the benefit of society with honesty and good faith is protected by law. The judicial protection of intellectual property involves maintaining an orderly, standardized, fair, competitive and energetic market that satisfies the principle of legal certainty. Intellectual property disputes often arise from a complex historical context. A division of interests and the balance of interests are often intertwined. Handling such disputes, we need to take full account of the historical causes and where possible respect the status quo. We must heed a variety of factors such as consumer awareness—in order to maintain good faith and respect for the basic principles of objective reality. When doing this we must strictly follow the guidelines of the law to reach a fair and reasonable solution.

The Supreme People's Court confirmed that both sides, without prejudice to the legitimate interests of others, may share the packaging and decoration rights. Both GPHL and JDB had positively contributed to the goodwill of the "Wong Lo Kat" brand and gained huge market shares while promoting corporate social responsibility. However, since the "Wong Lo Kat" trademark licensing relationship ended, the two sides continuously litigated against each other at great expense. The public showed concern and worry about this. The good faith of the corporations was damaged through their actions.

Because of this, the two sides should, through mutual understanding and good faith, take steps to fulfil this ruling, act in accordance with the principles of corporate social responsibility, cherish their trading results and respect consumer trust. They should make more efforts to strengthen their national brands and provide better products to consumers.

Article VI of the *General Principles of Civil Law* provide that a civil subject should follow the principle of fairness and the basic principles of civil law. Article II of the *Anti-Unfair Competition Law* also defines fair and honest business principles. In this case, the Supreme People's Court decided based on the facts and principle of fairness, that the two sides had made joint business investments and therefore shared relevant interests. This judgment not only implements the basic principles of competition law but also take into account the interests of operators and consumers. At the same time, it provides a clear judicial guidance to businesses that:

They should act in accordance with the principles of corporate social responsibility, cherish business results and respect consumer trust. They should make more efforts to strengthen their national brands and to provide better products to consumers.

In February 2025, in the unfair competition dispute between Shaanxi Xifeng Liquor Co., Ltd. and Huashan Lunjian Brand Management Co., Ltd. (plaintiffs) and Shaanxi Fengfu Liquor Co., Ltd., Deyang Shuxian Craft Liquor Factory, among others (defendants), the court affirmed the first-instance court's position that the assessment of product packaging and trade dress should be made from the perspective of an average consumer and within the context of real consumption scenarios. However, the appellate court pointed out that the first-instance court had narrowly limited the consumption scenario to the point-of-sale environment and concluded that consumers pay little attention to liquor bottle packaging and trade dress in that context, which was an incomplete view. The appellate court held that the consumption scenarios for liquor include not only purchase but also drinking and advertising. In drinking scenarios, consumers typically see only the bottle's packaging and trade dress, not the outer box. Even in retail environments, it is common for liquor bottles to be displayed independently. Furthermore, the packaging and trade dress of the liquor's outer box in this case featured a transparent window, allowing the internal bottle's appearance to be visible. Therefore, comparison of the products should comprehensively consider both the outer box and the bottle. The trial court's approach—evaluating only the product in the boxed state—was inadequate. The outer box and the bottle should have been compared separately.

The court further emphasized that in the market, product promotion is not limited to individual items; series-wide branding can shape consumers' perceptions. A series of products can develop common visual features that acquire distinctiveness through long-term marketing, which can influence consumers' perception even when encountering a single product from the series. Thus, in unfair competition cases, "packaging or trade dress with certain influence" is not limited to a single product. If the common features of a product series have gained market recognition through sustained promotion, they may qualify as "packaging or trade dress with certain influence" under the law.

In this case, the "Xifeng Liquor (Huashan Lunjian)" product series had gained significant recognition in Shaanxi Province through prolonged marketing and sales. Although individual products within the series differed slightly, they shared notable common features—particularly in bottle design: a slightly flattened round body, cylindrical long neck, specific body-to-neck ratio, a raised mountain shape at the bottle base, and a distinct three-dimensional cap design. These characteristics had formed a stable and recognizable impression among ordinary liquor consumers and distributors. Although the product "Xifeng Liquor (Huashan Lunjian) 10-Year Aged Banquet Edition (52% ABV)" had a relatively short marketing history, it retained the same distinctive design features. Despite its opaque red bottle, which made it difficult to observe the base structure, it still visually shared key characteristics with other products in the series, leading consumers to reasonably believe it belonged to the "Xifeng Liquor (Huashan Lunjian)" series. When comparing the alleged infringing product "45% Fulianfeng 10-Year Aged (Red Bottle)" with the plaintiff's "Xifeng Liquor (Huashan Lunjian) 10-Year Aged Banquet Edition (52% ABV)", both the outer packaging and bottle showed differences. However, they also shared the same prominent features: slightly flattened round body, cylindrical long neck, proportional structure, and a distinct cap design. These similarities were sufficient to cause an average consumer to believe that the defendant's product was part of the plaintiff's series or otherwise connected to the plaintiffs.

According to Article 6(1) of the Anti-Unfair Competition Law of the People's Republic of China, "A business operator shall not engage in the following confusing conduct that may mislead others into believing that a product is from another party or has a specific connection with another party: (1) unauthorized use of packaging or trade dress identical or similar to that of a product with certain influence." In line with Article 4(3) of the Interpretation of the Supreme People's Court on Several Issues Concerning the Application of Law in the Trial of Civil Cases Involving Unfair Competition, "In determining whether the name, packaging, or trade dress is identical or similar to that of a well-known product, reference may be made to the principles and methods used to assess trademark similarity." Regarding the outer packaging comparison between the new "Xifeng Liquor (Huashan Lunjian) 10-Year Aged (45%)" and "Fulianfeng 10-Year Aged (Transparent Bottle)", although there were differences in the shape of the window, top and bottom coloring, side element arrangement, label placement, content, and neck patterns, the visual distinctions were insufficient under ordinary consumer attention. Considering the use of distinctive elements like the character "凤" ("Feng") and overall stylistic similarities, consumers could be misled into believing a connection between the products. Similarly, in comparing the bottles of the older version "Xifeng Liquor (Huashan Lunjian) 10-Year Aged (45%)" and "Fulianfeng 10-Year Aged (Transparent Bottle)", despite differences in label text and cap shape, the general form, inward curvature, neck patterns, and color were alike. From a general consumer perspective, even when viewed through the packaging window, the visual differences remained insufficient to avoid confusion. Consequently, the appellate court concluded that the defendants acted with the intent to take advantage of the goodwill associated with Xifeng and Huashan Lunjian brands, amounting to "free-riding" and constituting an act of unfair competition (Beijing Municipal High People's Court 2025).

5.4.4 Substantial Similarity Judgment for Poster Design

Poster is the creative organic integration of the stills, painting, graphics, color, text and other elements. The graphic artworks with aesthetic significance belongs to the work of art in the copyright law, which are often seen in theaters, exhibitions, stations, parks and other public places. Poster design requires designer to put forward creative ideas which belong to the category of "thought". In the copyright law, there is a cornerstone principle, that is, "the dichotomy between thought and expression." It means that the copyright law only protects the expression of the work, but not the thought embodied in the expression. Therefore, in the perspective of copyright law, the creativity of poster design is not the object to be protected by law, but only the expression of creativity is the object of protection by law. As far as the macro creativity is concerned, an identical or similar idea does not constitute infringement of copyright. Therefore, the judgment on the infringement of poster design will be focused on the form of expression in the picture, that is whether the expression seems to be the same or similar.

In the case of Disney Enterprises, Pixar and Xiamen Blue Flame Film and Animation Co., Ltd, Beijing Base Film and Television Culture and Media Co. Ltd, and Shanghai Juli Media and Technology Co. Ltd (Shanghai Intellectual Property Court 2017), the Court of First Instance held that the animated images of "Lightning McQueen" and "Franzco" were original expressions through the combination of anthropomorphic eyes and mouths as well as specific colors, and that "K1" and "K2" in the movie and posters of "Cars" used the original expression of "Lightning McQueen" and "Franzco," which constituted substantial similarity and infringed Disney's and Pixar's copyrights. The Court of Second Instance ruled that the specific expression of anthropomorphizing a car belongs to the category of expression and can be protected by copyright law. The determination of substantial similarity in the case of copyright infringement should be based on whether the similarity between the two sets of animated images belongs to the category of original expression protected by copyright law. The court compared the similarities and differences between the animated images of "K1" and "K2" and "Lightning McQueen" and "Franzco", and held that the two groups of animated images were similar in the sense of being original expressions protected by copyright law. After comparing the similarities and differences between "K1" and "K2" and "Lightning McQueen" and "Fransco", the Court held that "K1" and "K2" were basically the same as "Lightning McQueen" and "Fransco" in terms of the choice of specific expressions. From the point of view of ordinary people, the creation of the former animated images would not be independent from the latter animated images, and therefore the two images constitute substantial similarity.

"Substantial similarity" is not a concept explicitly stipulated in China's copyright law. It was first raised in the judicial practice of the United States Court of Appeals for the Second Circuit, referring to "the cognition of the non-professional observer that the defendant's work has copied the plaintiff's copyrighted work". The following three methods have been developed in judicial practice to determine substantial similarity:

(1) Abstraction Test and Three-step Test

The abstraction test was born in the famous case of Nichols v. Universal pictures Corp in 1929. It involved two plays in which the children of different religious beliefs fell in love but were opposed by their families. Both stories ended in reconciliation.

The judge Hand holds that it is of course essential to any protection of literary property, whether at common-law or under the statute, that the right cannot be limited literally to the text, else a plagiarist would escape by immaterial variations. When the plagiarist does not take out a block in situ, but an abstract of the whole, decision is more troublesome. Upon any work, and especially upon a play, a great number of patterns of increasing generality will fit equally well, as more and more of the incident is left out. In such cases we are rather concerned with the line between expression and what is expressed. As respects plays, the controversy chiefly centers upon the characters and sequence of incident, these being the substance. The method to analyse the incident is called the abstraction test.

Subsequently, in the 1992 software copyright case of Computer Associates International, Inc. v. Altai, Inc., Judge Walker further developed Judge Hand's abstraction test into a three-step "abstraction-filtration-comparison" test. It is generally recognized that in the three-step test, "abstraction" refers to the process of separating out the idea; "filtration" will be imposed on public-domain information, and merging materials of some ideas and the expression; "comparison" is for the remaining part of the expression. "Comparison" will be processed on the remaining part of the expression.

(2) Overall Concept and Sensory Test

The overall concept and sensory test was first applied in the case of Roth Greeting Cards v. United Card Corp. The cards at issue were simple, which included original artwork with phrases such as "I love you" and "I miss you already".

Roth involved two greeting card makers. Roth claimed that United had copied a number of its cards. The short statements on the front and inside of the cards were virtually the same, as was their general placement. The art work was different (generally a cartoonish character under the words on the front of the card). In addressing the improper appropriation element, the court did not try to make a detailed determination of what was protected as expression and what was idea.

It appears to us that in overall concept and feel the cards of United are the same as the copyrighted cards of Roth. With the possible exception of one United card, the characters depicted in the art work, the mood they portrayed, the combination of art work conveying a particular mood with a particular message, and the arrangement of the words on the greeting card are substantially the same as in Roth's cards. In several instances the lettering is also very similar. "The test of infringement is whether the work is recognizable by an ordinary observer as having been taken from the copyrighted source."

The remarkable similarity between the Roth and United cards in issue (with the possible exception of exhibits 5 and 6 is apparent to even a casual observer.

Substantial similarity is judged by the court because the cards are same in total concept and feel. From the perspective of the ordinary observer, the defendant has indeed copied the plaintiff's works in terms of the idea, atmosphere, and expression, and unlawfully misappropriated the plaintiff's protected expression.

(3) Intrinsic/External Test

The extrinsic/intrinsic test emerged in 1977 as a result of the Ninth Circuit judges' development of the "total concept and feel" test. In the case of Sid & Marty Krofft Television Prods. v. McDonald's Corp, the court established a two-fold test. First, an "extrinsic" comparison of the similarity of ideas between the works; second, an "intrinsic" subjective test of whether the "total concept and feel" of the two works are substantially similar from the point of view of an ordinary and rational person. The "extrinsic test" requires the court, with the aid of expert testimony, to determine whether the ideas used in each work are substantially similar by objective analysis. The "intrinsic test" compares the overall expression of the two works, excluding expert testimony. The court affirmed as to infringement holding in addition to strong evidence of access, defendants commercials were based on the same ideas as plaintiffs' series and the expression of those ideas was sufficiently similar that a jury applying an intrinsic test could find infringement. The finding of infringement did not violate first amendment rights because the idea-expression dichotomy served to accommodate the competing interests of copyright law and the first amendment. The court reversed as to damages holding the parties did not intend the jury to consider the profits. The court held that the issue of "in lieu" damages should be properly addressed to the court, not the jury.

Although China's Copyright Law has no specific provisions on the connotation of plagiarism and judgment of infringement caused by plagiarism, "substantial similarity" has been applied in the trial of copyright infringement cases to judge whether the similarity between works is sufficient to constitute infringement. As a whole, it requires that the similarity between the allegedly infringing work and the original work reach a certain degree, but the degree is difficult to define accurately, which should take into account both the quantity and the quality of the similarities. For example, in this case, the animation image of "K1" and "K2" are basically the same to a certain extent to "Lightning McQueen" and "Fransco" in the color, eyes, nose, mouth, eyeballs, eyelids, teeth and other details of the expression. Moreover, these essentially identical expressions, i.e., the specific expressions of the anthropomorphization of the car, represent the original design of Disney and Pixar, which belong to expressions of originality protected by the copyright law. In addition, "K1" and "K2" are basically the same as "Lightning McQueen" and "Franzco" in terms of the choice of specific expressions. In the opinion of the ordinary observer, the two expressions reach a certain degree of similarity and that the former figures can not be created independently from the latter images. Therefore, it is sufficient to recognize that the animated images of "K1" and "K2" are substantially similar to the animated images of "Lightning McQueen" and "Franzco".

References

Azzi A, Battini D, Persona A et al (2012) Packaging design: general framework and research agenda. Pack Technol Sci 25(8):435–456

Beijing Municipal High People's Court (2018) Jiangling Holdings Co. Ltd. v. State Intellectual Property Office Patent Reexamination Commission Invalidation of Design Patents [2018] No.4169

Bloch P (1995) Seeking the ideal form: product design and consumer response. J Market 59:16–29

Chen RH (2016) Research on the characteristics and design principles of visual communication design. Constr Mater Decor 46:105–106

De Sousa MMM, Carvalho FM, Pereira RGFA (2020) Color and shape of design elements of the packaging labels influence consumer expectations and hedonic judgments of specialty coffee. Food Q Prefer 83:1–9

Guangdong High People's Court (2011) Dongguan Master Blackhand Laundry Products Co., Ltd. and Wang Huaguo et al. Appeal of Infringement of Design Patent Dispute [2011] No.223
Guo ZS, Zhao ZX (2010) Font design. Tianjin University Press, Tianjin, pp 49–51
He LH, Yan LM (2012) Individual computer fonts should not be protected by Copyright Law. Polit Law 6:113–120
High People's Court of Hebei Province (2021) Dispute over infringement of other copyright property rights between Zhanhuang County Zaoyuan Fruit Industry Co., Ltd. and Beijing Beifang Founder Electronics Co. [2021] No.205
Intermediate People's Court of Rizhao City (2023) Dispute over infringement of reproduction right of works by Guangdong Renzhiguan Food Co., Ltd. and Guangdon Siki Food Co. [2023] No.554
Jiangsu High People's Court (2012) Beijing Han Yi Ke Yin Information Technology Co. Ltd. v. Frog Prince (China) Daily Chemical Co. Ltd. et al. Dispute over Copyright Infringement [2012] No.161
Li HQ, Zhang QL (2016) Four issues on the protection of font copyright from the Fangzheng font infringement case. China Copyright 6:30–32
Liu GH (2020) Exploring the development history and theory of packaging design. West Leather 42(13):34
LYU JH (2022) Exploring the visual image of font design. Art Observ 2:156–157
Meyers-Levy J, Peracchio L (1995) Understanding the effects of colour: how the correspondence between available and required resources affects attitudes. J Consum Res 22(2):121–139
MMLC Group (2022) The Intellectual Property Protection of Fonts in China. https://www.hg.org/legal-articles/the-intellectual-property-protection-of-fonts-in-china-41356. Accessed 28 Oct 2022
O-M Bread, Inc. v. United States Olympic Comm., 65 F.3d 933
Rettie R, Brewer C (2000) The verbal and visual components of package design. J Prod Brand Manage 9(1):56–68
San Francisco Arts & Ath., Inc. v. United States Olympic Comm., 107 S. Ct. 2971
San Francisco Arts & Ath., Inc. v. United States Olympic Comm., 483 U.S. 522
Schifferstein HNJ, Fenko A, Desmet PMA et al (2013) Influence of package design on the dynamics of multisensory and emotional food experience. Food Qual Prefer 27:18–25
Shaanxi High People's Court (2025, Feb 13) The Case of Shaanxi Xifeng Liquor Co., Ltd. and Huashan Lunjian Brand Management Co., Ltd. v. Shaanxi Fengfu Liquor Co., Ltd. and Deyang Shuxian Craft Liquor Factory et al., Unfair Competition Dispute [2024] Shan Zhi Minzhong No.93
Shanghai Intellectual Property Court (2017) Shanghai Agricultural Production Materials Co. Ltd. v. CITIC Bank Corporation, Shanghai Branch and Other L/C Financing Disputes [2017] No.54
Supreme People's Court (2010) Copyright Infringement Dispute between Beijing Founder Electronics Co., Ltd. and Blizzard Entertainment Inc. et al. [2010] No.6
Two Pesos, Inc. v. Taco Cabana, Inc., 505 U.S. 763
United States Court of Appeals, Federal Circuit
Wan G (2021) Research on the aesthetic design of traditional techniques for food packaging. Daguan 7:57–58
What is visual communication design? (2022). https://blueskygraphics.co.uk/what-is-visual-communication-design/. Accessed 28 Oct 2022
Xie ML (2022) A study on the development trend of visual communication design in the new media era. Popul Liter Art 2022(08):54–56

Chapter 6
Service Design and Intellectual Property

6.1 Concept

6.1.1 The Concept of Service Design

Since the twentieth century, service design has gradually been discovered by designers. In 1991, Michael Erlhoff introduced the concept of Service Design. In 2004, the Köln International School of Design, Carnegie Mellon University, Politecnico di Milano, and others jointly established the Service Design Network. From a macro perspective, service design research is interdisciplinary, covering information and communication technology, design art, psychology, sociology, marketing, healthcare, etc (Luo and Zou 2018). From a micro perspective, service design is an important branch of design (He and Hu 2015), developing in fields such as computer technology, communication, industrial design, and management studies. Service design in developed countries in Europe and America aims to provide service for both private enterprises and public sectors, including healthcare and welfare, as well as data services.

As mentioned, service design involves interactions and collaborations from multiple disciplines, integrating various professional knowledge and research methods from different fields. It is gradually formed through cross-disciplinary innovation in management and design. By combining service design thinking with related design disciplines, new opportunities and paths for sustainable development of design can be generated. Initial research of service design focuses on the management and marketing behaviors and strategies outside of design fields to upgrade the existing service design framework. By comparing with research methods from other fields, the applicability of methods and tools in service design can also be enhanced. In product transportation, promotion, sales, and after-sales maintenance, comprehensive services are needed so as to guarantee the safe and sustainable market for the product throughout its lifecycle. This extensive and systematic service need has gradually catalysed service design, which provides a brand-new design strategy and

N. Jiang, *Design, Innovation and Intellectual Property*,
https://doi.org/10.1007/978-981-95-2042-8_6

business experience. With the aim of developing high-quality service, it integrates various service resources based on design strategies at different levels such as process optimization, systems, visuals, space, and products, forming an integrated service design strategy.

The Guiding Catalog for the Key Development Fields of the Service Outsourcing Industry (2018) points out that service design is user-oriented, and through multiple stakeholders' collaboration, it integrates innovations of personnel, environment, facilities, information, and other elements to achieve systematic innovation in service provision, processes, and touchpoints, thereby enhancing the service experience, efficiency, and value.

Birgit Mager, the President of the Service Design Network (SDN), believes that from the client's perspective, service design aims to achieve service interfaces that are more useful, usable, and desirable. From the supplier's perspective, it aims to ensure that service interfaces are effective, efficient, and distinctive. Stefan Moritz believes that service design can boost innovation or improve existing services; for customers, it makes services more useful, more accessible, and more satisfying; for organizations, services can become more efficient and effective. In all, service design is novel, comprehensive, interdisciplinary, and integrated.

Many scholars argue that service design can be understood as a sophisticated, human-centered, collaborative, holistic approach to enhancing existing or creating entirely new service systems and offerings (Yu and Sangiorgi 2017). At its core is the aim to understand contextual customer experience and anticipate new value propositions. It elevates design thinking by adding a service perspective. Furthermore, service design is, by nature, multidisciplinary, as it borrows from a range of theories belonging to different disciplines; for example, some suggest that it can be linked to service innovation. Service innovation is "a process of integrating resources in novel ways to enable new forms of value co-creation among actors (Lusch and Nambisan 2015)." Ostrom et al. (2015) argue that service design plays a significant role in service innovation because it brings new service ideas to life.

According to the new perspective, the meaning of the service design's concept has been extended to cover almost entirely the development of (new) services emphasizing the customer experience and the importance of design. The main differentiating factor between the approach of service development (e.g. NSD) and the approach of service design seems to be the extensive use of the methods of designers. We suggest that service design may bring new methods and approaches for the purposes of developing and innovating new services (Holopainen 2010).

Service design has been proposed as a transformative force that can go beyond enhancing service experiences to designing for more systemic transformation (Patrício et al. 2020). Initial efforts have advanced the design for networked service systems (Patrício et al. 2018), the development of platforms and capabilities for ongoing change (Karpen et al. 2017), and the design for institutional change in service systems (Vink et al. 2019; Vink et al. 2021). Service design embeds a betterment principle that illuminates the constant striving for the better, to increase well-being (Anderson et al. 2013; Sangiorgi 2011). The action-orientation toward creating better futures is central to the transformative potential of service design.

Taking a transformative view of service design as creating new service futures also requires acknowledging that designing goes beyond the sole action of design experts to a broader collaborative effort where everybody designs. Design experts, therefore, can leverage participants' creativity and culture to support a dialogic and collaborative approach to service design.

6.1.2 Service Design: Strategy and Focus

At present, there is still no globally unified standard for the process of service design. Many different organizations have put forward different views. The most famous one is the "Double Diamond Design Process" summarized by "the British Design Council," which turns the chaotic thinking into a prismatic thinking with divergent and convergent processes. In addition, the American "IDEO company" also proposed three stages of service design, that is, Hear, Create, and Deliver. According to the book, this is service design thinking, the four steps of the iterative process, "Exploration," "Creation," "Reflection" and "Implementation," are a basic method to form a complex design process. Among them, the creation process is a vital stage in generating ideas and strategies.

Service design emphasizes collective thinking. The key to the design is to integrate all relevant touchpoints as a whole according to the needs of specific customer groups. The effective way is to position peak touchpoints of the service delivery process which is conducive to determining the clear structure. The core of the service design strategy is to explore and create opportunities for cooperation to finally promote the value co-creation. Five dimensions of service design strategy including the peak touchpoints, destination branding, B2B collaboration opportunities, B2C and C2C co-creation opportunities are displayed along the horizontal axis (Gao et al. 2022).

An action-oriented, human-centered, collaborative approach to creating new service futures. From enhancing dyadic service interactions to: Collectively creating new shared visions and integrated systems and Creating conditions for diffusion and replication. From discrete service design initiatives to: Reforming institutions for long-term change and Continuous design, promoting the institutionalization of change. From designing for incremental change to: Challenging fundamental assumptions and beliefs and Visioning and experimenting with radically new futures.

Service design work centered on paradigmatic radicalness can also be found in design for social innovation. Here, design can contribute to experimental initiatives aiming to radically change citizens' dominant way of doing and seeing things (e.g. exploring the value of sharing instead of owning things) by operating as facilitator, trigger, co-designer, or activist (Manzini 2013).

Questioning fundamental assumptions and beliefs opens the ground for exploring radically new service system futures. Service design inherently involves a creative and iterative process that opens up new possibilities through the practice of "envisioning (Huotari et al. 2021)."

Service design is a new design discipline; moreover, it represents a new mindset. Service design thinking has emerged as an innovation management practice emphasising a human-centred innovation process of user interactions, creativity, and learning mindsets.

6.1.3 Design Thinking

The Design Division, the D.School of Stanford University and IDEO recently contributed to promoting design thinking. The most popular description of design thinking process is the D.School version as the process sequence of Empathize-Define-Ideate-Prototype-Test (D.School 2018). Design Thinking is well recognized as a mindset, process in design and in business innovation as well as diverse complex problem-solving tasks. Design thinking process is explained using visual thinking composed of seeing-imagining-drawing so that its interactive and iterative nature can be better understood. The visual reasoning model developed earlier to support visual thinking with underlying cognitive activities as well as schema and knowledge is used to characterize four specific imagining methods for service design. Further research would be desirable to justify the potential of the visual reasoning model as a framework in devising methods and tools to support design thinking.

Service design thinking combines the mindset and methods of design thinking together with embodiment strategies for creation of new services and customer experiences based on the perspectives of service dominant logic (Vargo and Lusch 2004) and experience economy (Pine and Gilmore 1998). With divergent strategy to expand servitization potential through empathizing, imagining and convergent approaches to realistic service strategies with defining and prototyping, design and delivery of value propositions to meet customer needs and wants are to be sought by creative integration of service activities and their elements. Active engagements of users are desirable in the use phase as well as pre- and post-use stages so that sustainable evaluation and management of customer experiences can be continued to close the loop (Kim and Park 2021).

6.1.4 Related Concepts

The concept of "stakeholder" originated from economics, and can be categorized into primary and secondary stakeholders. Their needs are the primary focus during the service design. Under the definition of stakeholder, individuals involved in service actions are called "participants." The concept of stakeholders is almost identical to the concept of "users" in service design for its collective and generic feature. Therefore, when conducting service design, it is necessary to understand the needs of all stakeholders and two key indicators need to be considered during analysis: the priority of stakeholder needs and the importance of stakeholders. A series of questions are important for consideration: how many types of stakeholders are involved in this service and what their respective needs are; which type of stakeholder is the primary stakeholder; and which type of stakeholder has a stronger connection to service.

During the initial plan and definition stage, stakeholder analysis diagrams can be drawn to present users, research activities, behavior models, aesthetic models, and other objects, and we can choose appropriate users at the right time to conduct contextual inquiries or scenario-based simulation surveys. At the initial stage of drawing stakeholder analysis diagram, designers need to brainstorm to fully explore user identities that may influence the service system. Based on the gathered information, the final stakeholder group can be settled down, as well as the motivations and needs of various users. Therefore, research on this target group is also referred to as "multidimensional user research". When the design and construction work of the service design prototype is completed, stakeholders can be invited to join the prototype field testing so that suggestions on feasibility can be collected and transposition thinking can be enhanced. This prototype validation method is called stakeholder walkthrough.

A fundamental aspect of service design is the involvement of key stakeholders, such as service providers and customers, in exchange relationships. Essentially, these relationships set the frame and roles of the actors involved in co-creation. Secomandi and Snelders (2011) suggest that service design requires a set of socio-technical resources. One of these resources is an effective customer relationship management process that is aligned with customer logics regarding behaviour and quality perceptions (Edvardsson and Olsson 1996). Aside from this, Shostack (1977) emphasises that the service provider must continuously monitor and manage the tangible outcomes of the service.

For service design, value is not simple relative utility, but rather a meaning system. Value proposition is the definition of this meaning system, a reciprocal commitment involving people throughout the entire service lifecycle. Co-creation of value refers to the unification of the subject and the object, such as participatory design training, visual workshops, "Achieving Together" creative exhibitions, and co-creation activities.

Apart from a few exceptions, most of the service design literature seems to be concerned with B2C environments. Furthermore, many researchers agree that the dark side of B2B relationships has yet to receive the adequate attention it deserves-in particular, aspects of relationship termination.

Understanding actor institutions and their effects on customer value assessment are critical for successful service design. Consequently, value co-creating actors need to respond by aligning and adjusting service design interfaces, infrastructures and actualisation mechanisms to customers' institutional logics of value assessment. Besides, by combining institutional theory with service design, Ostrom (2015) encouraged the advancement of service innovation research by "leveraging service design".

Our study shows that micro-level factors, such as personnel, can also influence institutions. By zooming in to the business relationship interface as the object of service design, we highlight that the design of the interface, infrastructures and actualisation mechanisms can influence actor institutions and, subsequently, their value assessment of resources (Struwe and Slepniov 2021).

Secomandi and Snelders (2011) define service design through touchpoints between actors. Touchpoints are characterised by three critical elements: the exchange relation, interface and infrastructure, and materiality.

The user journey is an experience of the user, rather than just touchpoints. It is the complete journey that connects touchpoints together. In practice, it requires designing multiple online and offline touchpoints.

The wide audience orientation of interaction design, service design, and product design has generated a higher requirement for user commonality and universality. Currently, they are transitioning from intuitive creativity to rational research and development. Interaction design includes the study of the behavior between people and devices, people and products, which involves visual interfaces, voice, brain-computer interfaces, and more. For IT, service design is encompassed within experience design. For example, the entire operation design of Taobao is service design. For industry or even in traditional service sectors, service design encompasses experience design, which is understood differently in different contexts and industries. Overall, service is the process, and experience is the outcome.

Evaluative research aims to discuss whether the design outputs meet the expectations of designers and users in a simulated environment, and obtain data crucial to drive precise and targeted behavior guidance, while also collecting data on aesthetics, emotional resonance, and human-computer interaction from the participants.

Service design can divide service creation into two domains: interface and infrastructure. The interface refers to sociotechnical resources that are directly related to the exchange between the service provider and the client. The infrastructure represents the resources indirectly related to the exchange. Secomandi and Snelders highlight that interface and infrastructure are inextricable counterparts in the exchange and integration relationship of sociotechnical resources. However, although service exchange relationships require infrastructure, ultimately, it is the interface that actualises service activities.

6.2 Features

6.2.1 Characteristics

The characteristics of service design are listed as follows:

First, service design is service-based innovation. Service is the object, and design is the method. Therefore, service design can be simply understood as providing services through design and design thinking, and solving various problems in services with the help of business models and multiple ideas and methods of design. Second, consumers prefer a certain function to a certain product. Service design is a transforming process from the physical to the non-physical, from the tangible to the intangible, which means shifting from creating to planning. It utilizes the functions generated and carried by objects. Third, service design is a multidisciplinary field that combines numerous methods and tools from different areas. Fourth, it is closely related to business. Service design must consider the business model, as the cost of providing a service should be reimbursed through other channels in order to gain profit. Fifth, service design can generate added value, provide a better and more excellent user experience, help businesses reduce costs, increase and facilitate return on investment, and enable systems to obtain more resources and opportunities. Six is about focusing on the entire process of service usage and the underlying system. Seventh, service design is for both users and businesses. Services become more useful, accessible, and satisfactory, or even exceed users' expectations through innovation and enhancement, ultimately improving user experience. Eighth, service design carrier can be diverse, including digital, physical, and interpersonal.

The difference between products and services is specifically reflected in the following aspects: products are produced, material, tangible, storable, and usually are not related with defects during or after manufacturing; services are performed, immaterial, intangible, unstorable, involve interaction with customers, and errors in production and behavior.

6.2.2 *Principles*

The book *This Is Service Design Thinking* mentions principles such as user-centered, co-creative, sequencing, evidencing, and holistic. The book This Is Service Design Doing mentions principles such as human-centered, collaborative, iterative, sequential, real, and holistic.

The user-centred principle holds that services should be experienced by users, and the entire service system should be examined from the perspective of user experience. Good services should come from and go beyond user needs to move users. The output of service design is often the design of specific touchpoints for a platform, application, or offline store.

Human-centeredness affirms that service design seeks to meaning-fully satisfy human needs by building upon deep insights into multiple actors' holistic experiences that inspire the generation of new service futures. Moreover, it means that service design involves users during the design process, while the design team facilitates the codesign processes (Trischler et al. 2018).

"Collaborative" means that all stakeholders should be involved in the service design. That is, service production and consumption happen simultaneously, and service providers should be involved in the service design. In a complete process of consumption, the consumer is the only person who experiences all the processes from beginning to the end. Service design aims for the overall system, which requires the participation of experts from various fields. For example, Google's autonomous driving service system is an integrated design that combines industrial, interaction, and system design.

The "sequential" principle means that service should be demonstrated through a series of interconnected actions. Service is a dynamic process that occurs within a certain period of time. It has logic and is presented visually in a rhythmic manner. Content, process, and rhythm are equally important and they can affect user emotions and user experience. For example, the user's boarding order and procedures, the time for each step, venue requirements, etc., should be considered to avoid rush of time or excessive waiting time. It's important to connect every point of user-service interaction with each other, and solve various problems in the service with design features, ideas, and methods. Thus, various characteristics of the service can be explicitly perceived by the user.

"Real" means that physical products should include intangible services. Service design is not just an idea, it must be conveyed and expressed through a certain medium. For instance, bicycles in bike-sharing are a medium. Service design needs to be guided by design thinking.

The principle of "holistic" means that the overall environment of the service should be taken into consideration, and holistic thinking should be emphasized. Every interaction and contact with the user should be taken into consideration to ensure the overall design, process, and interconnected links are optimized, including the user side and the organizational side. In this context, the term "front-end" or "front desk" refers to the specific services provided that customers, users, and consumers can see. On the other hand, the term "back-end" or "backstage" refers to the unseen services provided by companies, enterprises, governments, and other service providers. Service design involves designing the overall framework of a service, integrating various resources, restructuring various stakeholders to maximize benefits, and creating innovative business models.

6.2.3 Service Design: Process and Method

Many design process frameworks have been proposed in both research and practical application, encompassing three or more design steps. However, different terminologies are used to express the same concepts. In service projects or commercial design, the specific design process needs further clarification.

Company Engine's service design covers three parts. The first one, skills and strategy, includes initiation, research, and intention setting. The early research stage includes social environment, project background, and user research. The second part, design of the service, includes the concept, requirements, and plan. Thirdly, the implementation phase of the service includes design development, testing, and maintenance management of the design project.

Railway transportation is developing towards networkization. Railway passengers always need station transfers. Therefore, the transfer of large underground or surface railway transportation systems has become a research area and also a practical application in service design. Taking the case of "transfer service for rail transit" as an example for discussing service design methods and tools, the first step is exploration and discovery, which means user-centered participatory design. The second step is to determine the service content based on service requirements. The third step requires experiencing and verifying the service in a real environment.

In *This Is Service Design Thinking*, the service design process is divided into four steps, including exploration, creation, reflection, and implementation, the iteration of which is the fundamental composition of a complex design process.

Specific service design methods include collective sketching, mind mapping, KJ method (relationship diagram), task analysis table, service manual. Service requires collaboration. Simply adhering to principles and considering objects may not necessarily ensure satisfactory service for the user.

De Bono's 'six thinking hats' are composed of six different thinking hats, representing different thinking directions respectively. We discuss how thinking set comprised of individual hats coordinates the designer's designing activities. The conclusions can be applied in service design education as it can offer a new way to improve the students' designing creativity (Hu et al. 2021).

We propose an "extension service creation method" based on the "extension innovation four-step method," it can be effectively applied to the service design process and improve its efficiency. Under the background of economic transformation, service design has played a critical role in promoting the development of service economy. We aim to use extension in innovation method to guide the creation process of service design, expanding designers' thinking to generate systematic creative ideas. We propose an "extension service creation method" based on the "extension innovation four step method," and analyze it through a case study. The application has proved that the extension system can be effectively applied to the service design process and improve its efficiency. An Extenics-based method is used to expand service designers' thinking, so that they can view service design in a more comprehensive manner and generate creative ideas in a systematic way. The extension service creation model takes the "extension innovation four-step method" as the main framework and combines the tools and language of service design in form. In content, it follows the user-centered principle of service design. Starting from the users' pain points and the service status, it expands to other stakeholders and the entire service system through divergence, implication, and correlation analysis. From the individual to the whole, ideas are generated and the users' expectations are finally achieved. The extension innovation method provides a new way of thinking for the creation process of service design and opens up a new path for the realization of intelligent service design.

In order to realize the intelligence of service design, we will establish a users' basic-element database and extension service creation program. In addition, the database and program will be put on the Internet for more designers to use (Wang et al. 2022b).

6.2.4 *Tools for Service Design*

Tools for service design are still being explored and generally include the following:

Role ID reflects the consumer group's specific needs and expectations of the service through abstract crowd data with the help of visual technology.

The figure is the object needed to be closely observed by researchers and recorded by images, words, and pictures authentically and uninterruptedly.

"Five Whys" is a logical chain of inquiry tool for continuously tracing and digging deeper into the service providers' deficiencies hidden behind or on the surface during the service process.

A traffic flow diagram summarizes the detailed locations of all touch points present in the service, and aggregates in order of priority.

Contextual interview is the face-to-face observation of the researcher to understand the user, and get accurate information about the service process through the user's feelings, discourse, behavior and other factors at the scene.

Mind mapping is to devote time and energy to divergent thinking for a certain issue.

Plot storyboarding is to establish services and general contextual imagery based on obtained information.

Experience prototype is a simulation of the service experience that foresees some of its performances through the use of the specific physical touchpoints involved.

A service preview is a performance-based simulation of the service process that allows participants to experience service touchpoints.

Dynamic service blueprints are complex diagrams demonstrating relationships among the various phases, levels, participants, and service touchpoints of a service, and extrapolate the specific responsibilities of the service parties and the service flow.

6.2.5 *Functions for Service Design*

Communication refers to the process of exchanging and sharing information and ideas with the aim of establishing commonality and homogeneity between two people or in the organization. Communication happens at any time, and it is an integral part of service design. From the communication perspective, service design generally functions in the following three ways:

Firstly, it serves as a medium of communication between the people and the government.

Secondly, it improves the mechanism of internal and external communication of enterprises.

Thirdly, it enables direct communication between enterprises and users.

Service Design helps to innovate (create new) or improve (existing) services to make them more useful, usable, desirable for clients and efficient as well as effective for organisations. It is a new holistic, multi-disciplinary, integrative field. (This Is Service Design).

As service becomes an integral part of the product, the concept of design has been expanded to service design. Design's focus has also expanded from a single touchpoint (such as interface functions, etc.) to all aspects of user experience. Take Apple as an example, users can feel the meticulous service design of Apple products in all steps from purchasing, unpacking to use.

6.3 Types

Michael Erlhoff and Birgit Mager argue that the value of service design is not an adjunct, but independent of the product; service is a possibility of action; that product design is no longer function-oriented, but changes in accordance with the service provided; that the various terms for service design are repetitive, and that all the known design disciplines should be integrated.

The experimental nature of service design can foster and orient these service system innovation processes, combining small participatory experiments and framework projects (Manzini and Rizzo 2011), or promoting scalability by nodes. Structured interviews and questionnaires in the scope of service design can be used to understand the close relationship between waiting time and user satisfaction in the environment. Leddy et al. (2003) and Otani et al. (2010) also studied user satisfaction and demonstrated that environmental factors as well as privacy in the service space (e.g., response to service quality, interaction with service personnel, and overall experience of the visit) can affect user willingness to recommend or return. These related studies have focused on the service design methods of user experience.

Service design as practiced has also evolved from discrete interventions, to an ongoing and continuous designing process, with the aim of institutionalizing the change. This has been reflected in extending the service design role to the implementation stage in order to enhance the probability of success of the planned transformation (Norman and Stappers 2015). To this end, service design has adopted change management strategies to sustain endurance of transformation efforts, establishing closer designer-client relationships that can affect actors' perspectives and behaviors while facilitating organizational learning. Instead of merely introducing new service ideas in isolated projects, through the continued practice of designing new value cocreating systems and socio-material configurations, service design can assist in enduring transformation of institutional logics (Kurtmollaiev et al. 2018).

In terms of innovation in social issues, service design also gives rise to new business models, such as social innovation, the building of communities for left-behind children, and innovation in the life and learning for disadvantaged groups. At the same time, based on new technologies, new services and business models have come into being, such as location-based models like positioning, pushing, and taxiing. The product of service design is intangible, and are function and experience. It brings new experience and feeling and generates new values for users.

In the Spring of 2021, The Just Trust brought together IDEO.org, Sovereign Objects, and Some Days, a unique mix of creative agencies, to create a holistic vision, brand strategy, visual identity, and action plan that centered the voices of directly-impacted communities. To hold themselves accountable to their belief in centering local leaders and people who have been impacted directly (and most harmfully) by the system, The Just Trust gathered a group of 2021 Field Advisors as co-designers in their launch strategy. Centering the voices, experiences, and expertise of those most impacted by harmful policies must be central to any philanthropic strategy to achieving real and meaningful reform. Instead of neutralizing the needs of either group, we were able to help The Just Trust confidently enter the conversation with a rallying cry on common ground-one that honored the complexities of the movement.

6.3.1 Digital Service Design

The principles of digital service design involve leveraging design methodologies and creativity to ensure that products (services) effectively assist users. Simultaneously, it explores the collaboration between users and machines, seeking a common goal, allowing digital products to seamlessly integrate into the service design system to perform well. Logical thinking in design requires prioritizing the most important functions, maintaining consistency of product functions, and using appropriate design methods to clarify and meet the functional requirements and build user experience. Leveraging the advantages of digital technology further enhances the design of the service system.

The fast development of Cainiao logistics system in recent years is conducive to solve several pain points. Firstly, couriers need to resolve issues related to work efficiency and their income should be increased. Secondly, consumers require a more optimized parcel delivering experience. Specifically, when a package arrives at the Cainiao network station, NFC anti-counterfeit tracing labels are used to store a wealth of information, providing a comprehensive status of the parcel. Cainiao Network intelligently analyzes regionalized routes, automatically plans the optimal route, and provides navigation while intelligently avoiding congestions. They pre-notify users to pick up their parcels at Cainiao service stations, stratify users, segment them into areas, and customize service requirements. Users can identify the status of their parcels, such as fragility, privacy, and customed service needs, and notify the parcel owner via text messaging as fast as possible.

Alibaba Australia launched a Blockchain-based initiative called Food Trust Framework to improve cross-border food supply chain traceabilitylo. Alibaba joined forces with Australia Post, Blackmores Limited and PwC in 2017 to explore the use of Blockchain technology to address supply-chain fraud in the food industry. The system, which is being piloted in Australia and New Zealand, aims to ship food, especially dairy products, from Australia and New Zealand to China via Alibaba's Tmall Global platform. The system enables online shoppers on Taobao and Tmall to verify the authenticity of food products and avoid potentially dangerous counterfeits. In 2018, Tang Ren, Cainiao's senior technical expert for international logistics, promised: "With logistics data being uploaded from all parties, such as retailers and customs officials, buyers can cross-reference every detail of their purchases. Any attempts to conduct data fraud or add in counterfeit products will be as difficult as landing on Mars (Mostert and Jue 2018; Liang 2018)."

Servitization increasingly requires the use of digital technologies such as the Internet of Things (IoT), cloud computing, and predictive analytics. The study develops a new typology of digital service innovations (DSIs) groupings (Business enabler, Service enhancement, Digital service offering) demonstrating that DSIs have mainly enabling or service enhancing roles for manufacturers rather than one that is predominantly designed to create digital service offerings. The exceptions are "predictive maintenance" and "process improvement," which are radical/intermediate DSIs respectively and provide strong value for both manufacturers and customers (Raddats et al. 2022).

As governments look to reconfigure services-and often do so using abstract policy language-new frames of understanding of locality and place must be explored to deliver digital solutions that amplify the social and cultural dimensions that constitute a community. Through the digital, they can be configured to reflect the relational values and tacit knowledge that reside in communities and place. To maintain independent living and address the knotty issues surrounding ageing and ageing communities, the often invisible and informal daily practices that support as well as create community and place need to be understood (Alison 2018).

Digital libraries are evolving from content-centric systems to person-centric systems. Emergent digital services are interactive and multidimensional, associated systems multi-tiered and distributed. A holistic perspective is essential to their effective analysis and design, for beyond technical considerations, there are complex social, economic, organisational, ergonomic requirements and relationships to consider. Striving for simplicity, it is recommended that initial models be based upon simple input/output notation, and then extended as necessary. Such models will provide invaluable contextual understanding to future digital service analysis and design (Buchanan and McMenemy 2012).

6.3.2 *Public Service Design*

Service design in public services involves four levels of application, with increasing levels of difficulty. The first level involves simplifying and visualizing the processes of a specific public service and improving the touchpoints design of that service by using service design thinking, methods, and tools, so as to enhance the user experience. The second level entails improving service design capability as proficient as that required by public service departments and related agencies. The third level involves hiring professional service design companies or individuals to participate in specific service development and design projects within government departments. Through long-term collaboration, they provide possible advices for the policy-making of that service. The fourth level focuses on creating new social service ecosystems through service design, often led by design-driven government innovation labs. During this process, challenges may relate to user scale, internal organizational hurdles, constraints and regulations, and conservative resistance.

The stakeholders in social public services include residents, government departments, professional designers, community organizations, and the academic community. In practice, service design methods can be employed, such as passenger-involved optimization management with smart technology models, to create a tool for user "participation in design." This aims for establishing a comprehensive service design coordination mechanism and technological means to achieve intelligent interconnectivity across the entire public transportation service chain (Zheng 2014).

Public bicycle systems have attracted a great deal of attention in recent years, having been used as a new inner-city transportation mode that can be integrated with existing public transit systems in many cities. This study considers both the user's and the investor's point of view in addressing the design of public bicycle systems. The level of service provided to users is measured by the demand coverage level and travel costs, while the setup costs for bike stations and bike lanes are considered in the case of the investor. In considering the interests of both users and investors, the proposed model attempts to determine the number and locations of bike stations, the network structure of bike paths connected between the stations, and the travel paths for users between each pair of origins and destinations (Lin and Yang 2011).

E-Government projects are currently service oriented, focusing on the implementation and diffusion of digital public services through one-stop points of access for citizens. The route to e-Government is currently based on general and political plans, which do not include citizen or public administration expectations. As a result, what appears is the partial offering of digital public services and the definition of financial and commercial targets. The eGG(e-Government Groupware) system can succeed in involving civil servants in the e-Government era, can cooperate with current or future e-Government systems, and can be used in the participatory design of public services, in order for their discovery and improvement. The eGG can lead to the implementation of real one-stop e-Government portals, achieving citizen satisfaction and public administration modernization (Anthopoulos et al. 2007).

Service design is pursued by different types of public organisations with a multiplicity of aims. The organisations for which the public servants interviewed for this study worked include publicly-owned company, educational institution, government agency, municipality, and ministry. The aims of the service design procurements identified during this study ranged from improving service experience to innovating service systems (Junginger and Sangiorgi 2009). As one of the first efforts to examine briefing in public procurements for service design, this study focused on identifying the key steps involved in the process and unveiling the broad professional contexts. Accounting for the different organizational types in the public sector and the varying intentions in procuring service design was outside the scope of the inquiry. Future studies could investigate briefing in service design procurements with a specific intent and/or in a single type of public organisation and explore how professional contexts in this particular setting may impact the work of service design consultants. In doing so, the study unveils how the professional contexts of public servants and service designers impact briefing as well as explores the challenges and practical responses of practitioners in such engagements (Lee 2020).

6.3.3 Product Service System Design

Product Service System Design (PSSD) comes from service design. In 1999, Mark Goedkoop and others proposed that Product-Service Systems included products, services, the network of organizers, and supporting facilities. Over the years, PSSD's focus has shifted from production and products to an integration of products and services that can meet customer needs. According to the different proportion of products and services, Product-Service Systems is categorized into three types: product-oriented (including product-related services, information, and consultancy services), use-oriented (including product leasing, renting, sharing, and group buying), and result-oriented (including business management, pay-per-service, and functional outcomes). Agricultural economics emphasizes primary products, industrial economics focuses on commodities, and service economics places an emphasis on services, highlighting specialization and product functionality. New challenges include maintaining people's health, reducing energy and resource consumption, and assessed transportation schemes and flexible financial systems.

Service design focuses on creating better concepts from an experiential perspective through both tangible and intangible mediums to provide users with holistic services systems and processes. The entire business model planning is a service design system, a product (Hu 2017). New Retail refers to upgrading and transforming the production, distribution, and sales processes of goods on the Internet and comprehensively integrating online services, offline experiences, and modern logistics. Luckin Coffee's entry into campus and urban check-in activities and sports scenarios are examples of the New Retail model. Luckin's selling point may eventually be the brand's own lifestyle, which is also an example of experience economy.

Current Product-service systems (PSSs) are endowed with a market proposition that expands a product's functionality by unifying additional services to create value for customers and further build positive customer relationships for enterprises (Baines et al. 2009; Beuren et al. 2013; Kuijken et al. 2017). They are complex artefacts composed of products, services, business models, and a network of stakeholders who produce, deliver, and manage the PSS (Mont 2002). The design of PSS, therefore, requires a systematic approach to couple with the relevant components simultaneously (Chou 2021).

A PSS has many engineering characteristics (ECs), their design is a critical work in PSS planning, which has an important influence on the cost and quality of PSS. How to design a reasonable PSS-ECs scheme, and evaluate its life cycle cost (LCC) is a challenging task. Constructing a BN describing the uncertain relationships between PSS-ECs and LCC is the core of this research. By combining existing R&D data and expert experience, Bayesian estimation and arithmetic averaging are used to estimate the conditional probability in BN. The results show that the proposed method can effectively solve the problem of PSS-ECs design for LCC, it also shows that this method has positive significance in realizing engineering knowledge consolidation, assisting designers in exploring design space, and improving the rationality of design decisions (Wang et al. 2022a).

Service products are inherently coupled with service operations in order to leverage service satisfaction upon operations costs. This requires that design of personalized service products must be coordinated with service operations planning (SOP) within a coherent framework of joint optimization. This study proposes a hierarchical joint optimization (HJO) model for personalized service product family (SPF) design considering crowdsourcing of service operations by taking advantage of service resource family (SRF). A case study of personalized tourism product family design and tourism operations planning is reported to illustrate the feasibility and potential of the proposed joint optimization method (Zhou et al. 2022a).

To ensure sustainable value in a business model it is assumed that is considered both its production-related aspects and the customer's changes towards more sustainable and responsible consumption patterns. A sustainable value-focused PSS business model can be defined as a system of interconnected components that offers a superior value-in-use experience to customers. It aims at delivering superior value through resource use optimization, environmental benefits, long-term relationships, and constant revenue streams. PSS value network encompasses all stakeholders involved in the business model designed by the focal company to deliver the business value purpose. It involves cooperative partnerships and responsible, effective operational processes. There is a need to balance trade-offs in the value creation and keep in mind that the PSS design must be consistent with the characteristics defined in the PSS value proposition. Environmental aspects can be planned by considering value creation and delivery towards effectiveness. Social concerns are involved in the value proposition, which contributes to the development of more sustainable communities and can include benefits to the base of the pyramid (BOP). The proposed framework contributes to developing theory on PSS business models synthesizing sustainable opportunities regarding the business model structure. As most PSS business models have usually not been developed considering sustainable principles, this work adds to understanding value concepts related to PSS business models (Moro et al. 2022).

6.3.4 *Service Design Based on Local Culture*

Marco Lansiti and Roy Levien pointed out that no company can be fully self-reliant in the real world, and have to rely on larger systems beyond traditional value chains, which are business ecosystems. Local cultural resources are vital in these ecosystems and are a key focus of service design. Professor He Renke discussed the research, design, and cultural dissemination work conducted by Hunan University's School of Design and Arts in China's ethnic minority areas. They aim to modernize and internationalize intangible cultural heritage, creating a digital database and an intelligent design platform to empower the cultural industry. However, the ultimate goal is to help traditional culture thrive by contemporary design. Through the New Path Design and Social Innovation project, they use their expertise to address critical societal issues like targeted poverty alleviation. This involves creating brands, product packaging, and distribution channels tailored to each household's unique handicrafts or agricultural products, along with live streaming promotion services. For example, traditional weaving and patterns are exquisitely beautiful but may not necessarily align with today's market demands. The time-consuming process leads to high costs, making it hard to sell. Based on contemporary consumer aesthetic preferences and international trends, the research team reinterprets traditional patterns and intangible cultural heritage to create new product designs. The research and production base of Dong brocade has been set up in Wenpo Village where the product manufacturing can be carried out. Dong brocade has applied for commercial trademarks. Due to the limitation of technique, the woven Dong brocade can only as wide as about 40 cm. So scarf serving as the main product is sold on the international market. In addition to innovation in production, huge efforts to promote Dong brocade have been made, for example, taking advantage of offline and online channels for commercialization and promotion, participating in various competitions and inviting cultural celebrities to be its spokespersons in various areas of the world. Other design products based on local culture include Yao people's clothing, machine-knitted scarves, sleep stockings, Ya'an black sand, and Shanhai Wenyuan series of cultural and creative products (inspired by the Classic of Mountains and Rivers featuring rare natural history and geography customs).

6.4 Legal Protection

Services are intangible and heterogeneous. They can not be divided and only provide value within a certain period. Service design as an intrinsic economic factor in the exchange of products can effectively stimulate competition, which must be protected in a regulated and orderly manner in order to maximize the efficiency of economic development. The basis for the legitimacy of legal protection of service design is driven by economic factors and the realization of legal value. The realization of the value of service design is usually manifested in the process of its use as a knowledge product, in which the main body of creation is separated from the main body of use. The significance of the legal protection of service design lies in the goal of safeguarding different rights, constructing new order and maintaining public interest. The social relationship formed by service design is the core object of legal adjustment, characterized by rights and obligations. New practices in the field of design bring new concepts, new thinking and new programs for the protection of intellectual property rights, and service design is included in the scope of knowledge and information. Professor Zheng Chengsi has mentioned that the object of intellectual property rights is replicable, and that intellectual property rights belong to property rights because these rights can be embodied in the replication activities of certain products, works or other objects when they are utilized. The object of such rights can generally be reproduced by a certain tangible object, and service design innovation fits this description, and thus the intellectual property system can be applied as a tool for adjusting the social relations formed based on the creation, provision and utilization of service designs. In the high-tech sector, copyright is the primary method for protecting designers' innovations worldwide. Imitation of service designs may affect fair competition in the marketplace, which is precisely the kind of social relationship that the Anti-Unfair Competition Law upholds, and its underpinning provisions can address some of the complex situations in practice.

Indeed, a core part is the application of design thinking to legal design. The emphasis is on sharing the authors' practical knowledge of the demonstrated contribution of design thinking to legal practice. An important aspect of the authors' collective experiences is the difference between lawyer-think and designer-think. For example, whereas senior and older lawyers may be making decisions, it is the younger lawyers that more readily take risks and innovate. Mounting commercial pressure compels them to innovate on the services they offer. One example is the significant rise in the number of online and paralegal businesses offering higher services at lower cost. Imagine an online legal assistance service that helps people get their ticket refunds from airline companies. Their website's landing page could offer a simple, free online test for ticket refund eligibility, with the follow-through picked up for a fee by the lawyers behind the digital service. Service providers would be required to have sound legal knowledge and experience, and may offer an unconventional or innovative extension to legal practice. People may perhaps not realize the extent of the work and development that goes into solutions designed for users' needs. Developing seemingly simple products often takes a lot more effort than designing something obviously complex. The service might be so well designed, and the process so seemingly simple, that users may not even realize they are being given expert legal advice (David 2022).

6.4.1 Intellectual Property Protection of Digital Service Design and Countermeasures

(1) Interface Design

In the case of Tencent Inc. v. Kebei Networks (Hangzhou Railway Transportation Court 2018), the court held that Haiyi and Kebei had copied the User Interface (UI) of the WeChat complaint platform in order to falsely advertise the platform's products, i.e., the interface used by the defendant's platform was substantially similar to the WeChat complaint UI design interface developed by the plaintiff in terms of its initial layout, color, and the display of "submitted" after submission, which infringed Tencent Technology's copyright and harmed its commercial interests. As a result, Tencent Technology's claim was upheld by the court.

To achieve legal compliance in software development and application, avoiding the risk of copyright infringement is the primary goal. It requires that at the macro level, cautiously selecting open-source software to avoid the risk of infringement; in the long term, capabilities of the software development, including the programming language and other constituent elements can not be overlooked. Compared to copyright protection for works in general, copyright protection for software interfaces is particularly anti-competitive. Based on the huge online impact of mainstream platforms, such protection tends to discourage challenges from new entrants, consolidate software-based monopolies, and slow down innovation and competition in the software market. Therefore, to encourage free competition and restrict monopoly, the absence of copyright protection for application programming interfaces becomes a matter of course.

Although cloud offerings are often global and multi-jurisdictional, the copyright laws governing the services remain territorial and national. We divide the value of an application programming interfaces("API") copyright into two components: the API's "expression value" and its "standardization value." An API's standardization value is essentially the user switching costs that the right to exclude allows an API owner to appropriate. APIs are copyright-eligible works that allow their owner to appropriate standardization value, and thus copyright overcompensates API owners. Appropriation of standardization value is unnecessary to incentivize innovation, and actually causes many of the social harms that commentators have long associated with copyright on APIs. The Note discusses four legal regimes that prevent an API's owner from appropriating its standardization value and concludes that a variable-rate compulsory licensing regime has manageable transaction costs and provides creators with the closest-to-optimal incentives for innovation. In practice, however, many APIs cannot be adequately protected by trade secret or patent law. Thus, copyright provides the most reliable means of intellectual property ("IP") protection for APIs. IP protection of APIs has drawn criticism for decades. In particular, commentators have identified two features of APIs-network effects and switching costs that acting together can cause market monopolization and other negative externalities including spurring excessive marketing costs, increasing prices for consumers (generating deadweight losses), and increasing barriers to further innovation.

Few cases have addressed the fair use defense issue in the software area. Oracle v. Google, as the most important case in the software area, will have a great impact on the technology industry. The Supreme Court's decision in Oracle correctly applied the fair use doctrine because the Court did not apply the fair use doctrine narrowly, and it protected the software developer's creativity. The Supreme Court should have provided a clear standard for the fair use doctrine and discussed the standard in greater detail. The clearer approach would make the result more predictable and not impair software developers' ability to express their ideas and develop more convenient applications that can benefit humanity. It will also make it easier for the lower courts to apply the fair use defense (Gao 2021). As can be seen from the court decisions, fair use is a case-by-case analysis with less predictable results. Some scholars have argued that image-based and text-based programming are actually treated differently when dealing with API copyright issues, with the former left with only a meager layer of protection for the overall picture presentation, while the latter does not seem to lose its copyright altogether just because it is purely and ostensibly to allow computers to engage in functional instructions (Sun 2015).

(2) Existing Issues and Related Regulations for GUI

In the Patent Law, which was amended for the fourth time in 2020, the partial design system was recognized and formally established by the legislator. This stipulation injects a new impetus into the iterative updating of China's design patent protection system, and provides legislative support for the protection of graphical user interface (GUI) designs. However, GUI design patent infringement determination is challenged by many practical dilemmas: the scope of protection of the right of GUI design patent, product carrier system and software service manufacturer infringement determination, etc. still need to be perfected. GUI, as the theoretical and practical hot spots in recent years, has also ushered in the best time to reshape the protection rule system and respond to difficult and complex issues after being explicitly recognized as the object of the design patent authorization. The main function of GUI products is realized through human-computer interaction with the display screen panel, but the current problem is mainly how to define the object and carrier of GUI design patent protection, how to qualify the behavior of the software service provider in the case of separation of software and hardware, how to determine the infringement, what kind of legal responsibility should be borne, and how to better solve the problem in infringement litigation caused by unstable state of the rights. It also involves the penetration of indirect infringement in the field of design, which will ultimately affect the protection of GUI design patents. In the infringement determination of GUI design, there is no need to deviate from the framework of traditional rules, but to make corresponding adjustments after the introduction of the localized design system, in order to better meet the needs of GUI protection (Ma 2022).

The United States in the 1980s stipulated that the design was subject to the more stringent restrictions on the carrier of industrial products. Xerox's application for a computer software icon design during this period was rejected because it did not designate a specific industrial product as the object (Li 2014). In March 1996, the U.S. Patent Office included "Computer-Generated Icons" in the *Guidelines for Patent Applications for Designs Relating to Computer Graphical Interfaces*, and the revised *Patent Examination Guidelines* included the above provision as a new section (1504.01a) in the scope of design protection in July to supplement the "Statutory Subjects Matter for Designs." According to *Patent Examination Guidelines*, GUI design patents are examined as "computer-generated icons." If the GUI is displayed on a computer screen, monitor, or a part thereof, it satisfies the requirement of industrial product under Section 171 of the U.S. Patent Act (35 U.S.C. 171), and can obtain corresponding protection. In the early stage of the design development, the United States refer to "likelihood of confusion" in judging the infringement of the design, and thus the prerequisite for infringement judgment is the design of the product belongs to the same or similar types of products. The U.S. Court of Appeals for the Federal Circuit in the Avia Group International case pointed out that even in the case where the patentee has not yet produced any product containing the patented design, as long as the infringing product uses the design of the patented product, the infringement has been established.

According to design patent in the United States, GUI and GUI elements are defined as computer-generated icons for protection in the form of partial design. For authorization of protection, GUI must meet the requirement of being demonstrated in the display screen of an industrial product, and that it must be novel, non-obvious, and decorative. The infringement determination is based on the observation of ordinary people, to whom whether the same or similar design would be misleading. The "solid line" part of the partial design is the protected GUI, and the "dashed line" part is the unprotected product carrier. The U.S. requires that the GUI be combined with the applicable industrial product, that the GUI design not exist separately as an ornamental design, and that the GUI be the object of protection but not separated from the entity. The Patent Law in the formulation of the rules of damages is different from our country. In addition to the general rules, a separate provision of additional damages on the design is included, that is, whoever during the term of a patent for a design, without license of the owner, (1) applies the patented design, or any colorable imitation thereof, to any article of manufacture for the purpose of sale, or (2) sells or exposes for sale any article of manufacture to which such design or colorable imitation has been applied shall be liable to the owner to the extent of his total profit, but not less than $250, recoverable in any United States district court having jurisdiction of the parties. The European Union refers to Community Design Right, which protects partial design and design that considers GUI as a graphic symbol product. In order to be considered for registration, the design must be novel and unique, not necessarily in the form of physical products. Any commercial use or cross-class use of the GUI design constitutes an infringement. The EU Design Regulation determines the category of the product in the application file for the convenience of search and management, but it does not affect the infringement determination. In the infringement determination process, all the acts of copying the design which has been authorized by the design patent are recognized as infringement. It means that a design can be applied to all kinds of products, and the product category will not restrict the scope of protection of the GUI in the determination. Therefore, the scope of the protection of the design right is greatly extended. Japan follows Registered Design Right and provides protection for partial design and image design, that is, used for the operation of the equipment or to display the results of the operation. The design does not require a physical product as a carrier but it should meet the requirement of novelty, non-obvious design and industrial utility. Infringement judgment is determined by making comparisons with the GUI design, the "solid line" part of the protection of the GUI.

China's design patent right is adopted for product design with GUI. The design should be presented in the form of a product; meanwhile it should be novel, creative and decorative. In terms of the infringement determination, the protection for the product is limited to a certain scope, and the protection is also suitable for partial design. Article 2(4) of the Patent Law (as amended in 2020) states that a design means a new design of the shape, pattern, or a combination thereof, as well as a combination of the color, shape and pattern, of the entire or a part of a product, which creates an aesthetic feeling and is fit for industrial application. *The Patent Examination Guidelines* state that GUI design applications should be amended: the product design involving graphical user interfaces should be included; the product name should generally include "graphical user interface", reflecting the use and application of the product; the overall product design should be submitted; the dynamic GUI should involve the overall product design of at least one state, and the view of the remaining key frames, and the view of the remaining key frames. If necessary; provide statement for the use of the GUI, the area of the GUI in the product, the way of human-computer interaction, and the state of change. However, the pattern displayed by the product display device which has nothing to do with the human-computer interaction will not be protected, for the more emphasis is placed on the GUI design itself during the examination. *The Judicial Interpretation and the Guidelines for Determination of Patent Infringement (2017)* point out that it is necessary to first determine whether the product is the same or similar, and then determine whether there is a same or similar design. When trying infringement disputes related to partial design patents of GUI, the court shall take a flexible approach in the infringement determination, so as to break the unreasonable binding relationship between the GUI interface design and the product.

In the case of Beijing Qihoo 360 Technology co, ltd v. Beijing Jiangmin New Science & Technology (pending), the court held that the patent scope is limited to computer products. Although the accused infringing software is provided to users by the defendant, it is not a product in a same or similar category as computer. Therefore, the accused infringing software doesn't fall within the patent scope. With respect to contributory infringement, the court held that contributory infringement is premised on the fact that a user committed an act of directly implementing the patent in suit. But in this case, users only downloaded the accused infringing software to their own computers, and no one committed acts of making, selling, or offering for sale computers with the accused infringing software preinstalled. In view of this, no one committed an act of directly implementing the patent in suit, and therefore no contributory infringement can be found merely on basis of the fact that the accused infringing software is provided by the defendant (Beijing Intellectual Property Court 2016).

The fact that Jiangmin only partially copied the patented components also caused great damage to the interests of the originator. The infringement judgment should not be based on the same or similar product category, but should follow the infringement judgment standard of "overall observation and comprehensive judgment" to clarify the scope of patent protection, shorten the time of rights protection and reduce the cost. In the current GUI patent application, the product can be diluted and the interface highlighted, and use "be applied to… Product graphical user interface "as a patent name. GUI can be protected by diversification. For example, to protect highly original interface design as "works of art", to seek copyright protection for dynamic interfaces such as games as "works created in a way similar to film," and to apply for trademark for GUI with strong identification or visual elements. When the brand has a certain popularity, use the Anti-Unfair Competition Act to prohibit others from mimicking GUI (Jin 2018b). Take the case of Kingsoft v Mengjia and Kingsoft v Chubao as an example. The Court considered that the hardware, operation system and applications of a product containing GUI would normally be provided by different parties. In both cases, the allegedly infringing GUI designs were incorporated in the allegedly infringing software, and the allegedly infringing GUI designs would definitely appear when the end users were using the software on the mobile phones, which were also actively pursued by the defendants. Therefore, the defendants made substantive and irreplaceable contributions to the appearance of the allegedly infringing GUIs on the mobile phones, and the defendants' distributions of the software were the main causation of infringement in both cases. In conclusion, the Court determined that the distributions of the software in both cases amounted to patent infringement.

Another representative case involves a design patent infringement dispute. The plaintiff, Zhu, held a valid design patent titled "In-Vehicle Head-Up Display with Graphical User Interface." Upon investigation, it was discovered that the defendant, Fangzhou Dream Co., Ltd., had manufactured, offered for sale, and sold a head-up display product that was similar to the patented design without authorization. The Beijing High People's Court held that when a product of the same or similar type incorporates a design identical or similar to a patented design, such use falls within the scope of protection afforded by the design patent. The assessment of whether two designs are identical or similar should be based on the knowledge and cognitive ability of the ordinary consumer of the patented product. In determining similarity, the court should consider the design features of both the patented and allegedly infringing products, and make a comprehensive judgment based on their overall visual effect. If there is no difference in the overall visual effect, the designs shall be deemed identical; if there is no substantial difference, they shall be considered similar.

In this case, the patented design, titled "In-Vehicle Head-Up Display with Graphical User Interface," was valid and owned by Zhu. The accused product was a vehicle-mounted head-up display, which falls within the same product category as the patented design. Both the accused product and the patented product were rectangular cuboids with rounded corners and included a display screen. The graphical user interfaces of both products shared the following major similarities: a centrally located digital display zone; two semi-arc scale regions extending outward from the center; numerical display areas in the bottom-left and bottom-right corners; a small car icon in the center below; and various warning symbols scattered across the interface. The main differences were: the scale in the accused product's semi-arc area was rendered in long bar segments, while the patent used ruler-like markings; the patented design included thin side strips on the outer semi-arc; the car icon differed in position, size, and detail; the number of digits displayed in the bottom-left numerical zone differed; and the number and placement of warning icons were not the same. From the perspective of an ordinary consumer of head-up displays, the shared features between the two designs had a significant impact on their overall visual effect, while the differences were relatively minor and did not result in a noticeably different appearance. Therefore, the overall visual effects of the two designs were not substantially different, and the accused product was deemed to have an appearance similar to the patented design. The evidence presented was sufficient to prove that Fangzhou Dream Co., Ltd. had engaged in the manufacturing, offering for sale, and sale of the infringing product, which the company did not dispute. The court thus found the original judgment—holding that the defendant's product fell within the scope of the patent and imposing liability for infringement—was appropriate and legally sound (Beijing High People's Court 2022).

(3) GUI Protection

We investigate the graphical user interface and in particular the humble computer icon as the perfect metaphor for the challenge of technology to intellectual property analysis. In legal analysis, what is more important-its functionality or its look. Design law has its traditional role in protecting at the boundary between the aesthetic and the functional and we suggest that it could take a more prominent role in protecting graphical user interfaces (Brown and Cameron 2005).

It is well recognized fact that GUI has become an emerging area for countries to contribute to the economy by investing in the technology driven smart devices and its protection as an intellectual property. GUI can be protected under Copyright, Trade Dress, Patents and Design Rights under different jurisdiction. Overlapping of protection is not the issue as each IP is independent in its nature and has different eligibility criteria. The appropriate way to address GUI protection is through a sui generis law that is more adaptable to the evolving technological landscape. Enacting this type of law will serve the traditional purposes of promoting technology and improving general welfare. This law will also harmonize protections among distinct and, from a protection standpoint, disparate jurisdictions. A law that combines elements from various intellectual property schemes will have a better chance of adoption within international treaties, and be more likely to conform with the basic principles underlying all forms of intellectual property protection (Cruz 2017).

We analyze the legal structure among the developed and developing nations for grant of protection to GUI under design rights. The USPTO, EPO, KIPO and other jurisdictions has a wide range of registrations in the area of GUI protection and they have maintained the flexible structure of the legal system very intelligibly through providing space to future ventures in the area of technology. India being a developing nation is still reluctant to protect GUI under India Designs Act, 2000 because the nature of GUI does not establish the eligibility criteria required for acquiring design rights. The Act is more of a traditional approach ignoring the new ventures and innovations in the market. The rigidity of the Act does not allow protection of computer-generated elements and due to which large number of applications have been rejected. Improvement in IP management, performance and administration in the past few years along with amendments of Patents and Trademarks Rules, more techno-oriented reforms reforms and reengineering of IP procedures has resulted in better technology driven performance, decreased pendency and higher rates of disposal of IP applications (Prajapati 2021).

Copyright protects certain creator rights in intellectual property such as literary works, musical works and motion pictures. Conversely, software is utilitarian and technical, more like an invention than a creative work. More curious still, Congress, the courts, and international law have likened software to literary works-e.g. books and plays-when applying copyright law to computer programs. This application of a seemingly ill-fitting intellectual property doctrine, grounded in an imperfect analogy, has led courts to a divergence in software copyright decisions. The extent to which copyright law protects the "look and feel," specifically the user interface, of computer programs has been particularly controversial. Even the Supreme Court was unable to resolve the matter, deadlocking on whether Lotus Development Corporation could copyright its Lotus 1-2-3 spreadsheet software user interface (Castner 1997).

We draw on lessons from prior copyright disputes about GUIs. It first suggests that courts must act as gatekeepers, rather than allowing juries to determine which elements to disregard as functional. It then develops economic factors that can help the court determine whether a design element is functional, and whether to allow reuse by a competing program. Whether knowingly or not, courts have considered the importance of graphical user interface elements and have done their best to reach outcomes that incentivize future innovation while maximizing current benefits.

The doctrines of originality, merger, scenes a faire and functionality served to severely limit the number of protectable elements in Apple's GUI The limited number of protectable elements led the court to adopt the difficult standard of virtual identity. Both the district court and the court of appeals in this case applied these standards broadly to limit the scope of Apple's copyright. While it is possible that not every court will apply these principles so broadly, the reasoning behind the broad application may be used to similarly limit copyright protection in future cases. In addition, the court's broad application of these principles and rejection of the "look and feel" approach should prove important in future computer copyright cases.

Computer software developers who are the first to come up with an idea for a particular type of program will undoubtedly want to take note of the use of the traditional copyright limiting doctrines in *Apple I* Developers should recognize that for some new computer applications, especially GUIs, copyright protection may be more limited than the developer might anticipate. The knowledge of a possibility that copyright protection of an application may not be as extensive as once believed will allow for better planning by these developers. Counsel for software developers should also be quite interested in the use of traditional copyright doctrines in *Apple I* The court's analysis provides good insight into how a court may approach this type of copyright dispute.

Attorneys for litigants seeking to limit the scope of an opposing party's copyright will be able to use the reasoning of the court in support of their position. These attorneys will especially want to focus on the *Apple I* court's positions that many of the ideas in computer programs have a limited number of possible expressions and many elements of computer applications, especially GUIs, are functional. Attorneys who represent copyright holders may also benefit from a close look at *Apple I*. By examining the reasoning behind the broad application of traditional copyright limiting doctrines, these attorneys may be able to formulate new arguments to limit application of these doctrines. For instance, while the idea of graphically representing a document file on the screen has a limited number of possible expressions, another programming idea may arguably have a wider range of possible expressions. Such a difference may distinguish a case from *Apple I* sufficiently to prevent application of the limiting doctrines.

Developers wishing to provide more adequate protection for their computer applications may want to consider other legal avenues. One commentator has suggested that because of the unpredictable application of the "look and feel" test to GUIs, legal practitioners have begun to look to other areas of intellectual property law for protection. If courts begin to move away from application of the "look and feel" test as the Ninth Circuit has in *Apple I*, this search for new methods of protection will likely accelerate. Some alternate possibilities for protection include trademark, trade dress and design patent theories (Neville 1996).

The current duration of GUI protection is too long. Copyright lasts for more than seventy years, design patents last for fourteen years, or more through the use of continuation patents, and trade dress lasts indefinitely, so long as consumers continue to identify the "container of goods" with the specific source. For GUI designs, a shorter term of three years, for example, with the option to renew, would better maintain the balance between the GUI creators' interests (to recoup their investment) and those of the consuming public (to have works released into the public domain in a timely manner).

The GUI protection could be renewed every three years, with a maximum of, e.g., nine years, so long as the design remains in use in commerce and the design has not become a standard building block necessary for use in others' creations. This building block theory could be based upon copyright's merger doctrine, where if there is only one or a limited number of ways to achieve a certain function, that design element will not receive protection. The difference here is that under the new GUI regime, the original creator will have the benefit of exclusivity over the building block for the first three years of use (Stigler 2014).

(4) Patent Protection

Interface patents can also have "compatibility value." In other words, the patented technology is often essential to make products operate (i.e. compatible) with a particular interface (Chao 2016). The visual images created by software applications may be protectable as trade dress so long as those visual images are either inherently distinctive or have acquired secondary meaning; and are *de jure* nonfunctional. The holder of a protectable software trade dress would be entitled to relief if it were able to establish a likelihood of confusion between the "total images" of its trade dress and a defendant's trade dress. Because the visual image of the Macintosh GUI may be a distinctive and nonfunctional trade dress, it would appear that Apple Computer would be able to protect the total visual image of its Macintosh GUI as a trade dress (Caslowitz 1993).

Modern designers of graphical user interfaces, or GUIs, have obtained design patent protection for creative computer software displays, a realm previously limited to copyright. The difference in protection is important because design patents do not traditionally allow the same defenses like fair use associated with copyright. Apple's nearly billion-dollar judgment against Samsung, which included such a GUI patent, brought this issue to the forefront. Until now-few design patents have been asserted to protect a large portion of an interface, rather than a single icon (Risch 2014).

6.4.2 Data-Related Service Design IP Protection and Countermeasures

In the era of fast digitalization, information such as data and privacy in service design may be at risk of leakage at anytime and anywhere. As the total amount of data keeps increasing, the risk of consumer privacy and data security further upgrades (Jin 2018a). The digital industry is developing rapidly, and it is not rare for practice of data abuse by enterprises. However, at present, there is no sectoral law specifically regulating the rights and interests of enterprise data, with a lack of comprehensive legal protection of the rights and interests of enterprise data for the time being. Therefore, intellectual property rights infringements in varied cases are common in judicial practice.

(1) Related Regulations

Countries attach importance to the protection of data rights and interests through legal means at the level of theoretical research as well as at the level of actual legislation, justice and law enforcement. They have comprehensively strengthened the protection of data rights and interests through the promulgation of legal policies, improvement of organizational construction, and strengthening of supervision and law enforcement.

Data protection stems from the series of European regulations on personal information protection, the *Data Protection Directive* enacted in 1995. The implementation of the *General Data Protection Regulation* (GDPR) in 2018 has triggered extensive discussion and practice of data protection around the world (Chi et al. 2021). The system adopted by the EU is stricter than that of the U.S. For databases with actual inputs but do applied to the protection of the originality standard, the EU proposes special property rights protection rules. Further, the *Directive on the Legal Protection of Databases* was adopted in 1996, which protected this kind of dataset as a kind of proprietary property right. The Article 4 of the 2019 *Directive on Establishing an EU Framework for the Review of Foreign Direct Investments* states "...... Member States and the Commission may consider the potential impact on access to, or the ability to control, sensitive information, including personal data." This provision implies that the security of personal information, especially when it comes to large numbers of people and specific types of personal information, is not just about protecting the legitimate interests of individuals, but also about the deeper interests at stake. The European Commission's proposal for a *Data Act*, published in February 2022, provides an open-access use of data access rights. The *Data Governance Act* (DGA), formally adopted and published by the Council of the European Union (EU) in May 2022, focuses on the reuse of public data, data sharing between businesses, sharing of personal data for intermediation, and altruistic data use.

The United States has not established a unified data code at the federal level, mainly adopting the decentralized behavioral law protection mode. In the United States, protection of data is stated in various laws, such as the *Computer Fraud and Abuse Act* (CFAA), the *Video Privacy Protection Act*, the *Federal Stored Communications Act* and other laws. In the financial, children, health care and other special industries, special laws are developed for data protection by regulation in different categories, such as the *Financial Services Act Modernization Act*, the *Children's Online Privacy Protection Act*, the *Family Educational Rights and Privacy Act* and the *Health Insurance Distribution and Accountability Act*. The protection of corporate data and data sets through intellectual property laws is only applied to collections of data that constitute works and have originality. Patent protection needs to meet the criteria of novelty, non-obviousness and utility, so many enterprises turn to trade secrets to protect corporate data. Trade secrets and patents are in fact complementary. Although the combination of the two achieves the purpose of protecting data assets, but in the long run this may result in data monopoly. It should be understood that the protection of trade secrets is only a means of regulating the market order, and can not be fully consistent with the real needs of corporate data protection. In March 2018, the introduction of the *Act to Clarify the Lawful Use of Data Outside the Country* (the Cloud Act) had a certain impact on data protection. The U.S. judiciary attempted to take jurisdiction over enterprises not based in the U.S. The main focus is still to emphasize the safeguarding of the circulation and sharing of data, and to encourage the excavation and creation of the economic value of data. The *U.S. Federal Data Strategy 2020 Action Plan* proposes how the federal government can accelerate the use of various data in various specific tasks, services to the public and management resources, and protect security, privacy and confidentiality (Zhou et al. 2022b).

China's traditional legal framework grants a certain degree of protection for enterprise data and user data. The data rights framework is constructed to distinguish data rights and regulate its use for data right protection. Article 127 of the Civil Code only stipulates that "Where any laws provide for the protection of data and network virtual property, such laws shall apply," which lays the foundation for the construction of data rights and industrial development. The *Data Security Law* adopted in June 2021 is mainly a general provision for ordinary data (including governmental data). Some of China's model zones have proposed new rules on data ownership. In July 2021, Shenzhen issued the *Shenzhen Special Economic Zone Data Regulations*, which puts forward the concept of "data rights" and attributes them to individuals, the state and data market entities according to different data types. In November 2021, Shanghai passed the *Shanghai Data Regulations*, which aims to promote the circulation and exploitation of data, and to empower the digital economy and social development, while meeting security requirements. In 2022, the *Shanghai Key Work Arrangements for Open Public Data* proposed to promote data openness to empower epidemic prevention and control, focused on the needs of epidemic normalization prevention and control, and promoted data openness to empower the digital transformation of the manufacturing industry. In July 2022, the *Opinions of the Supreme People's Court on the Provision of Judicial Services and Guarantees for Accelerating the Construction of the Nation's Unified Large Market* specially mentioned that we should support the construction of a unified technology and data market and protect the property rights and interests of data products developed by data factor market players based on legally collected and self-generated data in accordance with the law.

(2) Existing Issues

The protection of copyright law is commonly granted to compilation works, but the protection is limited to the overall arrangement and structure, and has not extended to take different types of data and legal interests into consideration. To apply for the patent, the work needs to meet the requirement of novelty, creativity and applicability such as in the form of a big data computing or algorithmic program and other technical solutions. Its application combined with trade secrets usually results in data monopoly and will affect market competition. The problem of trade secret protection is reflected in the conflict between the social demand for data utilization and sharing and the form of protection of trade secrets. This problem may encourage the indecent behavior of data hiding and aggravate data monopoly, as well as leading to high cost and unfavorable transaction. Competition law protection aims to alleviate damage. As it focuses on the behavior and lacks clear standards for application, it is prone to deviate from the underpinning role of general provisions. While for contract law, its protection is too limited for data management.

Some operators utilize new technologies and means to fetch the collection of work data controlled by competitors, which gives rise to related litigation and the issue of legal protection of the collection of work data on Internet, such as the dispute against unfair competition involving the collection of work data of on Internet. The collection of work data in dispute includes the collection of work data formed by the review released by the users, the collection of work data formed by the short videos released by the users, and the collection of work data formed by the articles released by the users, and the work data collection formed by the audio and video procured by the internet platform (Diao 2021). The construction process of intellectual property data governance is also challenged by obstacles like insufficient institutional data carving, algorithmic ethics and data justice, legal attributes of data property rights, and regulation of data platform behavior.

(3) Practice Cases

In July 2020,the European Union Court of Justice issued a blockbuster ruling invalidating the EU-US data transfer agreement known as the Privacy Shield, based on a series of cases brought by Austrian lawyer and privacy activist Max Schrems v. Facebook. The Court of the European Union on the trial of the case is the political, diplomatic, national strength, policy of Europe and the United States of America multi-party competition. In addition to the legal space for discussion, more involved in the scope of public power between different countries to define, the judgment emphasized the government agencies to obtain and process personal data. In December 2020, the Irish Data Protection Commission fined the US company Twitter 450,000 euros for a data breach in January 2019.Twitter has revealed flaws in its "Protect your tweets" feature and that it failed to notify regulators within 72 h of discovering the breach and adequately document data breaches. In terms of enforcement practice, administrative fines under the GDPR do play a leading role. HiQ Labs, Inc. v. LinkedIn Corp., 938 F.3d 985 (9th Cir. 2019), was a United States Ninth Circuit case about web scraping. The 9th Circuit affirmed the district court's preliminary injunction, preventing LinkedIn from denying the plaintiff, hiQ Labs, from accessing LinkedIn's publicly available LinkedIn member profiles. HiQ is a small data analytics company that used automated bots to scrape information from public LinkedIn profiles.

The court ruled that HiQ had the right to do web scraping. However, the Supreme Court, based on its Van Buren v. United States decision, vacated the decision and remanded the case for further review in June 2021. In a second ruling in April 2022 the Ninth Circuit affirmed its decision. In a November 2022 ruling the Ninth Circuit ruled that hiQ had breached LinkedIn's User Agreement and a settlement agreement was reached between the two parties.

Shanghai Hantao Information Consulting Co Ltd. v Beijing Baidu Netcom Science Technology Co Ltd. is a recent precedent that applies Article 2 and 5 of the Anti-Unfair Competition Law. In this case, Baidu's map used technical means to grab review information from 'dianping.com' and its search results displayed these reviews with a link to the original comments. The court held that although Baidu's map, to a certain extent, enriched consumer choice, it was disproportionate as it did not take the measure that could be least harmful to 'dianping.com'. Moreover, Baidu's vertical search service replaced reviews generated from 'dianping.com', which not only undermined the interests of 'dianping.com', but also curbed the incentive to invest further in its content providing services, thus hindering the order of market competition (AnJie Broad Law Firm 2017).

In the unfair competition case between Tomi (Wuhan) Information Technology Co., Ltd. and Wuhan Beauty Evolution Information Technology Co., Ltd. (Hubei High People's Court 2022), the court found that both Tomi and Beauty Evolution are registered for cosmetics sales. The actual business activities of both included providing cosmetic ingredient data inquiry services to online users, so the two were competing operators in the same industry. In actual operation, Tomi provides the cosmetic ingredient data information it has collected and collated to online users after technical measures such as adding "Tomi" characters or watermarks, etc. However, the cosmetic ingredient data provided by Beauty Evolution to online users on its website and other commercial internet platforms for the same product also contains a large amount of "Tomi" or watermark used in the operation of Tom. Moreover, Beauty Evolution provided no evidence or reasonable explanations for the source of the cosmetic ingredient information with "Tomi" or watermark, so Beauty Evolution obtained the above cosmetic ingredient information through improper network technology and used it in operation. The behaviours of Beauty Evolution violated the principles of fairness and integrity, and compromised the competitive advantages and legitimate interests of Tomi as a cosmetics ingredient data service operator. Therefore, the actions of Beauty Evolution constitute unfair competition against Tomi. The court decided that Beauty Evolution Co., Ltd. stopped using data containing the "Tomi" logo and compensated Tomi 500,000 yuan (about $68,467) for financial losses (including reasonable expenses).

Reviewing the data-related lawsuits, it can be seen that most of the plaintiffs have won their cases. The applicable laws in judicial decisions are mainly concentrated in Article 2, 12, and 17 of the "Anti-Unfair Competition Law". Article 22, 41, 42, and 43 of the "Cybersecurity Law," Article 127 of the Civil Code, and the "Data Security Law" stipulate the data security system, data security protection obligations and legal responsibilities, etc.

The adjudication documents of various cases prove that due to the lack of legislation to determine the ownership of data rights and interests, the judicial authorities avoided making direct determinations on the ownership of data assets as much as possible. Instead, they first examined whether data products or data services held by enterprises can receive the protection of intellectual property law. Second, when an enterprise data product or data service cannot be viewed as a work protected by intellectual property law, the court will examine whether the enterprise has invested human or material resources in the data and whether the data has been processed, then determine whether the enterprise enjoys rights and interests in the relevant data. The court approves the relationship between competition law and data property interests and mainly uses the Anti-Unfair Competition Law for post-factual relief. Third, whether the relevant data forms the core competitiveness of the enterprise and whether it is the basis for the enterprise to carry out business activities will also influence the court's judgment on whether the enterprise enjoys data rights. Finally, the prerequisite for enterprise data assets to be legally recognized and valued is the legal compliance of the data itself and its quality assurance.

In the current data disputes, commonalities in court rulings include: First, the court affirms the value of data and information collected by enterprises and is worthy of corresponding protection. For example, the court once stated, "User information is an important operating resource for Internet operators." Second, the court protected enterprise data based on the "legitimate rights and interests of operators" in Article 2 of the Anti-Unfair Competition Law and determined that the defendant's acquisition or use of data or information constituted an act of unfair competition, thus supporting the plaintiff's lawsuit. Currently, academia and practitioners believe that data has a broad value. If an enterprise or individual infringes on the data interests of other enterprises, it will cause them certain losses, so they should be compensated accordingly. There is no determination whether the infringed user data is a property interest or a right. If the plaintiff files a lawsuit for enterprise data protection on the grounds of unfair competition, the court will use the provisions of the Anti-Unfair Competition Law as the basis for judgment according to the principle of discretion in civil procedures.

(4) Recommendations

The general provisions of the Anti-Unfair Competition Law are preferred when using existing systems to protect data assets. When creating the system, specific types of interests are regulated in the anti-competition law, and "data acquisition rights" are used to balance the relationship with the public sector. It is necessary to establish data-sharing rules, clarify the rights system for platform data, regulate the consent terms and scope of data collection, and establish a mechanism that balances data development and data protection to strengthen the supervision of data monopoly (Li 2021).

Academia tends to define enterprise data as property or intellectual property and calls for determining data ownership rules to break down core barriers to data transactions and circulation (Feng and Hu 2021). Some scholars believe that the object of exclusive data rights is derived data, that is, systematic, readable, and useful data formed by processing, calculation, and aggregation with algorithms after the original data is recorded and stored, and is not just a collection of data such as a database. They believe that exclusive data rights are property rights and are a new type of intellectual property right. Some scholars believe there is legitimacy to protecting enterprise data rights and interests. They also hold that constructing a new intellectual property and scenario protection model for enterprise data within the intellectual property system can help solve the problem of enterprise data protection (Liu et al. 2021). Theoretically, it is advisable to establish a data control right with moderate levels of exclusivity, which includes rights such as control, access, transfer, and deletion, as an intermediate part of the property rights spectrum (Jin 2022). To determine unfair competition involving a collection of work data, in addition to sections 2 and 12 of the "Anti-Unfair Competition Law," another two key points of analysis should be focused on: whether the dispute caused the work data collection to be replaced, and the Internet platform's investment in the work data collection creation process. At the judicial level, applicable regulations for adjudicating data property rights disputes have been introduced, focusing on outstanding legal issues in the case. Guideline and communiqué cases are published for reference by judges, lawyers, and the public.

When improving domestic data regulatory rules, judicial departments will enhance our influence in shaping international rules (Zhao 2022), align the domestic rule of law construction rules with extraterritorial rules, and establish a connecting mechanism for internalising international rules. Departments should cooperate to promote the system. At the government level, they should standardize institutional assessments, clarify the responsibilities of supervisory authorities, meet the actual situation and special security needs of different industries, prioritize according to the key levels and sensitivity of data, and establish a hierarchical classification and scenario-based data supervision system. For example, when applying the Data Security Law, it is possible to further clarify the specific meaning and judgment criteria for data types such as "important data" based on existing classifications, and coordinate the certification, authorization, and procedures for "important data". Specific data provisions or separate legislation on data protection in the anti-unfair competition law should be adopted as soon as possible. By clarifying the criteria for determining the legitimacy of data competition, the interests of market players in all parts of the data industry chain can be balanced.

A self-regulatory protection system for industry and enterprise data should focus on market regulation, combining government supervision with enterprise self-discipline. Enterprises should ensure the safety of data flow, give full play to industry advantages, and improve data security management capabilities. The government should require enterprises to strengthen cross-border data security monitoring, establish a multi-dimensional comprehensive privacy protection mechanism, encourage leading Internet companies such as Tencent, Alibaba, and ByteDance to participate in active technological innovation, continue to guarantee the free and safe flow of enterprise data, and bring the most economic benefits and value. The government seizes opportunities for data flow development to urge enterprises to strengthen connections and cooperation with domestic and foreign regulatory authorities and requires enterprises to seek help and guidance from data security advisors to apply for certification from extraterritorial supervisory authorities or third parties.

6.4.3 *Public Service Design Intellectual Property Protection and Countermeasures*

(1) Existing Problems and Suggestions of Medical Health APP

Recently, doctors, pharmacists, and companies have banded together to develop applications ("apps") that promise to redefine the way medicine is practised. It is hoped that apps will help users manage their health on a day-to-day basis. However, there are a number of concerns surrounding the use of apps in the medical field. Numbers quickly soared as developers released fitness and diet-related apps. The market was quickly flooded with a mix of beneficial and ineffective apps promising to do the same thing: improve the user's health and quality of life. These apps were developed and sold in a more or less unregulated market, and they were followed by allegations of misrepresentation-most recently against a company claiming their app could "treat" acne by causing the cellphone to emit a special light. Physicians and pharmaceutical companies have developed beyond one-sided monitoring, researching, and prevention of illness. They created a platform that has the potential to redefine the doctor-patient relationship (Fox 2014). Despite possible liability apportionment in common law remedies, the FDA must balance its new mobile medical app regulations to simultaneously protect the consumer and also encourage innovation. Even so, the mobile medical app industry will provide the most substantial oversight where FDA's budget and infrastructure are lacking. The bulk of the Final Guidance places a necessary level of responsibility on the mobile medical app manufacturer (Carroll 2014). The case-by-case review being utilized by the FDA is not an effective way of keeping up with the growing volume and demand for mobile medical apps. By giving app developers a quicker and cheaper alternative route to getting safe, reliable, and accurate mobile medical health apps to consumers, the mobile health field will continue to grow and produce high quality medical apps (Kilker 2016).

Liability assertions involving recommendation or curation are essentially informational, which raises the issue of whether and to what extent informed consent duties are implicated by health care app use. The advent of mobile health technologies does not necessitate the development of novel legal doctrines. Rather, existing doctrines are adequate to apply tort and privacy law to the development, use, recommendation, and prescription of mobile health products by healthcare professionals. Like any other new medical technology, mobile health products are likely to amplify existing uncertainties in the tort liability context, at least in the short term.

Mobile medical apps include applications that provide patients with medical consultation, health monitoring, and doctors with the latest medical knowledge as well as drug information. In this process, the network and informatization of medical data make the boundary of medical research data protection increasingly blurred. There is an obvious boundary between fair use, rights protected by intellectual property rights, and categories not protected. In particular, the infringement of facts on the Internet is becoming more and more common (Zhang et al. 2015). Some mobile medical application service providers publish medical papers without the consent of medical researchers through mobile software to achieve their commercial purposes, ignoring the protection of intellectual property rights of medical research achievements. Without the copyright owners' consent or authorization of the mobile medical APP, the pirated mobile medical APP makes copies of its source code that are not completely consistent with its source code for redistribution. The pirated mobile medical APP should first be decompiled to obtain the source code, and then be modified to restore a new APP with the same and similar functions as well as service interface as the original APP (Zhang and Wang 2017). There will also be subjects who make use of the mobile medical platform for false publicity, turning the mobile medical platform with consulting function into a platform for selling fake and substandard drugs through the media of the Internet, which brings a great threat to the personal health of patients. Mobile health care relies on a variety of acquired data for medical diagnosis, which involves personal privacy. If the stored data is easily lost or stolen, it will cause unnecessary information security problems (Yang and Feng 2016).

The top-level system framework of mobile health service is formed through legislation, it is included in the medical and health legislation as one of the chapters. Mobile medical services involve various legal issues such as the Internet, the Internet of things, medical institutions, consumers, third-party platforms and so on. It is necessary to clearly define the scope of their responsibilities and coordinate and manage relevant institutions. Ensure the legality and safety of hospitals and doctors engaging in mobile health services, promote the equalization of medical resources, and clarify the responsibilities of the regulated objects and the regulated subjects (Tu 2016).

(2) Existing Issues and Related Regulations for APP Privacy Issues

Many apps imitate influential signs of their competitors. "Squatting," "free-riding," and "hitchhiking," to name a few, are constantly emerging. If someone uses some prominent and well-known app names without permission, the act of squatting apps with the same name and uploading them to the app store constitutes trademark infringement and is also an act of unfair competition (Wang 2016). Some privacy policies have become manipulated by operators to restrict users' rights and shirk obligations, invisibly infringing on users' privacy. Since 2019, the Ministry of Industry and Information Technology has reported illegal apps found in the special rectification action on apps that infringe on users' rights and interests. Studies have shown that the overall privacy policy of social media apps is generally acceptable, but there are still some problems with the completeness and operability. Some apps pirate software or conduct other infringing acts. There is also disclosure of personal information and privacy. Regulations should be refined and supervision measures strengthened. When there is a conflict between rights regarding personal information, privacy, etc., to resolve the concurrence between different rights, it is necessary to set the boundary of rights by defining the applicable principles, building an independent privacy system or creating new rights. To effectively address this issue, there should be more theoretical research and case studies on solutions to rights concurrence.

The object of mobile medical legal relationship is a complex object, which also involves things, behaviors, intellectual property rights and personal rights. In terms of intellectual property rights, there are more types of mobile medical applications, such as computer software copyright in the form of copyright, patent rights in the form of invention patents, and design patents in the form of product appearance. The legal norms related to the protection of personal information are relatively sound, and there are still shortcomings in the legal regulations on the collection of personal information by apps. There are no special laws to regulate mobile health care in our country, and there are no corresponding industry norms. There are many varieties and uneven quality of mobile health care. With the increasingly vigorous development of the Internet, the impact of problems is easy to spread, and it is urgent to protect and regulate, and properly handle the corresponding disputes (Nissenbaum and Wang 2021).

The US adopts a decentralized legislation. Early laws enacted in the US focused on protecting privacy. Personal information was protected through industry and market coordination, and all states enacted laws relating to personal information protection. In 2016, the United States issued the "Application Privacy, Protection, and Security Act," which specifically regulates the collection and use of user information by apps. In 2018, California enacted the "Consumer Privacy Act," which establishes new disclosure obligations for relevant entities and introduces the right to access their data and the right to delete it. Consumers can refuse to sell personal information to third parties, providing a legal way for consumers to control personal information. In 2021, Virginia passed the Consumer Data Protection Act. In 2013, the European Union issued "Opinions on Apps on Smart Devices." In 2018, the General Data Protection Regulations granted data subjects seven message rights based on the principle of protecting the personal information rights of natural persons. In 2020, the European Commission issued the "Guidance to ensure full data protection standards of apps fighting the pandemic" to strengthen the protection of personal information of apps during the fight against COVID-19. Under the privacy theory of scenes, processing data is required to be consistent with the scene. When a mobile app collects personal data, it is determined whether it conforms to scene consistency in terms of participants, information types, and transmission rules to protect the interests of the information subject.

(3) Suggestions Related to APP Privacy Issues

To further improve and correctly implement the privacy policy, it is necessary to increase users' willingness to read the privacy policies, improve the content of the privacy policy text, and improve the social media privacy protection governance system. This means, under the Personal Information Protection Law and other legal provisions, a diverse collaborative governance system should be established under continuous supervision from government departments, self-regulation by industry organizations and operators, and active participation by users. In June 2022, the Cyberspace Administration of China issued the newly revised "Administrative Provisions on Information Services of Mobile Internet Application Programs." For applications that violate the new Administrative Provisions and related laws, regulations, and service agreements, application distribution platforms should take measures such as warnings, suspension of services, and removal in app stores by the law, keep records, and report to relevant authorities. As users of app logos, app developers should pay attention to preventing their own app logos from infringing on the legitimate rights and interests of others. When developing apps, they must search and screen for defects in rights such as trademarks and copyrights. App store operators should also strengthen management, review and file app developer information on time, sign relevant guarantee agreements, and clarify the rights and obligations of both parties. The government can improve the remedies for right holders, strengthen the multi-level and comprehensive supervision in aspects from management norms to law enforcement, and mobilise parties from right holders to the public (Chen 2020).

Some scholars put forward that the establishment of personal information security supervision department is the primary condition to ensure the security of APP users' personal information, and further refine the relevant supervision system. To clarify the scope of responsibilities of regulatory agencies and refine necessary regulatory measures, ensure that relevant legal provisions on personal information protection are effectively implemented in practice, ensure that the implementation of the legislative supervision system is as important as the operation mechanism and legislative activities, and take the consistency of power and responsibility, the violation of the law shall be investigated, and the infringement shall be punished as the basic principles of law enforcement. So as to effectively solve the current APP serious violation of citizens' personal data information problem (Liu 2020). To strengthen the protection of personal data information, it is necessary to strengthen the constraints on APP subjects. A series of measures can be taken to strengthen the legal regulation on APP subjects by improving the real-name system of APP development, design subject, APP subject filing system, APP subject market access system and so on (Chen and Hu 2021). It is suggested that regulatory departments should strengthen the inspection of APP privacy policies, distinguish the kinds of information that can be collected from those that cannot, so as to strengthen the protection of users' personal information in the APP (Zhang 2019). The establishment of unified privacy protection standards, the improvement of APP review process, and the stimulation of self-supervision awareness of the information industry, and the construction of a systematic control mechanism of APP privacy terms will effectively guarantee the security of APP users' information (He and Wang 2018).

6.4.4 *Intellectual Property Protection of Product Service System Design and Countermeasures*

(1) Existing Issues and Regulations for New Retail

In recent years, new retail models such as community group buying and live streaming have become mainstream, but some enterprises have little legal awareness and engage in unfair acts such as false publicity, low-price dumping, and price fraud. Many negative phenomena can be seen in digital stores, online retail, and live streaming. Moreover, there is still uncivilized shopping behaviour of consumers in self-service retail, which needs our further exploration of the impact of big data, retail technology, and face recognition technology on new retail. In December 2020, China promulgated the "9 Promises" for community group buying in order to improve the price behaviour of community group purchases and anti-unfair competition supervision in accordance with the law, stepping up enforcement and handling of cases, and maintaining order in the community group buying market. In April 2021, various departments jointly issued regulations such as the "Administrative Measures for Livestreaming Marketing (for Trial Implementation)" to control the negative phenomena in online retail. Existing new hotel retail services appear in the form of "hotel+". For example, MUJI HOTEL opened by Muji in Shenzhen in 2017 applies the "hotel+" mode. On 9 October 2018, China Industrial Economy News reported an article titled "Blue Ocean Business Opportunities for New Retail in Hotels - Magic Convenience Stores Bring New Consumption Channels in Guest Rooms," which introduced the form of "hotel + unmanned retail." However, the more typical new hotel retail in the industry is a "hotel+e-commerce" format in Lifease Hotel, where customers can truly experience and buy different products carefully selected by NetEase, bringing an experience of "using immediately after buying (Yan et al. 2020)". Changes in sales models will bring about many new problems and disputes. In new retail, some enterprises cannot innovate, and patent infringement issues are getting worse. To reduce costs and avoid solving technical difficulties, some enterprises ignore intellectual innovation, patent protection requirements, product quality and stability, directly copy products, and take a free ride. They seriously disrupt the market competition order. Patent infringement harms the interests of patent owners and consumers. Such behaviours also trigger unfair competition. Joint legal enforcement both online and on site should be strengthened.

As Amazon's role in the retail landscape continues to evolve and expand, it faces greater legal exposure. In recent years, Amazon has faced product liability challenges. Product liability law governs the "legal liability of manufacturers or sellers of goods to compensate buyers, users, and even bystanders for damages or injuries suffered because of defects in goods purchased." Since there is no uniform federal scheme that addresses product liability, jurisdictions faced with this issue have approached it differently.

(2) Existing Issues and Regulations for Artificial Intelligence

The widespread use of artificial intelligence comes with legal and moral risks. For example, in March 2018, an Uber self-driving car crashed into a pedestrian who was crossing the road and caused his death. This car accident triggered heated public discussions on autonomous driving and even shattered people's trust in artificial intelligence to a certain extent. The current written law system has no specific explanation for such accidents, which requires the current legal system to keep pace with the times and formulate corresponding judicial interpretations of AI technology (Wang and Lei 2018). Some researchers abstracts express delivery in intelligent logistics terminals into a multi-agent model, introducing a user-paid express delivery service process to ensure effective monitoring of the status of fresh food delivery and timely feedback to users with a minimum of energy consumption. Based on the updated data on the smart logistics terminal, the system can determine the optimal delivery route for express shipments. The results show that the smart fresh food logistics terminal system can improve the efficiency of sending and receiving express shipments and improve the user experience. Security and privacy can be well guaranteed in the system. The positioning and usage of courier boxes ensure the security and privacy protection of users and shipments. In terms of IoT application security, the system features passive tags, low cost, low memory, and only the tag ID is left on the label (Li et al. 2021).

In 2017, the US Self Drive Act proposed to protect the privacy rights of artificial intelligence autonomous vehicle users, incorporating the privacy protection of users and related entities into R&D requirements. Manufacturers must formulate corresponding plans for information protection and take strict protective measures to prevent the leakage of users' personal information. In 2016, the Economic Commission for Europe announced the enforcement of the amendments to the "Vienna Convention for Road Traffic" on autonomous vehicles. If the driving assistance system can be turned off, taken over by the driver at any time, or complies with specific international regulations (such as ABS, LDWS, etc.), it can be used. In 2017, the British "Vehicle Technology and Aviation Bill" stipulated that insurance companies, rather than manufacturers, should bear the liability of third parties in traffic accidents related to AI autonomous driving vehicles. The Bill provided strong protection for owners of artificial intelligence autonomous vehicles and accident victims. It also stipulated personal data protection in terms of AI autonomous driving. In 2017, Germany amended the "Road Traffic Law". Vehicle owners are still required to bear corresponding no-fault responsibilities. As long as an autonomous vehicle infringes on the property or personal safety of others, the vehicle owner must bear responsibility. The National Institute of Information and Communications Technology (NICT) of the Ministry of Internal Affairs and Communications proposed "symbiosis" between humans and AI as the first of the five concepts for AI development in the AI development guidance plan, which means "building a 'people-centred' society that respects human dignity and individual autonomy." (Ji 2019) In 2018, the German Federal Ministry of Transport and Digital Infrastructure (BMVI) formed an ethics task force with countries and organizations such as the United Kingdom, Austria, and the European Commission to publish a research report on autonomous driving. The report suggests prioritize human life as the primary value: "Of all our values, protecting human life is the highest value. Human life has unconditional priority in the event of unavoidable harm." Taking automatic driving vehicles as a typical case, the related responsibilities and obligations mainly involve the design of intelligent devices, the responsibility of use and the ethical obligation of group benefit. If there is no person responsible for the accident caused by the self-driving car and only the beneficiary's obligation exists, the relevant losses should be borne by the beneficiary group of the autonomous car in the form of obligation. The ethical bridge of the responsibility gap of AI application will form a virtuous circle between the application of AI and the realization of corresponding dividends (Wang 2022).

China actively improves its management of the autonomous driving industry. For example, the "Strategy of Development and Innovation of Intelligence Car (2018)" is a top-level plan for the intelligent car industry. The "Action Plan for the Development of the Intelligent Connected Vehicle (ICV) Industry (2018)" focuses on building an intelligent car industry system and proposes a medium- to long-term plan for the Internet of Vehicles. The "Development Plan for the New Energy Vehicle Industry (2021-2035)" (2020) proposed to develop connected and intelligent technology to build a technology supply system for key automotive components. The Supreme People's Court's report on how people's courts strengthen civil trial work by law and services to ensure sustainable and healthy economic and social development. The report also proposed legislative regulations on new issues such as the legal status of embryos, data rights, autonomous driving, copyright ownership of robot creations, and digital currency that have arisen along with the development of science and technology. When a driverless car is involved in a car accident, the information in the black box can be disclosed, which includes the user's privacy and other personal information. The protection of this type of data needs to be strengthened. Disputes and tort liability may occur after an accident involving a driverless car. Appropriate pre-prevention and post-factual supervision systems should be in place to avoid private information and data leakage so that protection and regulation can be carried out by operable provisions in laws and regulations.

Some scholars proposed establishing laws and policy regulations compatible with AI for its development. They suggest building a new social governance system and combining technology with law to establish a reasonable risk control mechanism relying on diverse value objectives with safety at the centre through discussions on laws, policies and ethical norms (Wu 2017). Some scholars pointed out that emphasis should be placed on the personal privacy and data protection of intelligent connected vehicles, exploring the protection of personal privacy and personal data security through technical methods such as federated learning, anonymization, and differential privacy. They suggest clarifying data property rights protection rules for intelligent connected vehicles and exploring mechanisms for sharing and disclosing data related to the safety of intelligent connected vehicles to jointly improve technical security and help the healthy development of the industry. Autonomous vehicle traffic accidents involve various legal relationships such as traffic accidents, product liability, and insurance. It is recommended that relevant judicial interpretations be formulated to guide the handling of accident disputes. A national autonomous driving data management platform should be established to supervise data collected by various car companies and ensure personal message security and national security. It can also provide data support for vehicle recalls, legal dispute handling, etc.

References

A criminal justice reform brand that defies party lines (2022). https://www.ideo.org/project/the-just-trust. Accessed 28 Oct 2022

Alison P (2018) Amplifying relationships through place and locality in the design of local government digital services. She Ji: J Design Econ Innov 4(1):47–59

Anderson L, Ostrom A, Corus C et al (2013) Transformative service research: an agenda for the future. J Bus Res 66(8):1203–1210

AnJie Broad Law Firm (2017) Competing fairly in the digital age-implications of new Anti-unfair Competition Law. https://www.lexology.com/commentary/competition-antitrust/china/anjie-law-firm/competing-fairly-in-the-digital-age-implications-of-new-anti-unfair-competition-law. Accessed 28 Nov 2022

Anthopoulos LG, Siozos P, Tsoukalas IA (2007) Applying participatory design and collaboration in digital public services for discovering and re-designing e-government services. Gov Inf Q 24(2):353–376

Baines TS, Lightfoot HW, Benedettini O et al (2009) The servitization of manufacturing: a review of literature and reflection on future challenges. J Manuf Technol Manag 20(5):547–567

Beijing High People's Court (2022, May 31) The case of Fangzhou dream (Beijing) Technology Co., Ltd. v. Zhu Yajun, Design Patent Infringement Dispute [2022] Jing Minzhong No.206

Beijing Intellectual Property Court (2016) Beijing Qihoo Technology Co. Ltd. et al. v. Beijing Jiangminxinke Technology Co. Ltd. Infringement of Design Patent Disputes [2016] No.276

Beuren FH, Ferreira MGG, Miguel PAC (2013) Product-service systems: a literature review on integrated products and services. J Clean Prod 47:222–231

Brown D, Cameron E (2005) Designing the interface. Int Rev Law Comput Technol 19(1):65–81

Buchanan S, McMenemy D (2012) Digital service analysis and design: the role of process modelling. Int J Inf Manag 32(3):251–256

Carroll NR (2014) Mobile medical app regulation: preventing pandemic of mobilechondriacs. Saint Louis Univ J Health Law Policy 7(2):415–448

Caslowitz C (1993) Trade dress and section 43(a) of the Lanham act: protection for total image of the visual displays of software applications. IDEA: J Law Technol 33(2):187–198

Castner M (1997) Copyright law: the software user interface. Adelphia Law J 12:33–92

Chao B (2016) Horizontal innovation and interface patents. Wis Law Rev 2:287–336

Chen CY (2020) On the identification of trademark infringement of app logo. China Trademark 8:61–65

Chen XP, Hu TJ (2021) Legislative regulation of APP subject. Adm Law 1:122–129

Chi YQ, Feng L, Qi JY (2021) Construction of enterprise data protection maturity model in the context of digital transformation. J Intelligence 40(09):133–140

Chou JR (2021) A TRIZ-based product-service design approach for developing innovative products. Comput Ind Eng 161:1–19

Cruz A (2017) International IP: harmonizing the protection of graphical user interfaces. Connecticut J Int Law 33(1):137–161

David D (2022) Review of the legal design book: doing law in the 21st century. She Ji: J Design Econ Innov 8:171–173

Diao YY (2021) The protection of unfair competition law on the collection of works data involving internet platforms. China Publishing 9:24–28

Edvardsson B, Olsson J (1996) Key concepts for new service development. Serv Ind J 16(2):140–164

Feng Z, Hu HY (2021) The protection of traditional factors of production rights and the construction of data rights brought about by new technology. In: Paper presented at the Shanghai Legal Studies—Collection of Chinese Articles on Emerging Rights and the Rule of Law 6:126–135

Fox B (2014) Mobile medical apps: where health and internet privacy law meet. Houston J Health Law Policy 14:193–222

Gao Y, Zhang Q, Xu XF et al (2022) Service design for the destination tourism service ecosystem: a review and extension. Asia Pacific J Tourism Res 27:225–245

Gao Z (2021) The sword of damocles: how the fair use defense application affects the computer programming area. Touro Law Rev 37(2):957–1000
Hangzhou Railway Transportation Court (2018) Shenzhen Tencent Computer System Co. Ltd. et al. v. Hangzhou Kebei Network Technology Co. Ltd. et al. Unfair Competition Dispute Case [2018] No.1020
He PY, Wang XR (2018) Security assurance mechanism of smartphone users' privacy based on "privacy clause" of third-party application. Inf Stud Theory Appl 41(10):40–46
He RK, Hu Y (2015) Research on design patterns and strategies in the concept derivation stage of service design. Design 1:40–49
Holopainen M (2010) Exploring service design in the context of architecture. Serv Ind J 30:597–608
Hu Y (2017) Design pattern and strategy of service design concept derivation stage. Hunan University Press, Changsha, p 2
Hu Y, Yu WY, Ren ZZ et al (2021) Coordinating role of six-hat thinking technique in design team during idea-generation phase of service design. Think Skills Creat 39:1–14
Hubei High People's Court (2022) Transparent Life (Wuhan) Information Technology Co., Ltd. and Wuhan Mei Zhi Cultivation Information Technology Co. [2022] No.500
Huotari KK, Patrício L, Zhang J et al (2021) Service system transformation through service design: linking analytical dimensions and service design approaches. J Bus Res 136:343–355
Ji WD (2019) The ideas, laws and policies for AI development. Oriental Law 5:4–13
Jin GZ (2018a) Artificial intelligence and consumer privacy. NBER Working Papers: 439–462
Jin Y (2018b) Design patent protection of graphic user interface (GUI): take the first case of GUI as an example. Creat Design 3:92–97
Jin Y (2022) The limits and possibilities of data property right under the logic of digital governance. Jinan J (Philosophy Soc Sci) 44(07):29–43
Junginger S, Sangiorgi D (2009) Service design and organisational change: bridging the gap between rigour and relevance. In: Paper presented at the IASDR09 conference, pp 4339–4348
Karpen IO, Gemser G, Calabretta G (2017) A multilevel consideration of service design conditions: towards a portfolio of organisational capabilities. J Serv Theory Pract 27(2):384–407
Kilker S (2016) Effectiveness of federal regulation of mobile medical applications. Wash Univ Law Rev 93(5):1341–1370
Kim YS, Park JA (2021) Design thinking in the framework of visual thinking and characterization of service design ideation methods using visual reasoning model. Des J 24:931–953
Kuijken B, Gemser G, Wijnberg NM (2017) Effective product-service systems: a value-based framework. Ind Mark Manag 60:33–41
Kurtmollaiev S, Fjuk A, Pedersen PE et al (2018) Organizational transformation through service design: the institutional logics perspective. J Serv Res 21(1):59–74
Leddy K, Kaldenberg D, Becker B (2003) Timeliness in ambulatory care treatment: an examination of patient satisfaction and wait times in medical practices and outpatient test and treatment facilities. J Ambul Care Manage 26(2):138–149
Lee SP (2020) Contexts of briefing for service design procurements in the Finnish public sector. Des Stud 69:1–39
Li XR, Jiang H, Gu JZ (2021) Design of internet of things intelligent fresh food logistics terminal under new retail mode. Comput Appl Softw 7:23–28
Li XW (2014) Design protection of graphical user interface (GUI) of electronic products. Intellectual Property Publishing House, Beijing, p 36
Li YJ (2021) Internet platform data monopoly: theoretical differences, governance practices and policy suggestions. Frontiers 21:56–66
Liang CY (2018) Tmall and Cainiao form blockchain alliance, SIXTH TONE. http://www.sixthtone.com/news/1001827/tmall-and-cainiao-form-blockchain-alliance. Accessed 28 June 2022
Lin JR, Yang TH (2011) Strategic design of public bicycle sharing systems with service level constraints. Transp Res Part E Logist Transp Rev 47(2):284–294
Liu SH (2020) On mobile phones automatic recording of user's movement track and personal information protection. Law Rev 38(05):101–111

Liu X, Jiang N, Ou ZH, Ma YW (2021) Research on the protection of enterprise data rights and interests in the digital economy era. J Intell 40(10):91-98+107
Lotus Dev. Corp. v. Borland Int'l, 516 U.S. 233 (Affirming through a nondecision the First Circuit's ruling denying Lotus a copyright in the user interface of their Lotus 1–2-3 spreadsheet program)
Luo SJ, Zou WY (2018) Research status and progress in service design. Pack Eng 39(24):43–53
Lusch RF, Nambisan S (2015) Service innovation: a service-dominant logic perspective. MIS Q 39(1):155–175
Ma YP (2022) Reconstruction of the protection path of graphical user interface under localized design system. Electr Intell Prop 6:66–75
Manzini E (2013) Making things happen: social innovation and design. Des Issues 30(1):57–66
Manzini E, Rizzo F (2011) Small projects/large changes: participatory design as an open participated process. CoDesign 7:199–215
Mont OK (2002) Clarifying the concept of product-service system-ScienceDirect. J Clean Prod 10(3):237–245
Moro SR, Miguel PAC, Mendes GHS (2022) Adding sustainable value in product-service systems business models design: a conceptual review towards a framework proposal. Sustain Prod Consump 32:492–504
Mostert F, Jue W (2018) The application and challenges of blockchain in intellectual property driven businesses in China. Tsinghua China Law Rev 11(1):13–42
Neville D (1996) Thermal windows: how well-insulated are software developers from copying of their programs' visual displays. Missouri Law Rev 61(1):203–214
Nissenbaum H, Wang Y (2021) Respecting context to protect privacy: why meaning matters. J Cyber Inf Law 1:3-28+236
Norman DA, Stappers PJ (2015) Design X: complex sociotechnical systems. She Ji: J Design Econ Innov 1(2):83–106
Ostrom AL, Parasuraman A, Bowen DE et al (2015) Service research priorities in a rapidly changing context. J Serv Res 19(2):127–159
Otani K, Waterman B, Faulkner K et al (2010) How patient reactions to hospital care attributes affect the evaluation of overall quality of care, willingness to recommend, and willingness to return. J Healthc Manag 55(1):25–37
Patrício L, Pinho NFD, Teixeira JG et al (2018) Service design for value networks: enabling value cocreation interactions in healthcare. Serv Sci 10(1):76–97
Patrício L, Sangiorgi D, Mahr D et al (2020) Leveraging service design for healthcare transformation: toward people-centered, integrated, and technology-enabled healthcare systems. J Serv Manag 31(5):889–909
Pine BJ, Gilmore JH (1998) Welcome to the experience economy. Harv Bus Rev 76(4):97–105
Prajapati V (2021) Intellectual property protection of graphical user interface. Int J Law Manage Human 4:2561–2571
Raddats C, Naik P, Bigdeli AZ (2022) Creating value in servitization through digital service innovations. Ind Mark Manag 104:1–13
Risch M (2014) Functionality and graphical user interface design patents. Stanf Technol Law Rev 17:53–106
Sangiorgi D (2011) Transformative services and transformation design. Int J Des 5(1):29–40
Secomandi F, Snelders D (2011) The object of service design. Des Issues 27(3):20–34
Shostack GL (1977) Breaking free from product marketing. J Mark 41(2):73–80
Stigler R (2014) Ooey GUI: the messy protection of graphical user interfaces. Northwest J Technol Intellect Prop 12(3):213–252
Struwe S, Slepniov D (2021) Conflict by design and why institutions matter in service design: a case of a German creative agency in China. J Bus Res 130:124–136
Sun YZ (2015) The copyright protection of computer software application program interface (API)-an appraisal of the infringement case of Oracle Corp. v. Google Inc. in the United States. China Copyright 5:61–66

Trischler J, Pervan J, Kelly SJ et al (2018) The value of codesign: the effect of customer involvement in service design teams. J Serv Res 21(1):75–100
Tu YQ (2016) China's mHealth service system and the improvement of its legal supervision. Wuhan Univ J (Philosophy Soc Sc) 69(06):107–118
Vargo SL, Lusch RF (2004) Evolving to a new dominant logic for marketing. J Mark 68(1):1–17
Vink J, Edvardsson B, Edman KW et al (2019) Reshaping mental models-enabling innovation through service design. J Serv Manag 30(1):75–104
Vink J, Huotari KK, Tronvoll B et al (2021) Service ecosystem design: propositions, process model, and future research agenda. J Serv Res 24(2):168–186
Wang J, Li R, Ding G et al (2022a) Product-service system engineering characteristics design for life cycle cost based on constraint satisfaction problem and Bayesian network. Adv Eng Inform 52:1–16
Wang JG, Guo HJ, Chen JW (2022b) Research on extension innovation model in the creation process of service design. Proc Comp Sci 199:992–999
Wang LF (2016) On attributes and trademark infringement of mobile internet app logos. J Shanghai Univ Finance Econ 18(01):109–116
Wang TE (2022) An ethical crossing of the "responsibility gap" in artificial intelligence application: taking the self-driving car as a typical case. Philosop Anal 13(01):15-30+196
Wang XQ, Lei SH (2018) Research on the impact of artificial intelligence on consumption and shopping experience in the new retail environment-based on the perspective of commercial retail reform and human goods yard system reconstruction. J Commer Econ 17:5–8
Watson, supra note 41, at 254 n.16
Wu HD (2017) Institutional arrangements and legal regulation in the age of artificial intelligence. Sci Law (J Northwest Univ Polit Sci Law) 35(05):128–136
Yan CX, Xiao DJ, Gong MS (2020) Research on new retail encounter service design for hotel scene-a case study of Netease Yan Xuan. Design 5:70–74
Yang XL, Feng XW (2016) Analysis of problems and countermeasures of mobile health service in China. Med Philos (A) 37(05):1-4+38
Yu E, Sangiorgi D (2017) Service design as an approach to implement the value cocreation perspective in new service development. J Serv Res 21(1):40–58
Zhang L, Wang Y (2017) Discussion on relevant legal regulatory issues of mobile health applications. J Qiqihar Univ (Philos Soc Sci Edn) 6:71-73+86
Zhang XB (2019) Collection of personal information: restricting the application of the principle of informed consent. J Comp Law 6:1–20
Zhang Y, Chen XY, Yang TW et al (2015) Ethical issues and countermeasures and suggestions for mobile medicine. Chinese Med Ethics 28(03):332–335
Zhao HL (2022) International legal conflicts and countermeasures for personal information protection from the perspective of data sovereignty. Contemp Law Rev 36(04):82–91
Zheng ZY (2014) Design standpoint extends the concept of service design. China Light Industry Press, Beijing, p 139
Zhou K, Du G, Jiao RJ (2022a) Personalized service product family design optimization considering crowdsourced service operations. Comput Ind Eng 166:1–18
Zhou WH, Wu Q, Tian X et al (2022b) A study on the practical framework of data governance in the U.S. Federal Government-policy-based analysis and implications. Modern. Intelligence 42(08):127–135

Chapter 7
Design Innovation and The Future of Intellectual Property

7.1 Emergence of New Technologies

Scientific advances have brought about new technologies which have impacted design in various ways. In this section, artificial intelligence, 3D printing technology and Internet of Things (IoT) technology will be introduced from three perspectives: the definitions, advantages and applications.

7.1.1 Artificial Intelligence Design

Artificial intelligence, or AI for short, is essentially a simulation of human thought processes, a concept that dates back to 1956. The research and application of robots has become an important symbol of measuring the level of scientific and technological innovation and high-end manufacturing of a country, and it is a strategic field to seize the opportunity of the development of an intelligent society.

(1) Relevant concepts

Artificial intelligence (AI) refers to the simulation of human intelligence in machines that are programmed to think like humans and mimic their actions. The term may also be applied to any machine that exhibits traits associated with a human mind such as learning and problem-solving.

Artificial intelligence leverages computers and machines to mimic the problem-solving and decision-making capabilities of the human mind. In the field of product design, AI has long since been accepted. Computers, in fact, have now designed furniture, bicycles, and even drones. The buzzword is "generative design". In this process, designers and engineers are no longer using computers simply as passive machines. Instead, they are using AI algorithms and cloud computing to rapidly develop solutions with an infinite number of alternatives.

N. Jiang, *Design, Innovation and Intellectual Property*,
https://doi.org/10.1007/978-981-95-2042-8_7

Artificial intelligence products refer to the content completed by or with the aid of artificial intelligence technology, including works, inventions, designs and other forms of expression. According to the degree of dependence on human beings in the creation process of artificial intelligence, the products of artificial intelligence are classified into products from human beings (the first type of products) and products not from human beings (the second type of products).

(2) The advantages of designing with AI assistance

In the coming years, people can expect AI to provide more services to consumers, businesses and the public sector, and many technology experts predict that people will use AI to do more design work. Here are a few ways AI can help design.

- AI stimulates creativity

The human mind's creativity is the biggest differentiator between machines and humans. Artificial Intelligence helps boost creativity for designers, by taking care of some usual work that saves time and efforts for the designer to spend on idea building.

AI is like a virtual assistant for the designer. It takes care of the stuff here and there, so the designer can focus on ideas and creativity. For example, an AI assistant will help collect data or find relevant references for you. Or find the best editing software for you. Adobe is already utilizing AI with its Sensei Stitch that identifies patterns in photos for patching.

- AI identifies user preferences

Artificial Intelligence is the uncrowned hero for analyzing user behavior and preferences. The algorithm identifies designs and platforms that users like spending time on. It provides designers with a pathway to follow, so a consistent, user-friendly, and effective design is crafted.

It goes beyond helping designers. Artificial Intelligence helps anyone and everyone in fostering a creative flare. It helps make designs by suggesting interesting tips and tricks for that added creativity.

- AI creates multiple variants

Artificial Intelligence helps designers create multiple variants after recognizing a pattern. The algorithm extracts colors and patterns of a design and then creates thousands of variants, within the range of identified colors and patterns.

This application is extensively useful for designers. Think of logo designing, for example. Designers can identify brand colors and abstract patterns. Artificial Intelligence can then use the patterns to create various different and unique designs while staying in the domain.

It is helpful for designers when they are struggling with creativity. The numerous visual options available can help designers and clients make a choice easily. Also, it opens doors to creativity and helps designers with different color combinations and patterns.

• AI helps non-professionals

Not everyone is a designer. Not everyone can become one. With AI-driven designing platforms, non-professionals can easily design, without any hassle. Logojoy is a perfect example. Not only does it create logos, but it also provides branding material such as envelopes, letterheads, and so on. The AI-driven algorithm crafts solutions for users, driven from the data.

Platforms like Medium have amazed authors with their simple and easy-to-use user interface. The numerous designs and templates give authors an exciting platform to share their content. The authors can customize the template to give it a personal touch.

(3) Cases of AI design

This section introduces two examples of AI design, one for business and the other for art. Despite their different fields, they all represent advances in AI autonomous design.

One of the latest examples that designing for AI has been popular is the Nutella packaging design. The project was named "Nutella Unica". It is a designing algorithm that pulled dozens of patterns and colors to create 7 million versions of covers. And it has been a huge hit and all these unique designs have been printed into jars, which made all the jars to be sold in just one month.

If these weren't designed without considering the empathetic context for the customer, selling these jars would have taken ages.

Next, the case of art. In the Netherlands, art experts used 3D scans to digitize 346 paintings by Rembrandt. They then fed the data into a deep learning algorithm and set a task that would test the program's ability to learn. On the basis of artificial AI, a picture was to be created depicting a "white, middle-aged man with facial hair" wearing "black clothes with a white collar and a hat."

The resulting image, made up of 148 million pixels and 150 gigabytes of data, was then 3D-printed to give it the same texture as an oil painting. The digital "painting" was so authentic-looking that even experts thought they were seeing an original Rembrandt.

What's certain is that we are experiencing a change - or even a revolution - in the processes involved in art and design. And if an algorithm can design, compose, and write copy, this is bound to change the work done in the creative professions.

7.1.2 3D Print Design

The 3D Printing technology was developed on the basic principle of Rapid Prototyping. Prototyping is the process of building an early-stage model, sample, or testing version of the actual product to be developed. Prototyping helps in the development process of the product and ensures the optimum output of the final product. 3D printing technology is also currently being used in the field of design as an important aid to mankind.

(1) Relevant concepts

3D printing, also known as additive manufacturing, began in the 1980s as a technology for additive rapid prototyping to manufacture products. Different from the traditional isometer or subtractive manufacturing, 3D printing has epoch-making significance in overcoming manufacturing bottlenecks, expanding manufacturing fields, and improving manufacturing capabilities.

3D printing design is the organic combination of 3D printing technology and design, in each stage of design with the advantages of 3D printing rapid prototyping, creative design or improvement of products.

(2) Advantages of applying 3D printing technology for design

Additive manufacturing, aka 3D printing, is the process of producing 3-dimensional objects from a computer file, where the part is built by adding material layer-by-layer.

Today, more companies in a variety of industries are embracing the 3D printing process as it presents many significant advantages over the more traditional manufacturing methods of subtractive manufacturing and injection molding.

- High efficiency

One of the biggest advantages of 3D printing technology is Rapid Prototyping. Rapid prototyping is the ability to design, manufacture, and test a customized part in as little time as possible. Also, if needed, the design can be modified without adversely affecting the speed of the manufacturing process.

Before 3D printing industry came to flourish, a prototype would take weeks to manufacture. Every time a change was made, another few weeks of time were added to the process. With shipping times figured in, fully developing a product from start to finish could easily take a year.

With 3D printing techniques, a business can design a part, manufacture it in-house on a professional 3D printer, and test it, all within a few days (and sometimes even less).

- Outstanding flexibility

Another big advantage of 3D printing is that any given printer can create almost anything that fits within its build volume.

With traditional manufacturing processes, each new part or change in part design, requires a new tool, mold, die, or jig to be manufactured to create the new part. In 3D printing, the design is fed into slicer software, needed supports added, and then printed with little or no change at all in the physical machinery or equipment.

3D printing allows the creation and manufacture of geometries impossible for traditional methods to produce, either as a single part, or at all. Such geometries include hollow cavities within solid parts and parts within parts.

- Strong market competitiveness

Because of the speed and lower costs of 3D printing, product life cycles are reduced. Businesses can improve and enhance a product allowing them to deliver better products in a shorter amount of time.

3D printing is conducive to saving energy and raw materials, and achieving social benefits such as environmental protection. It has the advantage of simplifying manufacturing procedures and shortening the development cycle. In addition, 3D printing can promote the manufacture and dissemination of products and increase consumer welfare.

(3) Cases of designs using 3D printing technology

There are many practical cases of 3D printing design, among which the application of 3D printing technology in the field of architectural design is the most common. In recent years, due to the ravages of COVID-19, the practice of this technology in the medical and health field has made remarkable achievements.

Cases of 3D printing design in the field of health care are as follows: Spanish brand Nagami Design has switched the use of its robotic arm from making furniture to 3D-printing face shields for medical staff treating coronavirus patients. Nagami Design usually makes objects such as 3D-printed chairs by Zaha Hadid Architects, but has converted its manufacturing process to address the shortage of protective equipment in hospitals. The brand's Covid-19 masks consist of a visor that is worn across the forehead and secured behind the ears with elastic. Clear plastic film is fastened to a second band attached to the visor, forming a protective shield that can be cleaned or replaced when it becomes contaminated. 3D printing has emerged as the ultimate tool for local manufacturing, reducing the production chain to the bare minimum. With COVID-19 emergency, this technology provides the opportunity to efficiently produce affordable tools, which are now essential to help save lives.

Besides, in Xianning, China, it would seem that additive manufacturing has facilitated this reorganization: Winsun has indeed 3D printed several isolation houses to accommodate quarantined people and medical staff and thus relieve the overloaded hospitals are facing.

The use of 3D printing in the construction sector is not new and has many advantages, including being able to provide a fallback solution in a crisis situation. Being faster, this method of manufacturing makes it possible to create temporary dwellings in an emergency, regardless of the area. Winsun has understood this and has used its 3D printing technology to address this global crisis. Originally, these small houses were intended for the tourism sector: as they are easily deployable in any location.

3D printing design cases in the field of architectural design are as follows:

Yinka Ilori has created vibrant patterns for the first public basketball court in Canary Wharf, London's financial district, which features a 3D-printed floor. The half-sized court is squeezed into a small lot in Bank Street Park and designed for three-a-side basketball, which sees both teams shoot into a single hoop. Unlike the hardwood or concrete floors typically used for the sport, Ilori's court is covered in 3D-printed polypropylene tiles produced by Hampshire company OnCourt. This allows the designer's kaleidoscopic court markings, which feature his hallmark geometric motifs, to be embedded into the material itself rather than just being painted on top. The technique is meant to ensure greater durability.

Construction technology outfit ICON and architecture studio Lake Flato have completed a 3D-printed, modern ranch-style home in Austin to be displayed during the SXSW festival.

The home is sited in a single-family residential neighbourhood in East Austin, Texas, and was built using ICON's Vulcan construction system.

The system uses 3D printing, a technology that dispenses layers of material mechanically based on a computer program, to lay the walls of the 2000-square-foot (186-square-metre) home. The 3D-printed wall aspects took 10 days to print.

The home was built using biophilic design principles, claiming that the soft curves of the 3D-printed support walls create "naturalistic circulation routes throughout the home". In addition to being able to build houses faster, the technology could mean that homes like this could be built at lower cost.

7.1.3 IoT Design

The seamless connection between machines, humans, and data means that IoT simplifies, improves, and automates processes. Sensors, coupled with connectivity and artificial intelligence, have the potential to make several systems more efficient. It cuts costs in areas that were historically not possible. Designing with IoT technology or thinking is also a sign of design innovation.

(1) Relevant concepts

The Internet of Things is an extension and expansion of the network on the basis of the Internet, which comprehensively applies various sensing technologies, through radio frequency identification, infrared sensors, global positioning systems and other information sensing equipment, in accordance with the agreed protocol, any item and the Internet are connected to exchange information and communicate. The Internet of Things can connect all objects to the network, facilitate identification, management and control, and bring more convenience to people's lives. The development of Internet of Things technology will drive the rapid development of related industries and applications, and realize the rapid development of Internet of Things terminals. Making use of the feature of "everything connected" to design and improve the product is the Design of the Internet of Things.

(2) The advantages of applying IoT technology for design

- Less energy and fuel consumption

Companies empowered by IoT monitoring systems report a reduction in energy consumption by 5–15% throughout the year. Insights from smart systems help to detect and eliminate resource leaks as well as find a new and smoother way for machines to operate.

The impact on energy consumption will account for approximately 1.8 PWh of electricity saved in 2030, and an additional 3.5 PWh of fuel. The electricity consumption in the United States, by comparison, was about 3.8 trillion kilowatt-hours (kWh) in 2020. The biggest contribution to electricity savings will be associated with smart electricity grids.

Besides the positive impact on consumption, IoT-based solutions have affected businesses by providing an opportunity for better waste management, including its monitoring and reduction.

- Boost efficiency and profits

As a result of machine downtime reduction, automatization, and less energy consumption, real-time data businesses experience growth in their efficiency and productivity. In addition, IoT can provide accurate data about the production process at different stages of manufacturing, hence allowing to identify bottlenecks in the process and increasing the throughput capacity of the production. Together all these benefits increase profits significantly.

The emergence of new business models: Technologies led to the Industrial Revolution also known as industry 4.0, which features high devices interconnectivity, IoT, enormous amounts of data, automation, machine learning, and Big Technology methods.

Wearable technology market: Smart devices like smartwatches, bracelets, and other accessories connected to the Internet are replacing traditional devices. They provide additional functionalities like NFC payments as well as gather meaningful information to users like step counting or sleep tracking. The Wearable Technology Market was valued at $27.91 billion in 2020, and the forecasting growth of the market size is expected to reach $74 billion by 2026, hence triple its value. This market is big and this IoT trend is on the rise.

7.2 Design Innovation Based on Social Issues

With the rapid development of digital technology, the application of technology has become an important part of daily design, forming a deeper connection between design and human needs, prosperity and well-being. Good design must be closely related to the society, which will be produced from the insight into society to solve social problems and increase social well-being. This section will introduce design innovation based on social issues from three aspects, namely: epidemic-based design innovation, design innovation in smart healthcare, and design innovation for ecological protection.

7.2.1 Epidemic-based Design Innovation

(1) Overview

The COVID-19 pandemic, also known as the coronavirus pandemic, is a global pandemic of coronavirus disease 2019 (COVID-19) caused by severe acute respiratory syndrome coronavirus 2 (SARS-CoV-2). The novel virus was first identified from an outbreak in Wuhan, China, in December 2019. Attempts to contain it there failed, allowing the virus to spread to other areas of China and later worldwide. The World Health Organization (WHO) declared a Public Health Emergency of International Concern on 30 January 2020 and a pandemic on 11 March 2020. As of 16 July 2022, the pandemic had caused more than 561 million cases and 6.36 million confirmed deaths, making it one of the deadliest in history.

COVID-19 symptoms range from undetectable to deadly, but most commonly include fever, dry cough, and fatigue. Severe illness is more likely in elderly patients and those with certain underlying medical conditions. COVID-19 transmits when people breathe in air contaminated by droplets and small airborne particles containing the virus. The risk of breathing these in is highest when people are in close proximity, but they can be inhaled over longer distances, particularly indoors. Transmission can also occur if contaminated fluids reach the eyes, nose or mouth, and, rarely, via contaminated surfaces.

The pandemic triggered severe social and economic disruption around the world, including the largest global recession since the Great Depression. Widespread supply shortages, including food shortages, were caused by supply chain disruption. The resultant near-global lockdowns saw an unprecedented pollution decrease. Educational institutions and public areas were partially or fully closed in many jurisdictions, and many events were cancelled or postponed. Misinformation circulated through social media and mass media, and political tensions intensified. The pandemic raised issues of racial and geographic discrimination, health equity, and the balance between public health imperatives and individual rights.

(2) Cases of designs for COVID-19

Six designers from China have created a series of conceptual products that aim to improve public health in the wake of outbreaks like the coronavirus, from an ultraviolet sterilising lamp to a DIY upper body capsule. In response to the current outbreak of coronavirus disease (covid-19), the series of six product concepts are designed to protect both the user and those around them from the spreading of infection and disease. The series is named Create Cures, which can be abbreviated to CC. This is a reference to the common unit of measurement of cubic centimetres that is used in medical treatments—a deliberate choice from the group of designers.

7.2.2 Design Innovation in Smart Healthcare

(1) The Concept of Smart Healthcare

Smart healthcare refers to the combination of information technology and medical information to facilitate medical research, health management and clinical treatment with the help of modern computer, network and mobile technologies, thereby improving the quality of healthcare and enhancing patient satisfaction.

Smart healthcare was born out of the concept of "Smart Planet" proposed by IBM (Armonk, NY, USA) in 2009. Simply put, Smart Planet is an intelligent infrastructure that uses sensors to perceive information, transmits information through the internet of things (IoT), and processes the information using supercomputers and cloud computing. It can coordinate social systems and integrate them to realize the dynamic and refined management of human society. Smart healthcare is a health service system that uses technology such as wearable devices, IoT, and mobile internet to dynamically access information, connect people, materials and institutions related to healthcare, and then actively manages and responds to medical ecosystem needs in an intelligent manner. Smart healthcare can promote interaction between all parties in the healthcare field, ensure that participants get the services they need, help the parties make informed decisions, and facilitate the rational allocation of resources. In short, smart healthcare is a higher stage of information construction in the medical field.

(2) Principles of smart healthcare design

The real novelty in smart hospitals is the integration of the aforementioned solutions into a coherent and synergistic technological ecosystem, which requires healthcare institutions to configure these facilities according to specific design cornerstones:

Smart healthcare harmonization: Hospitals are not just a bunch of technical assets, but rather complex systems combining technologies, processes, and professionals. Making healthcare digital is not that difficult, but turning it into a smart discipline requires a full harmonization of clinical functions, staff members performing such functions, and technologies deployed to streamline them. To do so, smart hospitals rely on centers of excellence to supervise this transformation, staff training to promote digital literacy, healthcare BPM to optimize medical processes, and knowledge sharing across departments to set up new care programs.

Patient-centric healthcare: Smart hospitals embrace an approach to medical care focused on patients' physical and psychological well-being. This can be achieved by configuring physical and digital spaces, along with crafting patient engagement strategies, that can actively contribute to enhancing the patient experience and speeding up recovery (the so-called healing environments). Think of mobile apps for self-service scheduling and 24/7 clinical record accessibility, AI-powered smart triage solutions, or health wearables and other telemedicine tools to constantly monitor patients from the comfort of their homes.

Data-driven medical care: Another staple of smart hospitals is physicians' experience and intuition complemented with solid data analytics solutions for more efficient risk identification and diagnostics. This requires collecting patient data from their EHRs or via wearables and processing it with machine learning-powered analytical systems to better understand their conditions. A similar logic applies to medical equipment, which can be monitored with proper sensors to spot any sign of malfunction and set up proper maintenance operations.

Healthcare decentralization: Smart hospitals are not monolithic, all-encompassing structures, but rather flexible hubs and data aggregators working in partnership and exchanging an ongoing stream of information with other facilities within the same digital ecosystem. These include tech companies providing their expertise and other healthcare actors, such as laboratories and clinics, sharing clinical data and the respective workloads. Service externalization and cooperation can be unlocked through technologies like EHR, health mobile app development, virtual care and IoT-powered health wearables.

Workflow automation: Another way for smart hospitals to mitigate their operational and administrative burden is through automation, be it physical (with actual robots) or digital (via RPA bots and digital assistants). The adoption of robotics and RPA to streamline clinical processes, coupled with the implementation of RFID technologies for medical asset management, remarkably enhances accuracy and efficiency while allowing physicians to better focus on patient well-being.

Please refer to Fig. 7.1.

(3) The application of smart healthcare

The service targets of sma7t healthcare can be roughly divided into three categories: clinical/scientific research institutions (e.g., hospitals), regional health decision-making institutions, and individual or family users.

The application of smart healthcare can be divided as follows, based on different needs:

- Assisting diagnosis and treatment

With the application of technologies such as artificial intelligence, surgical robots, and mixed reality, the diagnosis and treatment of diseases has become more intelligent. Using artificial intelligence to build the clinical decision support system, it has achieved certain results, such as the diagnosis of hepatitis, lung cancer, and skin cancer. The accuracy of artificial intelligence diagnosis results exceeds that of human doctors. Machine learning-based systems are quite often even more accurate than experienced physicians, especially in pathology and imaging. The most outstanding and representative product in the field of clinical decision support systems is IBM's Watson, an intelligent cognitive system that provides an optimal solution

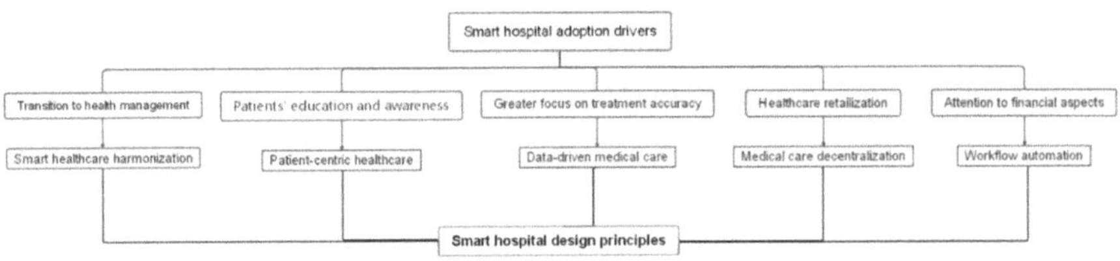

Fig. 7.1 Smart hospital adoption drivers and design principles. Note: Author independently created the Fig. 7.1 based on the book content

through in-depth analysis of all clinical data and literature data. The program has a great effect on the diagnosis of diabetes and cancer. Through the use of the clinical decision support system, doctors can give expert advice based on algorithms to improve the accuracy of diagnosis, reduce the incidence of missed diagnosis and misdiagnosis, and enable patients to receive timely and appropriate medical treatment.

- Health management

Since the beginning of the twenty-first century, chronic diseases have gradually occupied the top of the human disease spectrum and become a new epidemic. Chronic diseases have a long course of disease and are incurable and costly; therefore, the health management of the disease is particularly important. However, the traditional hospital- and doctor-centered health management model appears to be incapable of adequately dealing with the increasing number of patients and diseases. The new health management model under smart healthcare pays more attention to patient self-management. It emphasizes real-time self-monitoring of patients, immediate feedback of health data, and timely intervention of medical behavior. The emergence of implantable/wearable smart devices, smart homes, and smart health information platforms connected by IoT technology provides a solution to this situation.

- Disease prevention and risk monitoring

Traditional disease risk prediction is based on the initiative of the health authorities to collect patient information, compare that information with the guidelines of the authoritative organization, and finally release the prediction results. This method has a certain lag in time and does not provide accurate advice to individuals. Disease risk prediction under smart healthcare is dynamic and personalized. It enables patients and doctors to participate, proactively monitor their disease risk, and conduct targeted prevention based on their own monitoring results. The new disease risk prediction model collects data through wearable devices and smart apps, uploads them to the cloud through a network, and analyzes the results based on big data-based algorithms to feed back the predicted results to users in real time via short message service. These measures have been proven to be effective.

The prospects for smart healthcare are vast. For individual users, smart healthcare can facilitate better health self-management. Timely and appropriate medical services can be accessed when needed, and the content of medical services will be more personalized. For medical institutions, smart healthcare can reduce costs, relieve personnel pressure, achieve unified management of materials and information, and improve the patient's medical experience. For research institutions, smart healthcare can reduce the cost of research, reduce research time, and improve the overall efficiency of research. With regard to macro decision-making, smart healthcare can improve the status quo of medical resource inequality, push the process of medical reform, promote the implementation of prevention strategies, and reduce social medical costs. However, there are still some problems in the development process. The solution to these problems depends not only on technological progress, but also on the joint efforts of patients, doctors, health institutions, and technology companies.

7.2.3 Design Innovation for Ecological Protection

(1) Related Concepts

Eco-design, also known as green design, life cycle design, or environmental design, refers to considering environmental factors when designing to help determine design decisions. Eco-design requires that environmental factors be taken into account at all stages of product development, reducing negative impacts on the environment throughout the product's life cycle and ultimately leading to a more sustainable production and consumption system.

Green Design is an international design trend emerging in the late 1980s and it became the focus of modern design research in the 1990s. It represents people's reflection on the environmental and ecological damage caused by modern technology culture, and also reflects the return of designers' moral and social responsibility. With green design thinking, the design not only meets the indoor functional needs but also saves energy and protects the environment. It provides consumers with a healthy lifestyle, promotes the concept of green ecology, and promotes the sustainable development of the environment. It can be seen that green design is not only a design concept, but also an attitude to life, which requires people to set up a green consciousness of environmental protection to protect the environment, conserve resources, and do their best to improve the status quo of the environmental and ecological imbalance, to create a sustainable living environment.

(2) Principles of green design

- Prevention Instead of Treatment

It is better to prevent waste than to treat or clean up waste after it is formed. One of the central tenets of all green technologies is to make only the amount that is needed for the process at hand. From a business perspective, this makes absolute sense. If you purchase a quantity of a chemical, bit only use half of what was purchased, you will need to properly dispose of the remainder. You pay for the initial purchase and then pay the disposal costs, paying twice for something you didn't need in the first place. A related concept can be found in health care, in which we suggest vaccination to prevent disease. Better to get your flu shot in late fall than to suffer the agony of having the flu in the winter.

- Maximize Efficiency

Products, processes and systems should be designed to maximize mass, energy, space, and time efficiency. It is simplicity that will allow us, as a society, to become more sustainable. This is achieved by informing scientists and engineers to create designs that maximize efficiency in multiple areas such as mass, energy, space (i.e. real estate) and time. This is a simple and logical path that should be taken and the benefits gained can be quite significant. However, rather than focusing on these areas individually, by integrating these areas the benefits gained can be further increased. This is due to the high interdependence of one area on another.

- Meet Need, Minimize Excess

From sustainability point of view, building the manufacturing site to mostly like volume is preferred. If the demand is higher than the most likely volume, then one can manage the demand by adding over time or additional shift. If the demand is lower than the most likely volume, then consider product innovation actions (late point differentiators') to increase the demand to achieve the most likely volume. Also, designing with unnecessary capability will consume additional resources during all stages of the life cycle. For example, if the vehicle is designed to operate at all times in Alaska' December temperature, then the design will be inefficient and not optimal to operate in normal operating temperatures.

(3) Examples of green design

Green design plays a vital role in environmental protection and sustainable human development. This design concept is more often seen in the building sector, but there are also developments in the renewable energy sector.

- Green buildings

Green buildings today are some of the most beautiful works of architecture. They take inspiration from the natural world, and try to live with the environment not conquer it.

A Chicago firm, Urban Lab, built their home/studio to embody a plethora of sustainable features. It includes passive heating to take advantage of the sun in winter and shading from the sun in the summer. Care was taken in designing the site's water retention so to reduce the processing demand on the city. Large operable doors allow for ventilation when exterior temperatures allow reducing the demand for interior climate control, rain screens are also used to further sustainability.

Larger strides are being taken in high-rise construction as well. The global firm Perkins and Will is experimenting in building tall with timber. Trees capture carbon, and if replanted and harvested sustainably, have less embodied energy than steel.

As innovative architects like these lead the way, green architecture is becoming more mainstream in society. Everyone can benefit from the reduction in energy consumption and improved spaces green architecture creates—and it's in the best interest of our planet if we follow this philosophy.

When it opened a decade ago, the Pixel Building was Australia's first carbon-neutral office building, generating all its own power and water on site.

Among its energy-saving features are colorful, eye-catching panels that provide shade and maximize daylight as needed, supports that help process wastewater, a roof that captures rainwater, and a series of vertical wind turbines.

Shanghai Tower's graceful spiral is a site to behold—and its relatively low energy bill is another. The world's second tallest building at 2073 feet, Shanghai Tower is an architectural wonder as well as a sustainable one. A transparent second skin wrapped around the building creates a buffer of captured air that serves as natural ventilation, reducing energy costs, and 270 wind turbines incorporated into the facade power its exterior lights.

Thanks to measures like these, the tower uses significantly less power than other skyscrapers and has a platinum LEED certification.

Located in the heart of the largest city in China, the Shanghai Natural History Museum aims to tie Chinese history to the natural environment and to global ideas of sustainability. The gigantic, 749-square-foot construction includes a large oval pond, fed by rainwater collected atop the green roof, which promotes evaporative cooling.

The sustainable museum also has an "intelligent building skin" that reduces solar gain and maintains a comfortable room temperature at all times.

7.3 Design Innovation Poses New Challenges to the Intellectual Property System

The last two decades have seen an explosion of technologies that are transforming how we work and live in an increasingly interconnected digital world. The emergence and merging of frontier technologies is at the heart of what is sometimes termed Fourth Industrial Revolution or Industry 4.0. Frontier technologies are changing how we do business, how we innovate and create and the rate of change is increasing exponentially.

Today, new technologies are emerging that will have a significant impact on the existing IP landscape. While we do not yet fully understand all aspects of these technologies, it is possible to anticipate the major challenges that the IP system will face. It is also possible to anticipate significant challenges to development as a result of the wide variation in technological capabilities across the globe. But opportunities and challenges always follow each other. The developments that lead to these challenges are not in themselves negative. We just need to try to understand how these developments will affect the existing IP system and its future evolution.

7.3.1 Overview of Design Innovation and Intellectual Property System

(1) Establishment of Intellectual Property System

Intellectual property is a product of modern civilization and economic development. It originated in Italy, the center of an ideological and cultural emancipation movement, namely, the Renaissance(mid-14th century to the early 17th century). The Renaissance represented the anti-feudal struggle of the European emerging bourgeoisie in the field of ideology, emphasizing the respect for human nature and the concept of equality. The intellectual property system was born as a result of this technological and ideological progress.

In 1474, the Republic of Venice established the patent system which put forward three principles: protection of inventions, patent exclusivity, and infringement penalties. The exclusive protection for patents are granted by law: "Anyone else is forbidden to make a device identical with or similar to the invention without the inventor's consent and license for a period of 10 years. People who violate this law shall compensate the patentee with one hundred gold coins and the imitation should be destroyed immediately". Thanks to the patent system, Venice once attracted a large number of craftsmen from neighboring countries, who made great contributions to the prosperity of Venice's industry and commerce. Similarly, in the sixteenth and seventeenth centuries, under the influence of mercantilist policy, many European countries generally granted privileges, charters, franchises and licenses to inventors (craftsmen or industrialists), etc. In 1623, the British government promulgated the *Monopolies Act* which comprehensively stipulated the conditions for obtaining the subject and object of patent protection, the term of patent protection, the declaration of invalidity of patents, etc., and established the basic framework of patent law. Thus, the modern patent law was officially established and gradually spread to the U.S. and European countries.

The birth of copyright law is closely related to the invention and application of printing. Before the invention of printing, the concept of protecting author's right and their creativity has not been developed because works were copied by hand, which was a slow, time-consuming and costly process. After the German inventor Johannes Gutenberg printed the first Gutenberg Bible with movable type and mechanical printing in 1455, the view on the protection of works gradually changed. The invention of the printing in medieval Europe allowed publishers to print and sell large quantities of books, costing paper, ink, and less labor than ever before, because it only took the purchase of a machine and the cost of making plates for each book. Therefore, book publishing became an emerging business model. At this point, the value of the work itself has shifted from the traditional labor remuneration for manual copying to the profit of marketing the reproduced work by printing. Although the new business model was created and the cost of reproducing a work was lowered, publishers still had to invest a considerable amount of money in purchasing printing machines that were not affordable to everyone. So the object of protection was still the printed product rather than the author's original creation. In 1476, William Vaxton introduced movable type into England. In order to prevent the spread of opposition to the Crown through printing, the Crown required publishers to obtain permission from the government before printing, and all printed materials had to be inscribed with the name of the author and the place of publication, with the name of the printed material registered with the government. In 1557, the *Enabling Act* was enacted, which gave the right of licensing to printing to the Guild of Printers: the Guild would have the right of licensing, whose members were able to publish books and had the power to confiscate books that had not been licensed by the crown. From then on, professional writers' communities began to emerge and had a positive impact on the concept of safeguarding author's creation and the granting of property rights to writers. In 1709, after three years of lobbying by the Printers' Guild, the British Parliament passed *Queen Anna's Act* which became the world's first act centered on the protection of copyright holders.

(2) Interaction of Technology Innovation Practices and Intellectual Property System

In the seventeenth century, the first Industrial Revolution took place in England. Remarkable inventions in this period of time include the flying shuttle (1733), the "Jenny Spinner" (1765) and the improved Watt steam engine (1785). As the Industrial Revolution took place more than a hundred years after the establishment of the patent system, it may be indicated that the patent system may have been a key factor in facilitating the Industrial Revolution. During this period, publicly disclosed technical knowledge accumulated over time, gradually forming a huge public knowledge base, which laid a solid knowledge foundation for the emergence of the Industrial Revolution. Meanwhile, the exclusivity of patent protection also provided necessary institutional guarantee for the utilization of technology in the market. Take the steam engine as an example, Watt was not the first inventor of the steam engine. Rather, he worked on the basis of Newcomen-type steam engine and gradually improved its operational efficiency by trial and error. Further, owning to the patent on the steam engine, Watt received "venture capital" from entrepreneurs such as Baroque and Bolton, which in turn facilitated the marketization of steam engine technology. Thus, the patent system catalyzed the birth of the industrial revolution, and promoted the great development of industrial and machine-manufacturing-dominated economies. The technological innovation development went through the invention and application of the textile machine, steam engine and machine tools, gradually forming a more complete machine industry technology system.

In the second half of the nineteenth century, the establishment of electromagnetic theory and the invention of electric motors ushered in the era of electric power. Since steam power replaced electric power in industrial economy, technological innovation has also entered a new era where the development of the industrial economy was driven by breakthroughs in scientific theories. At the end of the nineteenth century, AC three-phase generators, electric motors, transmission and distribution transformers were invented one after another, and at the beginning of the twentieth century, high-power motors, electric locomotives and machine tools dragged by motors appeared. Notably, the whole industrial technological system underwent a fundamental change as inventions and innovations related to electric technology emerged in a large number of fields in various industries, and new technologies represented by electric power, internal combustion engines and synthetic materials developed rapidly. This period witnessed a great shift on the process of technological innovation which no longer relied on experience and skill, but more on scientific theoretical research and scientific experiments. In the second half of the twentieth century, information technology centered on computer technology has also developed rapidly, penetrating into various technical fields and even changing people's social life style. From then on, technological innovation has entered the era of information industry economy, in which innovation was characterized by the application of computer technology and electronic technology in various fields. In this period, a large number of technological innovations in new fields were emerging, such as atomic energy technology, space technology, laser technology, and especially microelectronics technology and gene technology after the 1970s. As a result, technological innovation has become the core driving force for enterprise development and national competition, and information technology, gene technology and nanotechnology have become the new power driving the world's scientific and technological revolution.

At various stages of technological development, the patent system has been continuously improved to meet new changes. In terms of the subject system, the demand for protecting technological innovation has triggered the transition of the subject of patent rights from natural persons to legal persons, which has also given rise to the service invention-creation. With the emergence of new technologies, scientific and technological innovation is gathering pace with the characteristic of high investment and high risk showed on technological innovation. In terms of the object system, the wide application of new technologies promotes a growing diversity on the object of technological innovation, as many subjects traditionally considered not belonging to the scope of patent protection are increasingly included. However, it leads to more conflicts between the traditional theories of the patent system and the innovation practice, adding to complicated challenges to the review of the object of patent protection. Besides, as human society has experienced different stages, from agricultural economy, handicraft economy, machine industry economy to scientific industrial economy and information industry economy, the process of technological innovation is becoming increasingly complex and the cost of technological innovation is getting higher, which lead to a longer cost-recovery period for investors. During the centuries-long development of the patent system, the term of patent protection has continuously been extended.

(3) Technology Innovation & Services Design Innovation

The process of design is a process of innovation, in which designers employ innovative thinking to stimulate their artistic inspiration and find new solutions to problems. It is indisputable to advocate and insist on innovation in design. Without the spirit of innovation and innovative efforts, designs will always be identical.

Design is subject to the influence of the science and technology development due to the changes in techniques, materials, tools, etc. There is a profound relationship between design and science and technology.

Technological advances have separated design from manufacturing. Before the Industrial Revolution, people tended to design by hand, and design can not be independent of manufacturing. While with technological progress, the emergence of mechanized mass production separated design from manufacturing and made it an independent profession. Machine production led to the standardization and integration of products, which helped lower the cost of design, such as the standard prefabricated unit components widely used in construction industry. These standard components were adopted to build the Crystal Palace exposition hall in 1851 and the Eiffel Tower in 1889.

New technologies will promote the development of design. For example, the technology of the copper plate camera invented in 1930 facilitated the adoption of photography in advertising design, and photography developed to become the foundation of today's photographic design. The emergence of movies and the employment of various new media such as radio and television accelerate the growth of advertising industry, and visual communication design is flourishing along with it. With the continuous innovation of communication technology, the expression methods of visual design have been greatly enriched, and the field of visual communication has been greatly extended at the same time.

Emerging information technology has caused epochal changes in design, production and model. With the development of computer technology and communication technology, computer software makes people's life more convenient. The design software represented by CAD has become the the tool used by majority of designers. Compared to the traditional hand-drawn method, this tool greatly improves the efficiency of the work, and facilitates network communication free from the limitations of the region. Design software allows graphic designers to freely use a large number of images, quickly foresee the effect of the work, so as to design excellent works. The traditional concept of design extends from the tangible material realm to the untouchable program realm.

It can be seen that the development of design is based on science and technology. At the same time, science and technology also depends on design to demonstrate its application. For a designer with a sense of social responsibility, the design should not only be closely integrated with science and technology, but also be added some characteristics of the times, such as sustainable design, green design, etc. Only for the benefit of the society and the interests of mankind can we prove the value of the design.

With the progress of science and technology, we have entered the era of Design 3.0, that is, with the aim to meet people's material and spiritual needs and promote ecological and environmental protection, try to provide design that realize harmony coordination of person, society as well as human and nature, and to achieve sustainable development design. In the cyber-physical and network computing environment that integrates Internet of Everything, Big Data, Artificial Intelligence, Cloud Computing and Cloud Services, Design 3.0 features green and low carbon, intelligent internet, and co-creation and sharing. Design innovation will contribute to social innovation in various perspectives. From the perspective of enterprise ecology, design innovation will improve the quality of manufacturing services, win the trust of users, gain competitive advantages in the market, create value, introduce new technology and new equipment, significantly improve quality and efficiency, and even trigger industrial changes, create demand, open up new markets, create a new ecology of the industry, and even create brand and cultural value for the enterprise. From the perspective of user experience, it can create new experience and value for users. From the perspective of social benefit, it can lead and promote the progress of social civilization and open up a better future.

In summary, the intellectual property system was established to protect scientific and technological innovations. Meanwhile, scientific and technological innovations, in turn, promoted the development of the intellectual property system. Since the twenty-first century, a new information technology revolution represented by the Internet, big data, and AI (compared to the previous traditional information revolution represented by telegrams, telephones, and television) has had a major impact on the world, profoundly changing the social form, appearance, and operating mechanism of all humankind. The latest technological innovations have also posed new questions for IP law and IP professionals. In this section, the author will introduce the challenges to the intellectual property system posed by the latest technology born in the Fourth Industrial Revolution.

7.3.2 Intellectual Property Protection for AI

AI becomes ever more powerful and efficient through rapid development and application. But it has posed many challenges to mankind in various fields. In the field of copyright law, AI can almost create content as fast as human creators. In the field of intellectual creation, humans are no longer the only creators of spiritual production. Since the end of 2022, general AI, represented by ChatGPT, has continued to emerge and has been widely used in economically and socially. People once again focus on the IP protection of AI. No matter how fast AI develops, the IP protection issues always revolve around data input, generated object definition and right holder.

(1) Legal Attribute of Data Entry Behavior

Machine learning requires massive amounts of data input by humans in advance. The data is knowledge and messages readable to a computer, which may cover works protected by copyright. Digitizing a work and entering it into an intelligent system is copying. Whether the copying is a lawful use or infringement is a legal issue involving data entry.

The copyright plans for reading old works and getting past knowledge mainly include licensing, statutory license system, and fair use. Licensing shows the exclusive effect of copyright, whereby creators can control the use of works by others, and receive cost rewards for intellectual labor through licensing, i.e. market transactions. Statutory licensing and especially fair use are a necessary restriction on copyright, because it divides the right boundaries between creators and users of works, reduces additional transaction costs for message resources, and ensures that users have reasonable access to copyrighted works.

In the age of AI, data entry, the boundary between fair use and statutory licensing, the technology support, legal regulations and implementations guarantees of statutory licensing are all difficult issues to be addressed. When choosing the copyright system, legislators in various countries mainly adopt the method of fair use but uphold different policy positions. Furthermore, based on the goal of encouraging intellectual creation and promoting the development of the machine intelligence industry, developed countries in Europe and the US have mostly passed written laws and case laws to establish copyright exceptions for text data storage and mining. But the scope of application and constitutive conditions for their fair use are different, showing the influence of their respective legal traditions and legislative policy considerations.

In a recent U.S. court decision, the issue of fair use in AI training was addressed in Thomson Reuters v. Ross Intelligence. On February 11, 2025, the U.S. District Court for the District of Delaware issued a summary judgment, holding that certain instances of infringement were clear and did not require a jury trial. The court found that Ross Intelligence had directly infringed Thomson Reuters' copyright by using annotated legal materials from the Westlaw database without authorization to train its AI-powered legal research tool, and rejected Ross's fair use defense.

The plaintiff, Thomson Reuters, is a global leader in legal information services and operates Westlaw, a well-known legal research platform that offers a vast collection of case law, statutes, and proprietary features such as legal annotations and the Key Number System, which classify and summarize judicial opinions. The defendant, Ross Intelligence, is an emerging legal technology company developing an AI-based legal search engine that directly competes with Westlaw. Ross initially sought a license from Thomson Reuters to use Westlaw data for training its AI models, but the request was denied due to Ross's competitive status. Ross then turned to a third-party service provider, LegalEase, from which it acquired 25,000 "bulk memoranda" as substitute training data. These memoranda were compilations of good and bad answers to specific legal questions, written based on Westlaw's legal annotations. Thomson Reuters alleged that Ross had copied Westlaw's case summaries in the process of training its AI system.

The court evaluated Ross's fair use defense based on the four statutory factors under U.S. copyright law: 1.Purpose and character of the use, including whether it is of a commercial nature or for nonprofit educational purposes, and whether the use is "transformative"; 2. Nature of the copyrighted work, focusing on the degree of creativity involved; 3. Amount and substantiality of the portion used in relation to the copyrighted work as a whole; 4. Effect of the use on the potential market for or value of the copyrighted work. After considering all four factors, the court concluded that Thomson Reuters prevailed on the two most important ones—the first and fourth factors—and thus rejected Ross's fair use defense.

First, the court found that Ross's use was clearly commercial in nature and lacked a transformative purpose. Ross had used the legal annotations to train its AI tool, which directly competed with Westlaw. The court emphasized that the functionality of Ross's AI tool closely mirrored Westlaw's—users would input a legal question and receive case law results through a mechanism similar to Westlaw's legal annotations and Key Number System. Because the use did not add a new or different purpose, it lacked transformative character, and its commercial, competitive nature weighed heavily against fair use. Second, the court found that Ross's copying negatively affected both the actual and potential markets for Thomson Reuters' work. It harmed Westlaw's current business and posed a threat to its potential market for licensing training data to AI developers—constituting a clear case of market substitution.

The court also addressed the public benefit argument, stating that even if Ross's use might benefit the public, this was not enough to qualify as fair use. While the public does have an interest in accessing legal information, the legal opinions themselves are publicly available. However, Thomson Reuters' curated legal annotations are original, copyrighted analyses. The court emphasized that public demand for access to such content does not justify copyright infringement. Moreover, copyright law aims to encourage the creation of socially valuable tools—such as high-quality legal research systems—and grants creators the right to receive economic returns for their work.

Recently, the Hangzhou Internet Court issued a judgment in a case involving the issue of fair use in the context of data training for artificial intelligence. The defendant, a smart technology company based in Hangzhou, operated the Chushou AI platform. Users of the platform could upload images and use them to train and share Ultraman AI models, which in turn could generate works that were substantially similar to the plaintiff's Ultraman character. The defendant, as a provider of generative AI services, charged fees for certain services on the platform. Although its user agreement stated that it did not review uploaded materials or generated content, the defendant actively encouraged users to publish their generated content. The court found that while the defendant did provide generative AI services, the infringing training materials were uploaded by users. Since there was no evidence that the defendant had co-created the infringing works with users, it did not constitute direct infringement.

However, the court held that the defendant failed to take necessary measures, appropriate to the technical level available at the time the infringement occurred, to prevent the infringement. By not fulfilling its reasonable duty of care, the defendant was found to have committed contributory (indirect) infringement. Although the infringing training materials in this case were user-uploaded, meaning the court did not directly address the most debated issue in the industry—whether the use of copyrighted works to train large AI models constitutes copyright infringement—the judgment nonetheless provided important reasoning on fair use in AI data training.

The court emphasized that, in order to promote the development of generative AI technologies, a relatively lenient and inclusive approach should be adopted when assessing infringement in the data input and training phase, while a stricter standard should apply to the output and use of generated content. This differentiated approach aims to strike a balance between innovation and protection. In principle, the court stated, the purpose of using others' works during the training phase is to enable the AI to learn and analyze the ideas, emotions, linguistic features, and stylistic elements expressed in prior works—thus facilitating the creation of new, transformative works. This use involves aggregating large volumes of existing works as analytical samples to improve creative capabilities, and is not aimed at reproducing the original expressions of those works. Therefore, in the absence of evidence showing that the generative AI system was trained with the intent to exploit the original expressive elements of copyrighted works, or that such training had negatively affected the normal use of the original works or unreasonably harmed the legitimate interests of rights holders, such training activity may be considered fair use.

(2) Protectability of AI-generated Objects

AI-generated objects are mainly divided into two categories: AI-generated works and AI-generated inventions. Depending on the conditions of protection, the protection provided by intellectual property law also varies.

Protectability of AI-generated works. Works under copyright law require originality and be able to be expressed in a certain form. This is the "protectability" of the work. Discussions on the "protectability" of intelligently generated content mainly focused on whether this type of work has originality. Some believe content generated by AI cannot be considered works within the definition of copyright law because they are all a result of algorithms, rules, and templates. Therefore, it cannot reflect the author's unique personality, or feelings. Although the generated content looks like a typical work, it lacks an internal personality foundation. Most scholars argue that the content generated by AI is copyrighted work and that the machine output is a product created by the will of the AI designer. The full participation of human beings in "algorithmic creation" brings about the personality elements in the work. The originality of the work can only be judged by the expression itself that has already been generated, that is, the determination of a copyrighted work should be estimated based on the expression results that have already been generated. Works generated by AI are indistinguishable from works created by humans in terms of the "form of expression of thought", that is, the appearance of the work. As long as they meet the requirements of originality, they can be "protectable".

The protectability of AI-generated inventions. In modern patent legislation and licensing practices, "protectable subjects" or new technological solutions that can be patented have always been adjusted and changed. The general trend is that the scope of "protectable topics" is gradually expanding. As a tool for generating new technology solutions, AI is in the upstream of invention and creativity activities, and itself is an outstanding technological innovation. Whether it is product innovation, method innovation downstream, or the innovation of the tools upstream, innovations are the purpose of patent law legislation. Therefore, they should be protected and encouraged by the patent law. The door to patent licensing should not be closed to an invention because it was created with AI, or that it was created independently by AI. If AI is excluded from "protectable topics", there will also be a few negative consequences. On the one hand, it fails to incentivize technological innovation through institutional design. If relevant inventions and creations fall into the public domain, "hitchhiking" will prevail. The spillover of benefits from new technology will make the profits of relevant industry players far below development costs, and the "lack of profit" in the market will eventually be expressed as the "lack of strength" in intelligent industry innovation activities. On the other, the open and commercial system for technological solutions is hindered. If the patent law does not protect AI-generated inventions, then the most valuable technical solutions generated by AI will tend to apply as a trade secret, which will lead to the closure of technical information and the waste of resources for repeated technology development. While AI generates inventions that do not or cannot adopt trade secret protection, no one wants to carry out industrial application or commercial development of these technologies because their investment expectations do not have effective protection of property rights. Therefore, patentable inventions can be protected by patent rights, but only if they are not exceptions to patent protection.

It can be seen that although AI-generated contents belong to a brand-new field, their intellectual property protection has not been excluded from the original framework. As long as AI-generated products meet traditional protection requirements, intellectual property protection can still be obtained.

The U.S. Copyright Office has repeatedly refused to grant copyright protection to artworks created solely by artificial intelligence. In the case of Thaler v. Perlmutter, the image in question, A Recent Entrance to Paradise, was autonomously generated by an AI system called Creativity Machine. The applicant, Stephen Thaler, made no modifications to the AI-generated image and submitted it as-is for copyright registration. The U.S. Copyright Office rejected the application on the grounds that the image lacked human authorship. The court affirmed this view, stating that "Human authorship is a bedrock requirement of copyright". In this case, the applicant neither provided creatively meaningful prompts to the AI nor engaged in any post-editing or processing of the output. As a result, the image did not meet the requirement of human authorship and was deemed ineligible for copyright protection.

Similarly, in the "Zarya of the Dawn" case, the U.S. Copyright Office once again denied protection to content generated by AI systems like ChatGPT. The Office reasoned that users cannot precisely predict or control the final output of tools like Midjourney through text prompts—they can only guide the direction of generation, but not determine the specific form of the result. In this decision, the Office emphasized that if the content is purely machine-generated or produced through automatic processes without human creative input or intervention, it cannot be registered as a copyrightable work.

In September 2023, the U.S. Copyright Office rejected registration for the work "Space Opera Theater", which was created using Midjourney, stating that the applicant, Jason Allen, had contributed only by providing text prompts to generate the image. Although Allen claimed to have issued at least 624 iterations and modifications, the final output still depended on how the AI interpreted his prompts. The Review Board acknowledged that some prompts might be sufficiently creative to qualify as literary works on their own. However, this does not mean that providing prompts alone "actually forms" the resulting image. Therefore, Allen's contribution did not demonstrate the "creative control" required for copyright protection. Moreover, although Allen used Adobe Photoshop and Gigapixel AI to edit the image generated by Midjourney, the Board found that such modifications did not add new expressive elements sufficient to reflect human creativity.

However, on January 30, 2025, the U.S. Copyright Office, for the first time, granted registration to a work entirely composed of AI-generated material—A

Single Piece of American Cheese—recognizing it as a compilation work protected by copyright. This decision marked a departure from the previously firm stance that "purely AI-created works" are not protectable. In approving registration, the Office stated that: "Keirsey's active selection, coordination, and arrangement of the AI-generated material contributed sufficient human original authorship, thereby satisfying the basic requirements for copyright eligibility". This case introduced the standard of "three-tier creativity", requiring the applicant to form an original expression by creatively selecting, coordinating, and arranging AI-generated elements—an approach analogous to protection for compilation works. This ruling reframes AI-generated output as a human-directed subject of rights, maintaining the centrality of human authorship while responding to the evolving challenges AI poses to the copyright system.

Accordingly, the current U.S. standard is that AI-generated content in itself is not copyrightable, but human-created compilations or collages of AI material—where the individual has made creative choices in structure, selection, or editing—may qualify for protection.

This landmark ruling does not abandon the fundamental position that purely AI-generated works lack protection. Instead, it uses the logic of compilation copyright to underscore a "human intervention-oriented" framework. Only when the human involved has made intellectually creative contributions in organizing AI material—such as by modifying structure, filtering content, or engaging in further processing—can the resulting work be recognized as reflecting sufficient intellectual labor to merit copyright protection.

In China's first copyright case concerning "AI-generated images from text prompts", the court explicitly affirmed that "creation by a natural person" remains a necessary condition for recognizing a work as copyrightable. The court held that the process of generating the image was not a case of "producing a work according to a fixed sequence, formula, or structure", but rather a process in which the AI generated an image based on the textual description input by a human. The AI acted in place of the human to draw lines and apply colors, giving tangible form to the human's creativity and ideas. The generation process, therefore, reflected the plaintiff's aesthetic choices and individual judgment. As a result, the court determined that the image in question possessed originality and met the requirements for copyright protection.

Another representative case is the "Banxin" case. The plaintiff created an image titled Banxin using a combination of Midjourney and Photoshop, later publishing it on the Xiaohongshu platform and registering it as a fine art work with the National Copyright Administration of China. The creation process involved repeatedly refining prompts in Midjourney to generate the image, followed by editing in Photoshop. The defendants later published an image highly similar to Banxin on Xiaohongshu and other media platforms. The plaintiff alleged that the defendants' image was substantially similar to their copyrighted fine art work and thus constituted copyright infringement. Midjourney's Terms of Service state that, except in limited circumstances, users own all assets they create through the service to the fullest extent permitted by applicable law.

The court held that Banxin, which features a cityscape, water, architecture, a heart symbol, and its reflection, displayed the author's unique choices and arrangement in terms of scene composition, environment, color palette, lighting, perspective, and the combination of these elements. As such, it possessed originality and qualified as a work of fine art protected under copyright law. The court found that the images used by the two defendants on platforms including Xiaohongshu, WeChat public accounts, video channels, and their 1688 online store were highly similar in the parts available for comparison, differing only slightly in aspects such as cropping, partial blurring, or the addition of text. These alterations were not sufficient to change the overall substantial similarity between the works. Without authorization, the defendants made the plaintiff's copyrighted work available to the public via the internet, thereby infringing the plaintiff's right of communication through information networks.

The court ordered Hangzhou Gaosi Air Membrane Technology Co., Ltd. to issue a public apology to the plaintiff Lin Chen on its Xiaohongshu account for three consecutive days, with the apology content subject to court review. Additionally, Hangzhou Gaosi Air Membrane Technology Co., Ltd. and Changshu Qinhong Real Estate Development Co., Ltd. were jointly ordered to pay the plaintiff RMB 10,000 in damages and reasonable expenses within five days of the judgment taking effect.

(3) Subject Qualification of AI Generators

Creating works using AI could have very important implications for copyright law. Traditionally, the ownership of copyright in computer-generated works was not in question because the program was merely a tool that supported the creative process, very much like a pen and paper. Creative works qualify for copyright protection if they are original, with most definitions of originality requiring a human author. Most jurisdictions, including Spain and Germany, state that only works created by a human can be protected by copyright. But with the latest types of AI, the computer program is no longer a tool; it actually makes many of the decisions involved in the creative process without human intervention.

The main part of intellectual property systems of different countries are established based on natural persons, and this kind of intellectual property system design has a deep ethical foundation. The Intellectual Property Law, as a law regulating various social relationships arising from the intellectual creations of human beings, should maintain the ethical order originating from the natural person. The design of the intellectual property subject system shall adhere to the principle of natural persons as the main subject, with legal entities or other organizations composed of natural persons as supplementary subjects, strictly restrict or even prohibit arbitrary expansion of intellectual property subjects, and adhere to basic ethical standards.

Within the framework of copyright law, AI cannot be identified as an author. AI generates ideas and expressions that can be seen as works through deep learning. This process of self-learning, self-reflection, and self-output of results may seem like creation in a sense, but it cannot qualify as a subject within the framework of copyright law. AI does not have the willpower of natural persons or legal entities.

Human-like "algorithm creation" is a product of machine learning. Its intelligent algorithm-driven behavior is different from rational or emotional behavior by human beings. At the same time, AI has no independent property or independent responsibility. In the end, it is the human behind who will take the responsibility. Some scholars maintain an open attitude on this issue and believe that the "machine learning" process is a human-like creative act. The generated content looks the same as a work with ideas and expression. Therefore, new perceptions and ideas about AI creation are required. Whether AI is qualified as a subject of law should be examined from the perspective of the copyright owner in the copyright system, rather than from the identity of the author. The author's non-subjectivity does not necessarily affect the subjectivity of the copyright holder, nor does it necessarily cause fundamental damage to the legal subject system. Conditionally admitting that AI is a "machine author" in algorithm creation does not prevent the law from assigning all copyrights to humans when allocating ownership. That is to say, the legal subject status enjoyed by humans as copyright holders will not be legally dissolved due to the existence of "machine authors."

In the field of patent law, some scholars believe that, unlike artificial machines in the past, AI is no longer just an auxiliary tool for humans. Instead, it may become an independent inventor. In the future, inventors defined by patent law will no longer be limited to natural persons. AI systems that creatively contribute to the substantive characteristics of inventions can also become inventors. Based on this, a "binary patent subject" structure can be formed. This structure separated the inventor from the patentee, which means it is possible to recognize that the intelligent robot is an inventor, but the ownership of patent rights, especially the legal consequences arising from acts authorized by the charging authority, can only be attributed to humans.

In summary, under the current legal framework, AI still cannot be the subject of intellectual property rights, but as AI becomes ever more independent, it may be identified as the subject of intellectual property rights in the future.

7.3.3 Intellectual Property Protection for NFT

A non-fungible token (NFT) is a unique piece of data that is stored on a blockchain. More specifically, NFTs are digital files such as photographs, videos, or audio files that can be bought and sold with cryptocurrency. In many cases, NFTs are large files and, thus, a link to the actual photo, video, or audio file is what is stored on the blockchain rather than the actual piece of artwork.

(1) Legal Attributes of NFT

There are different opinions in academia about the legal attributes of NFTs. First, NFTs are regarded as virtual property. Although section 127 of the Civil Code stipulates the protection of data and online virtual property, there are no specific laws that clarify them. Some Chinese scholars define virtual property as something in an online environment or cyberspace, simulating real things in a digital form, something relatively independent, and can be exclusively enjoyed. In this sense, the virtual carrier marked by NFT meets the requirements for the certification of virtual property. Furthermore, there are views that an NFT is simply a piece of software code with a specific function identified by a unique identifier. When users buy NFTs, they don't get the digital assets linked to the NFTs. Instead, they bought a long list of hash values composed of numbers and letters. Others believe that the high liquidity of NFT can be applied to the "upper chain" of physical assets such as real estate and automobiles. By using NFT as an asset authorization symbol, it is possible to achieve rapid circulation of assets and save transaction costs. There are also opinions that NFT is an application of Coase's theorem in digital assets, a new economic tool for commercializing the intellectual achievements of intellectual property owners. NFT is currently developing in full swing, but current legislation in related fields in China is still vacant. Therefore, regulations on NFT should be further strengthened in the future.

(2) Copyrightability of NFT

While NFTs are relatively new and may be an unfamiliar type of art, copyright law will treat NFTs the same as any other traditional artwork. If an artist creates a new piece of artwork, they will automatically acquire a copyright of that new artwork. There are certain rights that are acquired by a copyright owner automatically upon creation of a copyrighted work. A copyright owner has exclusive rights to reproduce the work, prepare derivative works, and distribute copies of the work. Thus, a copyright owner has exclusive rights to make an NFT based on an original piece of artwork because "creation of an NFT can be categorized as a copy or even a derivative of the original work".

For example, let's imagine that I own the copyright to a famous piece of art. Because I own the copyright, I have the exclusive right to reproduce the work, prepare derivative works, and distribute copies of the work. I can create an NFT based on the artwork and I will be able to sell that NFT without transferring the copyright to the underlying piece of art just as I would be able to create and sell a reprint of the underlying piece of art. Because my rights are exclusive, I can also ensure that others do not infringe on my rights by bringing suit for copyright infringement if anyone creates art, such as an NFT, that is copying or infringing my copyrighted work.

Digital artwork is still artwork as it has always been, and copyright owners and their licensees are the only ones who should be creating NFTs based on copyrighted artwork.

(3) Legal Attributes of NFT Trading Behavior

If a copyrighted work is sold after being cast as an NFT digital work by others without permission, the interests of the copyright holder and infringes on copyright will be damaged. However, there are different views on which exclusive rights the copyright holder enjoys should be controlled by this type of behavior, and whether the sold NFT digital works are subject to the patent exhaustion rules or whether they can continue to be resold without permission from the copyright holder.

Some believe that the transactions of NFT digital works should be controlled by distribution rights. Because the sale of digital works can achieve the same legal effects as the purchase and sale of offline tangible works. Specifically, "NFT technology makes the work, work carrier, and work transfer specific. The content of each transaction is a copy of a specific digital work at the time of casting. While the public obtains copies, the number of copies does not increase because of the NFT transactions. The entire transaction process is transparent and traceable, so the transaction of NFT digital works is, in its nature, a distribution act". In other words, the distribution rights should apply to the internet works so that the tokenized sale of other people's works can be controlled under the distribution rights. Based on the analysis above, the patent exhaustion of distribution rights can also be applied to NFT digital works transactions.

According to the first NFT copyright infringement decision made by the Hangzhou Internet Court in April 2022, with reference to Art. 10(6) Copyright Law, the court reasoned that the transfer as part of a sale transaction should require the transfer of ownership of an original or copy of the work "in tangible form", which the court then rejected to exclude infringement of the right of distribution. Through this approach the Court further rejected the defense of first sale and exhaustion of right raised by the defendant Metaverse. The decision argued that "according to the relevant provisions of the Copyright Law, when the original or copy of the work is transferred as an object, the ownership is transferred, but the copyright of the work is not transferred. Under the NFT trading model, the act of the minter (seller) of NFT digital works copying and uploading the NFT digital works to the platform for trading falls under the control of the reproduction right (sic!) and the information network transmission right in the Copyright Law respectively. Therefore, the minters of NFT digital works (the seller) should not only be the owner of the copy of the work, but also the copyright owner or licensor of the digital work, otherwise it will infringe the copyright of others."

Chinese scholars who doubted this view argue that instead of circumventing the situation where the distribution right in the Copyright Law does not apply to the transaction of NFTs due to the lack of "tangible carriers" transfer, it is more reasonable for the court to take into account the characteristics of NFT that cannot be tampered with or copied arbitrarily, and give an expansive interpretation to the distribution right, so as to control the sale and resale of NFTs minted without authorization. At the same time, the principle of one-time exhaustion of the distribution right can be applied to restrain smart contracts that arbitrarily prohibit resale.

NFT transactions also involve liability of the platform. The majority of NFT transactions are on mainstream platforms, which, therefore, should assume the responsibility of pre-transaction qualification check. However, current trading platforms such as OpenSea fail to fulfill their responsibility to conduct legal examinations on the qualifications of sellers, the source of products, or the legitimacy of NFT transaction history. They only provide a reminder on the website for buyers to conduct due diligence before purchasing NFTs. However, China's Regulation on the Protection of the Right of Communication to the Public on Information Networks states a very important "safe harbor" principle for dealing with infringement cases of online copyright, which is the "notice and removal" obligation of platform service providers. When the trading platform receives a notification from the buyer and believes that the NFT transaction may involve copyright infringement, it should bear the obligation to remove and take it down. In the scam of blockchain transactions, it is difficult to recover the defrauded funds as they are permanently transferred from the buyer to the seller. The buyer may lose both money and property.

7.3.4 Digital Economy and Intellectual Property

With the vigorous development of a new round of information technology revolution, digital economy quickly becomes an important driver for economic recovery and social progress. Taking China as an example, the scale of China's digital economy reached 39.2 trillion yuan in 2020. The proportion of the digital economy in China's GDP rose to 38.6 percent, up 2.4 percent compared to 2019. The digital economy has become a new engine for economic growth. Existing studies' description of the characteristics of the digital economy share common points. For example, Kang Wei et al. point out the interconnection of all things, knowledge intelligence, data elementization, and wealth virtualization. Meng Hongtao indicates the free characteristic of digital economy on internet and economic order. Wang Hua et al. (2022) mention data-orientation, coordinated online and offline innovative models, and low innovation costs. This book believes that, in the context of highly developed digital technology, the digital economy has the following characteristics: shorter innovation cycles; diverse innovation outcomes; data at the core.

Digital economy is closely related with the intellectual property system. On the one hand, the cost of innovation in digital economy is reduced and efficiency is improved, which requires more efficient protection and incentives of intellectual property rights. On the other hand, digital economy gives rise to new technologies, new businesses, and new models, for which the intellectual property rights system needs to provide guidance. In addition, the synergy between digital economy and IPR will play a significant role in promoting economic growth. Zhang Jincan et al. find that the promotion of intellectual property protection on high-quality development of foreign trade is influenced by digital economy: when digital economy reaches a certain level, the promotion of intellectual property protection on high-quality development of foreign trade is enhanced.

The development of the digital economy also brings a series of challenges to intellectual property rules. Due to the inherent lag of the law, problems arise in the intellectual property system for lack of effective regulation in digital economy. Thus the intellectual property system needs to keep pace with industrial development to achieve a healthier and more rapid growth of digital economy through rebalancing innovation protection and incentives.

(1) Digital Economy Brings Challenges to the Copyright System

The challenges brought by the digital economy to the copyright system mainly manifest as rampant online infringement and imbalanced interests in copyright law.

Digital technology has contributed to rampant online copyright infringement and difficulties in protecting rights. Huang Ji points out that in the digital age, piracy is no longer relied on physical carriers and its cost is low, which make it difficult to combat piracy. Wang Hua points out that online P2P, online music services, etc. are the areas most affected by online copyright infringement; the nature of cloud storage makes it difficult to determine and prove infringement. Scholars believe that the above issues can be resolved by leveraging blockchain technology.

The digital economy can also cause imbalanced interests in copyright law. The Fourth Industrial Revolution has arrived, and the Internet and digital technology industries have achieved explosive growth through the extensive use of open innovation, which is becoming a key driver of digital economy. Industry connects universities, design companies, suppliers, and global integrators through open innovation, forming an innovation ecosystem and technology community. However, there is a natural conflict between open innovation and intellectual property protection. Taking copyright law as an example, as internet sharing and creation is important for knowledge acquiring and entertainment, the copyright system should encourage the creation and internet dissemination of new types of works, in order to maintain a balance between the rights of copyright holders and users, and promote the development of the digital economy. From the perspective of balancing interests, Zhang Jin believes that digital economy advancement has disrupted the balance of interests highlighted by copyright law. There are two reasons for the imbalance: first, the expansion of copyright leads to increased protection, but exceptions and limitations have not developed synchronously; second, the licensing system has not played its due role. Xiong Qi (2014) reckons that the conflict between copyright holders and internet service providers constitutes the biggest crisis for copyright in the digital era: copyright holders hope to continue controlling the dissemination of their works through copyright law, while internet service providers want to provide works as much as possible. For written works, this contradiction is even more prominent because of their special attributes: first, the rights ownership of written works is more dispersed, which leads to an increase in digital costs; second, the diverse applications of written works make it difficult to form a relatively unified licensing agreement, resulting in high negotiation costs. In the digital era, overly strict protection of intellectual property rights can lead to technological monopolies and market crowding-out effects, which are not conducive to technology diffusion and economic growth, and will hinder the development of the digital economy.

(2) Digital Economy Brings Challenges to the Patent System

The challenges to the patent system caused by the digital economy include the patentability of digital technologies, the high number of low-value patents, and the low patent resource conversion rate.

The patentability of certain digital technologies is a key issue. Internet product innovation, online services, etc. generally only provide computing solutions and no longer produce and sell physical products. Therefore, software, business models, and services have become key parts of the digital economy business. The development of the digital economy has also given rise to new combinations among software, solutions, and business models. The patent law is amended to expand protection to new business, which emphasizes that technical features can be patented.

The development of digital technology has led to a large number of low-value patents. In some low-cost digital technology fields, technology imitating enterprises lack the ability to identify technological opportunities. They rely on imitating innovation and filing patents that depend on core patented technologies of others, thus leading to a large number of low-value patent applications. Low-value patents would increase the operating costs of enterprises and reduce overall social efficiency. On the other hand, these imitative applications will trigger high vigilance and excessive reactions from competitors, known as defensive patent strategies. Companies applying for patents for defensive purposes rather than innovation contradict the original intention of the patent system to incentivize innovation. The surge in patent applications related to digital technology has led to backlog of unexamined patent applications for major patent offices worldwide. According to a report from the UK Intellectual Property Office, it would take 10 years to cope with the current patent surge at the existing examination speed of the European Patent Office (EPO).

The rapid growth of the digital economy has raised higher requirements for the utilization of patent resources. The technologies in the digital economy highly overlaps with those in patent-intensive industries. The patent thicket strategy in the global electronics market leads to low efficiency in examination and technology transfer, resulting in prolonged application and transfer. Therefore, the sharp increase of digital technology patents and the additional waiting time for authorization weaken the motivation, decision-making, and action of innovators. Deng Peng believes that it is difficult to meet the demand for patent resource utilization, which is mainly manifested in the disconnection between the technical classification system of patent literature and industry applications; the improper use of patent technical terms; inconvenient patent retrieval and outdated patent information.

(3) Digital Economy Places Higher Demands on Intellectual Property Protection

In the digital economy era, improvements in digital property rights and protection efficiency and effectiveness are a necessity for IPR protection.

The core of the digital economy is data, and how to protect data is a hot topic. Currently, the views of Chinese scholars can be divided into two categories. One is rights recognition, which regards data as the object of statutory rights or rights protection. As for the scope of protection that data should fall under, property rights and intellectual property rights are more representative choices. For example, Wang Hua et al. believe that a specialized property rights protection system should be established for the most fundamental data. The second category is behavioral regulation. Scholars who hold this view believe that there are disadvantages in legislating data ownership, such as legislative difficulties and blurred boundaries of rights. Therefore, regulating the legal use of data from a behavioral perspective is a more preferable method of protection. Some scholars disagree on both of the viewpoints, believing that we should start from legal interpretation, reuse existing laws, and adopt a "three-step" approach to protect data.

Higher efficiency of intellectual property protection is required in digital economy. Deng Peng believes that in order to adapt to the fast development of digital technology, the IPR system needs to improve protection efficiency and adapt to shorter innovation cycles to meet protection needs. Currently, our country has shortened the examination period for several major intellectual property rights. For example, the examination period for invention patents has been reduced to within 20 months; high-value patents to within 16 months; average examination period for trademark registration to within 4 months; software copyright registration to 1–2 months.

The digital economy requires more effective protection of IPR. Ji Hongfen (2022) points out that due to the lack of a sound and comprehensive intellectual property legal protection system, it is impossible to achieve effective protection for the current new economic forms. In addition, there is a lack of experience in intellectual property protection, and the administrative protection mechanism is also absent. The lack of versatile talents in intellectual property management and protection has further weakened the strength of intellectual property protection in digital economy. Jiang Hong et al. (2018) further propose requirements: during the development of the digital economy, not only strong intellectual property protection is required in foundational supporting technologies such as big data and 5G, but intellectual property protection system needs to be elevated to become a standard. Only in this way can the leading market position and the coordinated development of the digital economy and intellectual property protection be achieved. Some scholars also analyze the challenges faced by the IPR system from a macro perspective. As Xu Shi (2021) believes, under the context of digital economy, intellectual property protection mainly faces domestic and international pressure: "First, it is the requirement for the development of domestic scientific and technological innovation; second, intellectual property instrumentalism caused by the complex changes in international trade situations is prevalent." "Internally, we need to establish the concept of intellectual property protection, improve the protection system, make efforts in independent innovation, and lead technological progress." For example, it is necessary to establish a mechanism for industry-university-research cooperation to integrate innovative resources, concentrate innovative forces, and solve key technical problems. At the same time, it is necessary to build a countermeasure system in IPR based on laws such as the Anti-Foreign Sanctions Law to combat the abuse of intellectual property tools. Internationally, it is necessary to adhere to the principle of putting national interests at the core, actively join hands with the world, especially with countries and regions that share common interests and cooperation desires. Moreover, we need to strengthen cooperation, build synergies to form a new force in the international rules-making of IPR, and construct a "community of shared future for intellectual property rights".

New technological revolution is being driven by information, rather than by the industrialized processes of earlier periods. Accordingly, the ways in which we develop, use, store, and communicate information with technology has become a major driving force for our economic and social lives. Intellectual property law plays a central role in this new technological revolution because it is a legal regime for controlling information. Indeed, this technological revolution has brought a certain prominence to intellectual property law, and every area of intellectual property (copyright law, patent law, trademark law, and trade secret law) is now closer to the consciousness of the public, legislators, and courts as a result. An important, yet unaddressed, broader question presented by the merger of technology and intellectual property is how best the two areas should co-exist.

7.4 Meeting the Challenge: Building a New IP System

Today, intellectual property rights are more important than ever in this global, highly-connected digital landscape. With all of the good the rise of the internet has done for the sharing of information and ideas, it has unfortunately become easier for ideas and works to be stolen, which can be damaging to both national economies and innovation.

Intellectual property protection varies from country to country, but countries that have strong IP laws recognize the important impact original works, designs, inventions, etc. have on the overall economy. Almost every country that has a dependence on international trade takes strong measures to protect their intellectual property rights. A strong IP system is necessary to meet the challenges of IP in the technological age.

(1) A new system must strike the right balance between the production and the distribution of new ideas.

To develop new products and processes, individuals must have a financial incentive to undertake the costs, risks, and efforts of developing new knowledge. Not surprisingly, bigger incentives lead to the production of more knowledge than do smaller incentives.

At the same time, once any piece of knowledge exists, the social incentives are reversed 180 degrees. The wider the use and the faster the distribution of that new knowledge, the greater the benefit to society. Free usage leads to the widest and fastest distribution.

Any system of intellectual property rights must make a trade-off between these two inherently conflicting objectives—more production versus faster distribution.

To accomplish society's interest in expanding knowledge as rapidly as possible, certain classes of knowledge ought to be in the public domain and freely available to everyone. One can argue that basic scientific knowledge should be public while those who develop products from that knowledge should receive private monopoly rights. But the line between scientific principles and the knowledge that is necessary to allow products to be built is, in practice, hard to draw. Here again, the issue is a judgment call.

There are other reasons for keeping knowledge in the public domain. A society may determine, for example, that its interests in educating the young justify placing some types of knowledge—educational technologies, for example—in the public domain. And egalitarian democracies may want, say, lifesaving technologies to be generally available to everyone, not just to the rich.

Such considerations mean that we need principles to determine when knowledge should be publicly available and when it should be kept private. This does not mean that patents or copyrights should be forbidden in areas where there is a social interest in allowing general access to knowledge at little or no cost. That would be unacceptable because no one would have the incentive to produce such generally useful knowledge. Inventors who happened upon such discoveries would have an enormous incentive to keep them secret. We must ensure that those who generate knowledge in the public domain get paid.

The solution to this problem is found not in the patent system itself but in the establishment of some public agency—perhaps a branch of the National Science Foundation. Armed with funds and the power of eminent domain, the agency could decide to buy knowledge for the public's use when it seemed warranted. If the seller would not agree to sell at a reasonable price, adjudication principles very similar to those used in eminent domain land-acquisition proceedings could be used.

As monopoly power wanes and social interests in encouraging the development of new intellectual property grow, the balance in our system should shift toward encouraging the production of new knowledge and be less concerned about the free distribution of existing knowledge. Tighter or longer-term patents and copyrights would seem to be warranted.

(2) Laws on intellectual property rights must be enforceable.

Although the need for the protection of intellectual property has never been greater, the same technologies and developments that have made intellectual property rights more central to economic success have also made enforcement of those rights much more difficult. Laws can be written, but they are meaningless—and should not be written—unless a technological choke point exists to make enforcement is possible. Laws that cannot or will not be enforced make for neither good law nor good technology policies. The honest end up being suckers who pay more precisely because they are honest. And a law that is widely violated leads to disrespect for the law and more violations. Put bluntly, if someone cannot think of how a legal right can be enforced, it should not be a legal right.

(3) The system must be able to determine rights and resolve disputes quickly and efficiently.

Many of the problems with the patent system flow from the lack of consistent, predictable, rapid, low-cost determinations about intellectual property rights and a means of quick, cheap dispute resolution. The first problem is easily solved, at least in part. In the United States, people who file for patents pay user fees that exceed the costs incurred by the patent office. Those fees are put into the general budget, and Congress then appropriates funds—less than the amount collected in fees—to run the patent office.

One easy change is to establish a system in which the user fees directly finance what they are supposed to finance but are set high enough to ensure speedy decisions. Like an income tax, fees could be adjusted to reflect the income levels of the applicants and equalize the burdens on large corporations and on small, individual inventors. The relevant agencies should be taken out of the civil service system, and salaries should be set high enough to attract and keep the people who could run the system efficiently and speedily.

For inventors of technologies that have very short useful lives, making use of today's system of dispute resolution—with its delayed, lengthy, and expensive court trials—is equivalent to losing one's rights. In seeking an alternative approach, the U.S. system for settling water rights disputes in irrigated areas might serve as a model. Federal water masters are given the authority to allocate water in dry years and to settle disputes quickly because crops die quickly.

A nation's ability to innovate, attract foreign investment, and develop valuable businesses offering products and services that can compete on a global scale is intrinsically linked with intellectual property (IP) and its supporting innovation ecosystem.

Appropriate IP policies, an effective legal framework, robust operational infrastructure and effective education are key elements of this innovation ecosystem that leads to an innovative and competitive nation.

The advent of the new scientific and technological revolution and industrial revolution has not only brought about changes in the technological base, production methods and lifestyles, but also changes in management and social resource allocation mechanisms. All countries in the world are shifting the focus of development from production to innovation, and innovative design has become the core of a country's advantage in fierce international competition. As a national design policy integrated into the national design innovation system, its policy orientation, the positioning of design in sustainable socio-economic development, and how the design industry can develop in harmony with the manufacturing industry, and thus form a strong advantage in promoting national socio-economic development and international competitiveness, are all realistic issues that must be addressed when formulating a national design policy.

A well-developed IP legal framework is the cornerstone of an effective design innovation ecosystem. Not only that, but it is the foundation of an enabling environment that encourages entrepreneurs and businesses to invest in developing solutions to the technological challenges facing humanity and creators to develop exciting new forms of cultural expression.

(1) Strengthening IP system

Intellectual property is a special kind of property right, the object of protection is the results of intellectual activity. The creation, scope, exercise and protection of intellectual property rights are all subject to the provisions of the law. Legalisation is the basis and guarantee of IPR protection, and the rule of law for IPR protection goes hand in hand with IPR protection work. Taking China as an example, the progress of China's IPR legal system in recent years is reflected in three aspects. First, the protection of intellectual property rights has been increased through legislation. On the one hand, the scope of IPR protection has been expanded, the protection provisions have been refined and the duration of protection has been extended. On the other hand, the fight against IPR infringement should be intensified, and the rules of evidence should be improved to provide legal support for rights holders to defend their rights. Secondly, we promote the implementation and application of IPRs through legislation. Thirdly, to improve the level of public services for IPRs by the government through legislation. Against the backdrop of the fourth technological revolution, the intellectual property system is assumed to adapt to the needs of the flourishing development of new technologies and new industries, strengthen research on issues related to intellectual property protection in emerging fields such as big data, artificial intelligence and gene technology, and improve the intellectual property protection system in emerging fields.

(2) Supporting judiciaries

The judicial administration of IP plays an important role in innovation. Given that the speed of technological innovation tends to outpace legislative and policy responses, judiciaries are often on the front line of confronting novel legal questions that may significantly impact innovation stakeholders not only in their own countries, but also beyond national borders. The development and enforcement of IPR makes it possible for the United States to continue being one of the most innovative countries in the world. American scientists, engineers, and entrepreneurs invented the microchip, created the Internet, invented the smartphone, started the biotechnology revolution, sent astronauts to the Moon, and saved millions of lives through innovative medicines. America's creative artists—authors, musicians, film directors and gamers—have captivated the imagination of people all over the world.

A strong system of IP rights assures inventors, industrial designers, and creative artists that their ideas will be protected. They can receive payment for the use of their creations and continue to invest in future innovations. Also, they are incentivized to make their innovation available to others, and share knowledge that enables others to come up with other novel and advanced solutions.

Innovation exists widely throughout the world. Anyone who finds challenges and seeks solutions can create IP. It is important to encourage innovation both domestically and internationally. By encouraging the implementation of strong IPR systems and enforcement around the world, IP protects the ideas and rewards of innovators as well as stimulates the creativity of inventors and artists everywhere.

(3) Training and further education

In addition to the necessary IP policy, legal and technical infrastructure, it is essential that government officials, researchers and business people be aware and knowledgeable about the use and administration of the IP system. To build an innovative country, the key is in talents, especially in innovative scientific and technological talents. To cultivate and create innovative scientific and technological talents, we should fully implement the policy of respecting labor, respecting knowledge, respecting talents and respecting creation, and take the demand of building an innovative country as the basis, use the cause to gather talents, use the time to create talents, use the mechanism to motivate talents, use the legal system to protect talents, continuously develop and expand the scientific and technological talents team, and strive to form a vivid situation of practical talents training. The legal system of intellectual property is the most effective mechanism to stimulate and guarantee independent innovation, and it is also the most optimal mode to stimulate talents with the mechanism and guarantee them with the legal system. In the process of building an innovative country and cultivating innovative talents, the intellectual property system is the accelerator, and the cultivation of intellectual property professionals is the first task in the cultivation of innovative talents. In addition, the active building of IP service institutions is also part of the talent strategy. China has previously had patent agencies, trademark agencies and other service providers, and continuing to strengthen these will enable better implementation of the IP system.

(4) Dispute resolution

There are various ways to resolve IP disputes, such as settlement, arbitration, litigation, etc.

In a mediation procedure a neutral intermediary, the mediator, helps the parties to reach a mutually satisfactory settlement. Any settlement is recorded in an enforceable contract. An advantage of mediation is that parties retain control of the dispute resolution process. This can help to preserve good business relations with the other parties involved.

In an arbitration procedure, all parties agree to submit the dispute to one or more arbitrators who then make a binding decision on the dispute. The arbitration procedure is private and less formal than court proceedings. An award of damages obtained through arbitration is also more easily enforceable internationally than an award through national court proceedings.

Where IP infringements persist, you could seek the assistance of law enforcement and initiate judicial proceedings. Depending on the national law, a range of remedies are available to protect your IP. As a provisional measure, a court can, for example, order the preservation of evidence of the alleged IP infringement. Once the infringement has been established, a court can order the infringer to stop the infringement and pay compensation for the damages that you may have suffered. In addition, infringing goods may be seized and disposed of outside the channels of commerce, and, in many countries, the infringer may be ordered to identify third persons involved in the production and distribution of the infringing goods and their channels of distribution.

Where an IP infringement amounts to a criminal offence under the applicable national law, such as in cases of trademark counterfeiting or copyright piracy committed wilfully and on a commercial scale, you can alert the authorities and request that the matter be investigated.

WIPO offers options outside the courts, Alternative Dispute Resolution (ADR) such as mediation and arbitration can empower parties in an IP dispute by enhancing their control over the dispute resolution process. The consensual nature of the process often results in a less adversarial experience, allowing parties to solve disputes in a less acrimonious manner. In offering these benefits, ADR contributes to the optimal development and use of IP assets in the economy. To a certain extent, it also helps unburden national court systems.

References

Ji H F (2022) Research on the challenges and countermeasures of intellectual property protection in the era of the digital economy. Jiangsu Science and Technology Information 39(15): 14–17

Jiang H, Wu Y H, Gao S P (2018) Research on the relationship between technical standardization and knowledge management: A lifecycle perspective. Science and Technology Progress and Policy 35(13): 18–27

Wang H, Zhang R Z, Yang W (2022) Research on the challenges and countermeasures of China's intellectual property rights system in the digital economy. Science and Technology Management Research 42(11): 145–151

Xiong Q (2014) Large-scale digitization and innovation of collective management system for copyright. Legal and Business Studies 31(02): 100–107

Xu S (2021) Comparative study and prospect of intellectual property protection in the context of the digital economy. Journal of Beijing University of Aeronautics and Astronautics (Social Sciences Edition) 34(05): 43–44

Index

N. Jiang, *Design, Innovation and Intellectual Property*,
https://doi.org/10.1007/978-981-95-2042-8

MIX
Papier aus verantwortungsvollen Quellen
Paper from responsible sources
FSC® C105338

If you have any concerns about our products,
you can contact us on
ProductSafety@springernature.com

In case Publisher is established outside the EU,
the EU authorized representative is:
Springer Nature Customer Service Center GmbH
Europaplatz 3, 69115 Heidelberg, Germany

Printed by Libri Plureos GmbH
in Hamburg, Germany